DarkLore

Daily Grail Publishing

Darklore Volume 4

ISBN: 978-0-9807111-1-0

Daily Grail Publishing
Brisbane, Australia
userhelp@dailygrail.com
www.dailygrail.com

Contents

’Tis the old secret of the gods that they come in low disguises.

- *Ralph Waldo Emerson*

If you would like to be notified of future releases of *Darklore*, please send an email to darklore@dailygrail.com. Please be assured your contact details will not be used for any other purpose.

Editor's Introduction

Recently I read a blog by a well-known skeptic in which he noted his excitement about the growth of the modern skeptical movement. It was, he said, a step in the right direction; a further move towards rationality and the end-game of cleansing the general population of its interest in 'woo': UFO sightings, conspiracy theories, belief in ghosts and the afterlife, and so on.

I can't help but think though that these 'New Skeptics' have got it seriously wrong. The human attraction to mystery is built-in to our minds, a fact regardless of whether you think the 'mind' is simply an accidental by-product of a squishy wet lump. The innate drive to understand is at the root of these 'woo' subjects, and if anything it's something that should be *encouraged*. And before I get shouted down by the vociferous CSICOPians that haunt my every step, I'll take some support from one of the 'gods' of the New Skeptics, Richard Dawkins. "I think that the appetite for mystery, the enthusiasm for that which we do not understand, is healthy and to be fostered," Dawkins once said. "It is the same appetite which drives the best of true science, and it is an appetite which true science is best qualified to satisfy." I agree wholeheartedly with Dawkins on this point, even if I differ on other philosophical points.

Card-carrying skeptics should put less emphasis on belittling people interested in 'woo' topics, and more on engaging them and encouraging critical thinking in evaluating claims and evidence of the paranormal. In that spirit, in Volume 4 of *Darklore* we've got a number of articles which take the knives to some cherished 'woo'. Don't think we've gone all negative though – there's still plenty of high strangeness and heretical theorizing in the latest release. I leave it in your capable hands to separate the wheat from the chaff.

the temple of EDEN

the truth behind the mythic landscape of gobekli tepe

by *Filip Coppens*

Five millennia separate us from the birth of ancient Egypt around 3100 BC. Add another five millennia and we are in 8100 BC, coincidentally the start of the Age of Cancer. Add another millennium and a half, and we have the date when Göbekli Tepe, in the highlands of Turkey near the Iraqi and Syrian borders, was constructed.

Archaeologically categorized as a site of the Pre-Pottery Neolithic A period (c. 9600–7300 BC), the world's oldest temple sits in the early part of that era and so far has been carbon-dated to 9500 BC. It is the time-frame when Plato's Atlantis civilization is said to have disappeared. And it was built an incredible 5000 years before the rise of what many consider to be the "oldest civilization", Sumer, not too far south of Göbekli Tepe as one goes down the River Euphrates and leaves the highlands of the Taurus Mountains in Turkey.

Göbekli Tepe is an incredible site. David Lewis-Williams, Professor of Archaeology at Witwatersrand University in Johannesburg, says that "Göbekli Tepe is the most important archaeological site in the world". It is a small hill on the horizon, 15 kilometres northwest of the town of Şanlıurfa, more commonly known as Urfa – which has been linked with the biblical Abraham (some claim that Urfa was the town of Ur mentioned in the Bible) and which once hosted the Holy Mandylion, linked with Christ's Passion. Once also known as Edessa, Urfa is on the edge of the rainy area of the Taurus Mountains, source of the river that runs through the town and joins the Euphrates. Urfa was (and still is) an oasis, which could explain why Göbekli Tepe was built nearby. A life-sized statue of limestone that was found in Urfa, at the pond known as Balıklı Göl, has been carbon-dated to 10,000–9000 BC, making it the earliest-known stone sculpture ever found. Its eyes are made of obsidian.

An old Kurdish shepherd, Şavak Yildiz, discovered the true nature of Göbekli Tepe in October 1994 when, after spotting something, he brushed away the dust to expose a large oblong-shaped stone. A survey of the site had been carried out by American archaeologist Peter Benedict in 1963, but he identified the area as a Byzantine cemetery. When German archaeologist Harald Hauptmann and Adnan Misir and Eyüp Bucak of the Museum of Urfa began excavations in 1995, they soon learned that the site was so much more.

Göbekli Tepe is a series of mainly circular and oval-shaped structures set in the slope of a hill, known as Göbekli Tepe Ziyaret. "Ziyaret" means "visit", but this is often left out of the name. And though some translate "Göbekli Tepe" as "Navel of the World" and "Gobek" does mean "navel" or "belly" and "Tepe" means "hill", the most correct translation of the site's name should be "bulged-out hill".

The more sensationalist media have made attempts to link Göbekli Tepe with the biblical Garden of Eden. Göbekli Tepe is indeed old, but it is not unique; nor was it a garden. However, over the past 50 years the time-frame for the beginning of civilization has been gently pushed back from the rise of the Sumerian civilization to the construction of Göbekli Tepe. Alas, it has been a voyage that has not received the attention it should have had.

Pushing Back the Birth of Civilization

The discovery of the biblical town of Jericho and its stone walls, dated to approximately 8000 BC, was the first to push back the date of the birth of 'civilization'. 'Ain Ghazal is often seen as a sister site of Jericho and, with its 15-hectare area, is the largest Neolithic site in the Middle East and four times as big as Jericho. American Gary O. Rollefson, its principal archaeologist, was able to date the town to 7250 BC, and there is evidence of agriculture in the area dating back to c. 6000 BC – later than the establishment of the town itself. In its heyday, 2000 people lived at 'Ain Ghazal. However, by 5000 BC the town was completely deserted. Thirty statues have been found there, measuring between 35 and 90 centimetres; they are human in appearance but may represent deities or the spirits of ancestors.

Jericho's discovery added weight to the argument that the Bible is history, not myth. But when it was next learned that there are even older sites than Jericho, "unfortunately" not located in Palestine but further north in Anatolia, southeast Turkey, media interest in these new discoveries seemed to wane.

The most famous of these sites is Çatal Höyük. It was discovered in 1958 by British archaeologist James Mellaart, who began excavations in 1961 and eventually dated the site to 7500–5700 BC. It is the largest and best-preserved Neolithic site found to date. Mellaart described it as "a Neolithic Rome", and it is indeed worthy of the name 'town'. Its constructions show clear signs that its inhabitants possessed a religion – labeled by some as a Mother Goddess cult, although this theory has been the subject of much controversy. What is known is that the dead were buried beneath the floors of the buildings, and that several of these structures contain depictions of bulls. Some people have gone so far as to suggest that there may be a common origin between Çatal Höyük and the Minoan civilization on Crete, despite the fact that 3000 years separate the two.

Çatal Höyük was the first of several discoveries to slowly unveil the Turkish region's ancient history. Göbekli Tepe is but one of several extremely old sites and is the oldest discovered so far. However, the existence of these sites has only been reported within the specialised press, although each site has a 'wow factor'.

The site of Çayönü, located around 96 kilometres from Göbekli Tepe, conforms to a design that is known as a "grill plan", as it looks like a grill. This reveals that careful planning went into its construction. Americans Linda and Robert Braidwood, together with Turkish archaeologist Halet Çambel, began to excavate Çayönü in 1964 and found that the floors of the buildings were made of terrazzo (burnt crushed lime and clay), even though at the time of the discovery it was thought that this had first been used by the Romans. The site also revealed the use of metals and the earliest evidence of

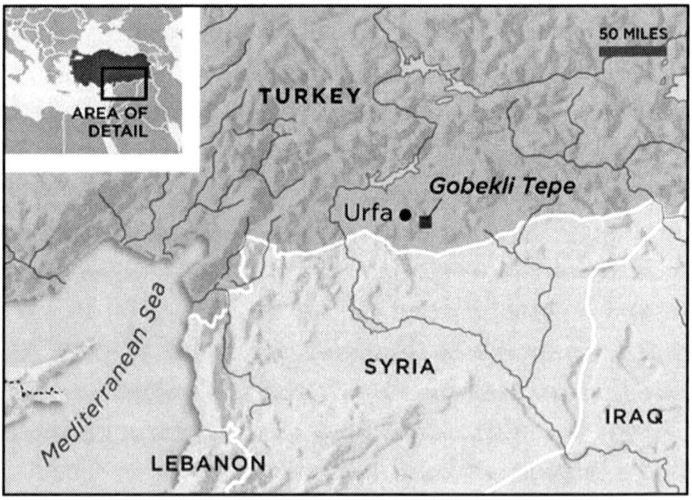

the smelting of copper, though some nevertheless argue that the copper was originally cold-hammered rather than smelted. The use of copper should not come as a total surprise, as the site is within range of copper ore deposits (as well as obsidian) at Ergani in nearby Diyarbakır Province. And all of this in a site dated to 7500–6600 BC. Çayönü is often seen as the site that began the epoch that would culminate in Çatal Höyük.

Çayönü offered evidence of the first farmyard pigs, but it also revealed a hoard of human skulls, one found under an altar-like slab and stained with human blood. Some have concluded that this is an indication of human sacrifice, while others have been unwilling to go that far based on a single type of artefact. Other archaeological evidence suggests that some people were killed in huge death pits, while children were buried alive in jars or roasted in large bronze bowls. Çayönü is therefore civilization, but perhaps not as we like to know it.

Another important site is Nevalı Çori, in Hilvan Province between Diyarbakır and Şanlıurfa. Here, Harald Hauptmann began excavations in 1979 and was able to uncover large limestone statues. In 1991, the site was submerged with the construction of Lake Atatürk Dam. It shares many parallels with Göbekli Tepe and is dated to 8400–8000 BC. All the artefacts retrieved are now in museums, including a life-sized egg-like head with crude ears and a carved ponytail, found in a niche at the centre of a north-western wall. Interestingly, the ponytail is actually a curling serpent that ends in a mushroom-like cap. Whatever being the figure is meant to represent, German archaeologist Klaus Schmidt believes it was worshipped as a deity.

Nevalı Çori set the stage for Göbekli Tepe: shortly after its disappearance under the waters, Göbekli Tepe emerged from the sands. Many people highlight the T-shaped pillars of Göbekli Tepe as the 'signature' of the site. However, such T-shaped pillars were also found in Nevalı Çori. Site-wise, Nevalı Çori is more square than circular in design, although a square precinct has been found at Göbekli Tepe, too. Although there are several parallels between the two sites, Nevalı Çori's pillars are nevertheless smaller and its shrine is located inside a village.

The Göbekli Tepe Site Revealed

In comparison, the site of Göbekli Tepe is small. British author Andrew Collins has compared its size to that of "three tennis courts". Its principal excavators are Klaus Schmidt and Harald Hauptmann of the German Archaeological Institute in Istanbul. All of the complexes in Göbekli Tepe that they have unearthed so far are typified by structures containing T-pillars.

These pillars were used as "drawing boards" and many depict animals, with an apparent preference for boars, foxes, reptiles, lions, crocodiles and birds, as well as insects and spiders. Most of these were carved out of the flat surfaces of the pillars. However, some are three-dimensional sculptures, including one find, made during the 2006 excavation season, of a reptilian creature descending on the side of a T-pillar, demonstrating that whoever created this had mastered the art of stone carving – on a par with much of what we would see thousands of years later in Sumer and Egypt.

So far, four circular/ovalshaped complexes have been excavated. The walls are made of unworked dry stone and the floors of terrazzo. The interior of the walls usually have several T-pillars set along them in a radiating pattern, the depth of the pillar normally against or near the wall so that the two main surfaces of the pillar could be carved and seen by whomever was inside the complex. A low bench runs along the entire exterior wall of each complex.

The structures are situated on the southern slope of the hill, orientated roughly north–south with their entrances to the south. All the T-pillars were excavated from a stone quarry on the lower

Image credit: Gevork Nazaryan

southwestern slope of the hill. One pillar remains *in situ* in the quarry; it is seven metres long and three metres wide, and if fully excavated would have weighed around 50 tonnes, underlining that building with stones that weigh tonnes did not begin in Egypt or in England with Stonehenge.

Complex A, the first circular structure to be excavated, is nicknamed "the snake column building" because depictions of the snake somewhat dominate the carvings on the T-pillars. One is of a 'net' containing snakes. Another pillar, however, depicts a triad of bull, fox and crane, positioned one above the other. Some pillars only feature a bull, others only a fox, and so on.

Complex B measures nine metres in length when measured from east to west, and 10 to 15 metres north to south (part of it is still to be excavated). It is nevertheless the only complex dug to floor level, revealing the terrazzo floor surface. Two central pillars have a large fox depicted on them. One central pillar, no. 9, is 3.4 m high; pillar no. 10 is 3.6 m high; their weights are 7.1 and 7.2 tonnes respectively. The complex was clearly built to 'house' these monolithic pillars, which prove how well-versed our ancestors were in working with gigantic stones; not merely in quarrying them but in shaping and decorating them as well. Archaeologists believe that 200 T-pillars originally stood at Göbekli Tepe. If each weighed 'only' five tonnes, it would still mean that 1,000 tonnes of pillars were excavated and decorated, and it highlights the importance of the site and the effort that went into creating it.

Complex C is nicknamed "the circle of the boar", as it depicts various wild pigs. There remain nine pillars around the wall, but several were removed at some point in the past. One pillar shows a net of birds. As later cultures are known to have caught migratory cranes in nets, could this be a custom that was practised much earlier than assumed? Complex C is also of interest because a U-shaped stone has been found there which is deemed to have been the access stone. This stone has a central passage 70 centimetres wide, and one side of the U is topped with a depiction of a boar; the other side unfortunately is missing. Again, the U shape and the boar underline the craftsmen's technical expertise in carving, which is shown even more so on pillar no. 27, featuring the earlier-mentioned three-dimensional reptilian creature. This intricate sculpture could be regarded as being on a par with Michelangelo's statue of David.

Complex D is nicknamed "the Stone Age zoo". Pillar no. 43 has scorpions, and some pillars are indeed so profusely decorated with animals – much more intensively than in the other complexes – that the description is quite apt. Once again, there are two central pillars (nos 18 and 31), though other pillars reveal symbols, like one in the shape of the letter H as well as one with an H turned 90 degrees. The site has revealed other symbols, specifically a cross, a resting half-moon and horizontal bars – evidence that the origin of writing is likely to be much older than is currently assumed. Pillar no. 33 is the 'star' of the complex. Schmidt states that the shapes on this pillar come close to the Egyptian hieroglyphs, hence he posits the existence of a pictographic language in the 10th millennium BC.

Combined, these four complexes – and others, still unexcavated – are a series of ovals and resemble the layout of the oval-shaped Stone Age complexes found on Malta. This is all the more remarkable as Malta's oval shapes were considered unique, though some of the megaliths on Sardinia also display some oval-like tendencies but not as profoundly as at Göbekli Tepe.

A 'rock temple' lower down on the slope is equally oval in shape and has an opening to the "burial chamber". Whereas at other sites these openings are so narrow that a human could not navigate to the interior, here it is wide enough to enter. Elsewhere on the site, on the northern slope of the hill, there is a rectangular complex named "the lion column building". Its four pillars have depictions of leonine creatures, which could also be tigers or leopards. One pillar has a 30-cm-high graffito of a squatting woman who appears to be giving birth.

Speculation on Göbekli Tepe

Excavations at Göbekli Tepe are still ongoing; only a quarter of the suspected 200 T-pillars have been discovered so far, and not all the structures have been unearthed. In short, further surprises may be in store. It is therefore early days to draw major conclusions, but what could it all mean? The site definitely demonstrates that things which we thought were much more recent are far older – and all present in one site, sitting in a region which shows that a civilization worthy of that name existed there in the 10th millennium BC, thousands of years before anyone would have dared to guess until recently.

Klaus Schmidt has labelled Göbekli Tepe "the first temple" and "a sanctuary of the Stone Age hunter". He sees the site as part of a death cult, not specifically linked with a sedentary group but a type of central sanctuary for several of the tribes living in the region. The carved animals are believed to have been there to protect the dead. At

Çayönü, as previously described, one structure has a cellar that was found to contain human skulls and bones. So far, though, Göbekli Tepe has no evidence of habitation and therefore appears to have been purely a religious centre.

Once again, it appears that, just as the ancient Egyptians did, the civilization that constructed Göbekli Tepe had far greater regard for their religious buildings than for any structures of a practical or more materialistic nature. Still, with only Complex B excavated to floor level, no tombs or graves have been found to date.

Some have voiced criticism as to whether hunter-gatherers could have created such a structure as Göbekli Tepe. The many flint arrowheads (and the lack of construction tools) found around the site would seem to support this criticism, and one could even see these artefacts as part of sacred hunts rather than as part of the daily activities to put food on the table – if indeed tables even existed then.

Schmidt maintains that the hunter-gatherers convened at the site at certain times of the year. Whether these meetings were determined by solar or lunar cycles is anyone's guess, but it is nevertheless an interesting question to ponder. Equally, one could logically conclude that those who constructed the site lived there and were a dedicated resource supported by others who sustained them with dietary and housing needs. Archaeologists have estimated that up to 500 persons would have been required to extract the 10- to 20-tonne pillars and move them from the quarry to their destination, a distance ranging from 100 to 500 metres. However, Schmidt actually believes that maintaining the community of builders was the real reason behind why our ancestors 'invented' agriculture: they began to cultivate the wild grasses on the hills to sustain this sedentary population. In short, he believes that "religion motivated people to take up farming".

As well as appearing to have ritual significance, Göbekli Tepe, with its large and exquisitely decorated stone blocks, reveals that its creators had an extraordinary ability and familiarity with stone masonry and carving. That our ancestors in 10,000 BC were so skilled is an archaeological discovery that is wiping out long-cherished beliefs about the origin of civilization.

As for the carvings, why were certain animals chosen? Why do the depictions seem to have no clear or apparent organisation but appear to be a rather random collection? Truth is, we don't know. In later civilizations, all of these animals were given divine attributes. Some cultures chose to depict snakes because these animals shed their skin, which they saw as a symbol of rebirth. Others opted for the same animal for different reasons. So far, there is no way of knowing what beliefs the creators and users of Göbekli Tepe held.

Some observers have pointed out that some of the cranes are depicted with human-like knees and have suggested that a form of shamanism was practised inside this temple. Sister sites have revealed sculptures of a mixture of animal and human, specifically that of the body of a bird with a human head. As it happened, thousands of years later the ancient Egyptians used this symbol as a hieroglyph to depict the *ba*, the human soul freed from the body at death or during shamanic flight.

Andrew Collins has specifically underlined the shamanic potential of these sites in modern-day Turkey. The image of the previously mentioned naked woman depicts her hair in the shape of a hemispherical mushroom cap. The side of one pillar at Göbekli Tepe features a series of serpents with mushroom-shaped heads, four winding their way downwards and a fifth one climbing up to meet them, while the other side shows several interwoven serpents wearing mushroom-like caps, eight emerging at the top and nine at the bottom. Is this evidence of a ritual involving hallucinogenic mushrooms or similar mind-altering substances?

The bones of vultures have been found at Nevalı Çori, Göbekli Tepe and Jerf el-Ahmar (in Syria). A communal cave site, Shanidar, in the Upper Zagros Mountains of northern Iraq, contained a series of severed birds' wings covered with red ochre. The remains have been dated to c. 8870 BC. The wings are believed to have been used in some ceremony, but precisely in what manner remains unknown. However, it is known that, in the distant past, the people of this region placed the bodies of the dead on high constructions and let vultures eat the flesh of the dead. Depictions of such a Neolithic excarnation tower have been found on a mural in Çatal Höyük. Interestingly, human bones have recently been found in the soil that once filled the niches behind the megaliths at Göbekli Tepe. Schmidt argues that "...the ancient hunters brought the corpses of relatives here, and installed them in the open niches by the stones. The corpses were then excarnated." Not just vultures but wild animals seem to have taken part in this ritual. This may explain why so many animals are depicted on the T-pillars: perhaps the people who constructed these sites felt that 'something' of the dead lived on in these animals.

Cradles of Civilization

What is known is that Göbekli Tepe and its sister sites have pushed back the age of monolithic building much further in time. Previously, we looked to the likes of Stonehenge and the Egyptian pyramids, but now we find that our ancestors were hauling massive stones to build their constructions around 12,000 years ago. Even if a structure like the Sphinx were suddenly found to be 10,000 years old, the immediate reaction might now perhaps be: "So what? It is not that unique." Furthermore, if the dates for some of these sites in Turkey pre-date the assumed time-frame for such events as the disappearance of Atlantis or the Great Flood, it means that these ancient ancestors cannot be neatly placed as "survivors from a deluge".

Our ancient history has grown much more interesting and complex. The cultures that followed the establishment of Göbekli Tepe had domesticated pigs, sheep, cattle and goats and cultivated wheat species such as einkorn. Indeed, recent analysis has shown that the first cultivation of domesticated wheat occurred at Karacadağ, a mountain 32 kilometres from Göbekli Tepe. Other domesticated cereals such as rye and oats also originated here. According to Schmidt, this adventure began c. 8000 BC.

It is easy and tempting to label this region as 'the cradle of civilization', but the fact of the matter is that it has already been proven that corn (maize) was engineered in Mexico at the same time, only underlining how the frontiers of 'civilization' are being pushed back on both continents. In fact, there is evidence of Barbary sheep being cultivated by our ancestors in North Africa as early as 18,000 BC. Furthermore, several grains of emmer wheat have been found at the Palestinian site of Nahal Oren, suggesting cultivation of this crop occurred there as early as 14,000 BC.

In any case, it is clear that Göbekli Tepe is not alone. It may be receiving much of the focus, but another site, Karahan Tepe, 63 kilometres east of Urfa in the Tektek Mountains, deserves attention. Discovered in 1997 and investigated by archaeologist Bahattin Çelik of the Turkish Historical Society, it has been dated to c. 9500–9000 BC. It has a number of T-pillars as well as high reliefs of a winding snake and other carvings similar to those at Göbekli Tepe. Covering an area of 325,000 m2, Karahan Tepe is much bigger than Göbekli Tepe. The stone pillars are spaced 1.5 to 2.0 metres apart and protrude

above ground level, waiting for an archaeologist to expose them fully. Other carved stones include a battered torso of a naked man and polished rock with forms of goats, gazelles and rabbits.

It is too early to draw any extraordinary conclusions from these sites, apart from the fact that our history is no longer as we know it. But just as Jericho proved in part that the Bible contains historical facts, these sites may yet substantiate some of the Sumerian myths which claimed that agriculture, animal husbandry and weaving had been brought to mankind from the sacred mountain Du-Ku, which was inhabited by the Anunna deities. Though it's unlikely that this mountain was Göbekli Tepe, we are probably in the correct general vicinity here at the frontier of the Taurus Mountains.

Around 8000 BC, descendants of the creators of Göbekli Tepe turned on their forefathers' achievements and entombed their temple under thousands of tonnes of earth, creating the artificial hill – a 'belly' – that we see today. Why they did this is unknown – doing so would have required an extraordinary amount of time and effort – though ultimately it was a decision that preserved the monument for posterity. Schmidt argues that the local landscape began to change around that time: as the trees were chopped down, the soil began to lose its fertility; the area became arid and bare, and the people were forced to move elsewhere. Could it be that they began to make their descent and, millennia later, established what is known as the Sumerian civilization? Such a scenario is just one possibility.

Even in ancient Egypt, religious constructions were often abandoned if not dismantled after a while because they belonged to a particular 'cycle' of time that had since passed. If that were the case with Göbekli Tepe, it would mean that knowledge of astronomy is older by millennia. The past five decades have so radically reshaped our understanding of the period 10,000–4000 BC, specifically the level of 'civilization' our ancestors had achieved in those days, that this shouldn't at all come as a surprise. And it seems that it's a given that somewhere, even older towns are waiting to be uncovered.

However, it is equally clear that entering into the mindset of these hunter-gatherers—how they saw these animals and what they believed happened to the dead—is a difficult subject which will require years of study. Alas, it is an area where few archaeologists dare to tread, and in all likelihood they will hop from one site to the next, as they've done for several decades, to 'only' uncover the fact that civilization is much older than we've assumed. Already, other sites are vying for Göbekli Tepe's fame. The previously mentioned site of Jerf el-Ahmar, located along the Euphrates in Syria, has been dated to 9600–8500 BC. Other sites will certainly soon submit their applications. It's likely they will all reveal that they are part of our history, but not as we know it.

Philip Coppens is an author and investigative journalist on topics ranging from the world of politics to ancient history and mystery. He is the former editor-in-chief of the Dutch magazine *Frontier* and is a frequent contributor to various publications. Since 1995, he has lectured extensively across the world. He is the author of *The Stone Puzzle of Rosslyn Chapel*, *The Canopus Revelation*, *Land of the Gods*, *The New Pyramid Age*, and the recently released *Servants of the Grail*. His website is www.philipcoppens.com.

Nightmares on the Edge of Reason

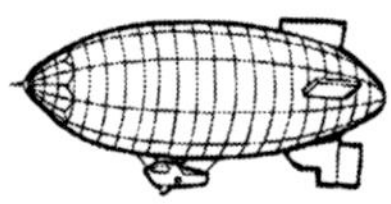

Men in Black, Phantom Airships and UFOs

by *Nigel Watson*

Men in Black (MIB) are thought to be part of a dirty tricks operation to discredit witnesses and to stop people revealing the 'truth' about UFOs and alien operations. Traditionally MIB go around in gangs of three and drive old (yet mint-condition) black Cadillacs or Buicks. They are regarded variously as agents of the Government, agents controlled by aliens, or even as robots or aliens in human disguise.

The alien nature of MIB is emphasised by the fact they seem to act and speak in an odd manner; they know a lot about the witness and what they have seen but have no social skills or awareness. They are described as having a swarthy complexion with slanting eyes giving the overall impression of a 'gypsy' or oriental-like appearance. Classic

MIB wear dark sunglasses, Homburg hats and smart black suits, but on occasion they pretend they are Air Force or government officials. When they visit they show suitable identification, but when this is checked it is found that they are not known by the agency they say they came from.

Men in Black have been associated with UFOs and aliens since the start of the modern-day era of flying saucers, which began with Kenneth Arnold's sighting of strange objects skipping over Mount Rainier on 24 June 1947. Within days of the concept of flying saucers getting worldwide publicity, the Maury Island case took us down the route of conspiracy, sinister plots, MIB, abduction, double bluffs, sabotage, death and assassination. All these elements were to be integrated into mainstream ufology by the 1980s.

Buicks and Crashed Planes at Maury Island

At about 2pm on the afternoon of June 21, 1947, Harold A. Dahl, his teenage son Charles and two (unnamed) crew members were in their boat off Maury Island, Washington, when they observed six large "doughnut-shaped objects" high above them. One of the craft appeared to be malfunctioning, and began ejecting material which fell from the sky. According to Dahl, slag-like material began hitting the boat, damaging parts of it and slightly injuring his son, as well as killing his dog which was on the decks. They beached their boat and took several pictures of the craft. They gave the dog a burial at sea, and upon their return Dahl showed his sceptical boss, Fred Crisman, samples of the slag-like rock as evidence. The photographic evidence did not help though as the pictures were ruined by what looked like exposure to X-rays.

The MIB encounter allegedly took place at 7am the next day when a man, aged about forty-years-old, turned up at Dahl's home asking about buying salvaged timber. The man, who was dressed in black, took Dahl – in a new 1947 model, black, Buick sedan – to breakfast at a smart diner in Tacoma. Here the MIB recounted the full details of Dahl's UFO encounter and went on to warn him to keep quiet; otherwise, something might happen to him or his family. Dahl ignored this advice.

Kenneth Arnold was asked by science fiction magazine publisher Ray Palmer to investigate the case. Arnold invited United Airlines Captain E.H. Smith to accompany him to Maury Island, but on arriving was unimpressed with Dahl's evidence. Nevertheless, Arnold asked Captain William Davidson and Lieutenant Frank M. Brown of the United States Army Air Corps to help him with the case, as they had been the officers who had originally interviewed him about his own flying saucer sighting. After being shown the UFO slag the officers were equally unimpressed, and at 2am on August 1 they departed for their base at Hamilton Field, California. On the way the aircraft caught fire and crashed, killing Davidson and Brown.

Only hours before the crash, a mysterious phone caller told *The Tacoma Times* all about Kenneth Arnold's meeting with the two investigators. After the crash, but before the details of it were made public, the caller told the newspaper the names of the men who were killed and recalled that the B-25 aircraft had been sabotaged or shot down by a 20mm cannon because it was carrying fragments of a flying disc. This seemed to indicate that the caller had bugged Arnold's room, yet after a thorough search, no bug was found.

Was the caller the mysterious MIB who had warned Dahl about dabbling with UFOs? So far, two men and a dog had lost their lives, and Kenneth Arnold was nearly added to the list. When he took off from Tacoma, his engine failed and he had to make a crash landing. On checking his aircraft, he found that his fuel valve had been switched off.

Another strange incident occurred not long after the UFO sighting when Dahl's son went missing. He was out of contact for a week until he was found at Lusk, Montana (some accounts say Colorado). He had no memory of how he got there. Perhaps if he was hypnotically regressed he might have recalled an alien abduction – or was he just being a wayward teenager? Certainly, no one at the time, including Arnold, thought it had anything to do with the UFO sighting.

In her book *MIB: Investigating the Truth Behind the Men In Black Phenomenon*, Jenny Randles was in general favour of the idea that Kenneth Arnold was set-up in some sort of elaborate hoax that got out of hand.

The Federal Bureau of Investigation (FBI) took an interest in this case due to the allegation of sabotage to the B-25 and to discover any details about the recovered debris. On 6 and 7 August 1947, a FBI special agent was dispatched to Tacoma to conduct an investigation. He interviewed a newspaper reporter who was sent by the *Seattle Post Intelligencer* to speak with Howard Dahl about the flying disc story sometime in June 1947. In the kitchen of his home, Howard Dahl had told the reporter about seeing five or six discs, one of which fluttered to the earth and disintegrated, causing the death of his dog. Dahl spoke in a low voice and was acting suspiciously. His wife appeared and angrily declared that the whole story was a plain fantasy concocted by Dahl, and she made him admit it was a hoax. Given the enraged behaviour of the wife, the reporter quickly left and told the *Seattle Post Intelligencer* that Dahl was a 'mental case' and that they should not carry the story.

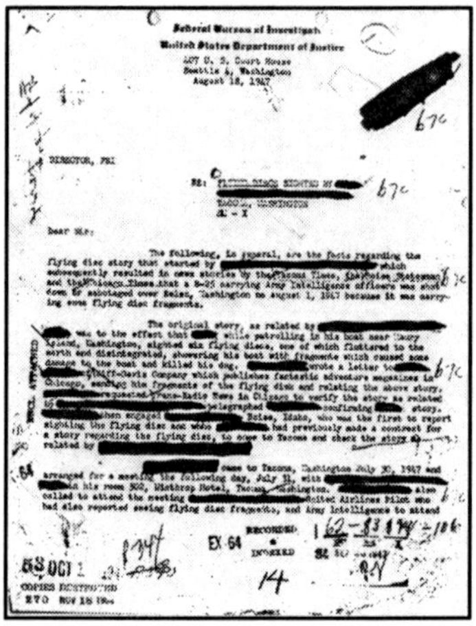
Federal Bureau of Investigation
United States Department of Justice
Seattle 4, Washington
August 18, 1947
DIRECTOR, FBI
Dear Sir:

Maury Island FBI Report

The FBI agent spoke to Crisman and Dahl, who were evasive and at a loss to explain how the rock fragments became connected with the story of flying discs. After much questioning, they admitted that they had sent Ray Palmer some rock fragments that were found in a gravel pit on Maury Island in early June. It was their contention that Palmer asked if the rocks were connected with flying discs and they told him it was a possibility. They had merely told him what he wanted to hear.

The FBI documents show that the B-25 was not sabotaged. It was their opinion that rather than the hotel being bugged, Crisman had probably been the anonymous caller to *The Tacoma Times*. Although they had no solid evidence, they thought he made the calls to make the story more important, thereby increasing his payment from Palmer.

The files make no mention of the MIB story though they do suggest how it might have originated. Captain Smith told the FBI agent that on the morning of August 2, he, Arnold, Dahl and Crisman had met at a coffee shop near the Winthrop hotel. At the meeting was an unknown man who discussed lumber with Dahl and left after breakfast. To me this sounds like a prototype for the more elaborate MIB story. At the coffee shop Dahl was asked about the photographs of the flying discs; he said the negatives were in his car's glove box. When he went to get them there was no sign of them anywhere in his car. It was equally frustrating when they went to his boat to visit Maury Island. Here they found no evidence of it having been showered by hot lava rock; furthermore, it would not start, so the trip was abandoned.

As we can see, the story quickly became complex and convoluted and over the years has gained more erroneous and exotic details. Dahl and Crisman are often claimed to be part of the local Coast Guard harbor patrol, when in reality Dahl used his boat to collect unmarked logs to re-sell, and to carry out security patrols for owners of beach cottages. The FBI files noted that Crisman went to work with Dahl as a pilot for his private plane. When investigating Crisman for a job application, the FBI found that he was generally of good character. His faults were that he had a poor credit rating and lacked good judgment. It also mentioned that Dahl was rumored to have dabbled in the black market during World War II and that he stole the idea of running the boat from Crisman. Since it was Crisman who tipped off the press and told Palmer about this case, we can wonder if he did it to set up Dahl as a form of revenge.

UFOs and Disinformation

It seems likely then that the Maury Island case was a hoax, rather than aliens or a cover-up. That is not to say though that governments and intelligence agencies are not above employing disinformation when it comes to certain reports of flying objects. For example, from November 1944 to April 1945 the Japanese launched approximately 9000 bomb-laden balloons at the United States. U.S. intelligence listed six reasons for this campaign:

1. Bacteriological or chemical warfare, or both.
2. Transportation of incendiary and antipersonnel bombs.
3. Experiments for unknown purposes.
4. Psychological efforts to inspire terror and diversion of forces.
5. Transportation of agents.
6. Anti-aircraft devices.

Fortunately only a fraction of these high-altitude balloons actually reached the United States; they caused little damage and just a handful of fatalities.

However, what is interesting is that the U.S. government kept the balloon flights secret, because they did not want the Japanese to get any feedback about the success rate of this operation. It was only when one of the balloons exploded after being found by a group of picnickers that the government felt it needed to tell the public about them. The cover-up of the recovery of these balloons, and suppression of related witness statements about weird things in the sky, quickly established in the minds of the public that the government would do the same things with flying saucer wreckage and sightings.

If we go further back in time, rumored activities of German secret agents were very much linked in the public mind with the British phantom airship sightings of 1909 and 1913. This kind of link, and other stories recorded during these periods, appear to be very similar to some of the more bizarre aspects of the contemporary UFO scene. The ambiguity and bizarre nature of some of the airship sightings, the fear of 'alien' invasion, the existence of foreign spies and mad inventors, allied with secret government investigations, parallels the modern day UFO phenomenon closely, in which we find witnesses with strange encounters, the fear of alien (extraterrestrial) invasion, men in black, and secret government involvement.

Alien Airships and Hovering Strangers

The British airship wave of 1909 started getting press attention on May 15 and fizzled out in early June. The same can be said of the accompanying spy scare. One particular scenario which reveals a combination of airship and spy elements was played out in Clacton-on-Sea, Essex, when Mr Egerton S. Free, in the early part of May, saw an airship hovering near his home. He said:

> ...I looked up, and in the sky I saw a long, torpedo-shaped balloon, high up in the air overhead. It was a clear, fairly light night, and I could see everything most distinctly. The airship was travelling swiftly in the direction of Frinton and showing two bright lights. I stood and watched it for some time until it disappeared.[1]

The next day an india-rubber bag, which was presumed to have been dropped from the airship was found. Mr Free said:

> When I got to the cliff-edge at the top of the steps I saw a most curious shape sticking up in the sandy grass. It looked like a large,

> slightly flattened football, with a steel bar pushed right through it. I picked it up – it was not very heavy – and brought it into the house. The contrivance is about five feet long from end to end. The central bar is of hollow steel, with an end round and flat like the buffer of a railway engine. The ball part is about three feet long, oval-shaped, made of hard grey rubber, and corded net-fashion with twine, while the words "Muller Fabrik Bremen" are painted on the ball in black letters. The steel ends project about a foot on either side of the ball, and when I found it the sharp end was sticking in the grass and the ball was on its side.[2]

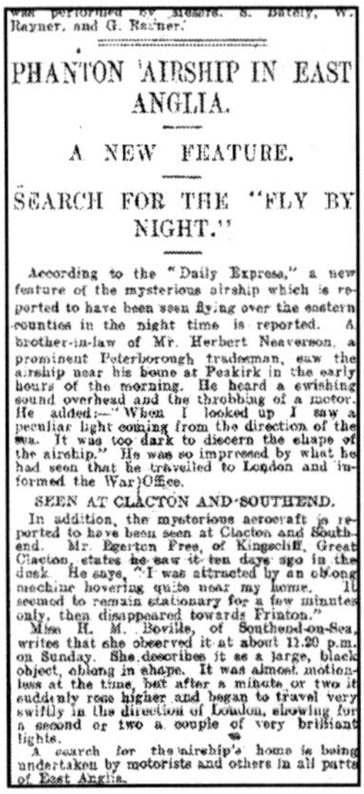

was performed by Messrs. S. Bately, W. Raymer, and G. Rayner.

PHANTON AIRSHIP IN EAST ANGLIA.

A NEW FEATURE.

SEARCH FOR THE "FLY BY NIGHT."

According to the "Daily Express," a new feature of the mysterious airship which is reported to have been seen flying over the eastern counties in the night time is reported. A brother-in-law of Mr. Herbert Neaverson, a prominent Peterborough tradesman, saw the airship near his home at Peakirk in the early hours of the morning. He heard a ewishing sound overhead and the throbbing of a motor. He added:—"When I looked up I saw a peculiar light coming from the direction of the sea. It was too dark to discern the shape of the airship." He was so impressed by what he had seen that he travelled to London and informed the War Office.

SEEN AT CLACTON AND SOUTHEND.

In addition, the mysterious aerocraft is reported to have been seen at Clacton and Southend. Mr. Egerton Free, of Kingscliff, Great Clacton, states he saw it ten days ago in the dusk. He says, "I was attracted by an oblong machine hovering quite near my home. It seemed to remain stationary for a few minutes only, then disappeared towards Frinton."

Miss H. M. Boville, of Southend-on-Sea, writes that she observed it at about 11.20 p.m. on Sunday. She describes it as a large, black object, oblong in shape. It was almost motionless at the time, but after a minute or two it suddenly rose higher and began to travel very swiftly in the direction of London, showing for a second or two a couple of very brilliant lights.

A search for the airship's home is being undertaken by motorists and others in all parts of East Anglia.

The Navy took the bag away for examination; a few weeks later they identified it as a 'reindeer buoy' that is used as a gunnery practice target.

On May 16, the day after Mr Free's sighting became publicly known, two strangers investigated the vicinity of his home. They looked at the area where he had seen the airship, and, according to Mr Free:

> The men hovered about my house persistently for five hours, that is until 7 o'clock in the evening. When the servant girl set out for church she heard them conversing in a foreign tongue. Finally they came up to her, one on each side, and one of the men spoke to her in a strange language. The girl … was so frightened that she ran back to my house, and would not again leave for church.[3]

UFO researcher David Clarke noted that:

> The clear implication was that the 'foreigners' were German agents who had been dispatched to recover the 'buffer' dropped by the

> Zeppelin and so remove evidence of its spying mission. Cold water was later poured on these claims by a reporter from the *East Essex Advertiser*, a Clacton paper, who noted how a respected local amateur photographer had innocently gone to the house to take a picture of the object on the beach. It added: "The next day it was reported that a foreign looking gentleman with a camera had asked permission to take a photograph of the 'find'."[4]

Paranoia about possible German military and spying operations was certainly in the air at the time. On May 19, 1909, Sir J. E. Barlow asked in the House of Commons if the Secretary for War knew anything about the 66,000 trained German soldiers in England, or about the 50,300 stands of Mauser rifles and 7,500,000 Mauser cartridges stored in a cellar within a quarter mile of Charing Cross. Mr Haldane dismissed the story as ludicrous, saying that lowered the nation's reputation for common-sense abroad.[5] Mr Haldane might not have wanted to say anything, but the *Daily Telegraph* did reveal that these arms were probably the 500,000 arms stored by the Society of Miniature Rifle Clubs, in a sub-basement of Lloyds Bank in the Strand.[6] Another story said that in the garrison town of Colchester the police had been receiving many reports of foreigners who were seen to be noting the whereabouts of crossroads and buildings throughout the neighbourhood. The police themselves noted several incidents of a similar nature.[7]

For some peculiar reason, Grimsby. Lincolnshire, was greatly affected by a bout of spy scares. Perhaps this was a compensation for the lack of airship activity in this locality during 1909. However it could not be disputed that Grimsby was located at a vulnerable point of the East Coast. If the Germans wanted to invade England, the town of Grimsby would offer them strategic command of the Humber estuary. This factor no doubt hovered like an airship at the back of the minds of its citizens, as the thought of war loomed on the horizon.

The first citizen of Grimsby to become anxious about a possible invasion was the town's Member of Parliament, Sir George Doughty. On May 12, 1909, he asked Mr McKenna, the First Lord of the Admiralty, in the House of Commons, if he knew anything about the story that the German Army had suddenly commandeered two steamers at Hamburg, loaded them with soldiers before crossing the North Sea, then steamed up the Humber with them before returning to Hamburg. Mr McKenna replied that he had no information about this war exercise, and that he would be pleased to have any further information about the episode.[8]

The next day a rumor circulated in Grimsby which claimed that two foreign spies had been caught trying to steal Admiralty codebooks from the nearly completed Admiralty wireless telegraphic station in Humberstone Avenue. Official sources said that some men had been cleared out of the station by guard dogs. Another variation on the story was that a few weeks earlier, a servant was attacked by two men who were thought to be tramps. The wildest report alleged that a servant girl had been captured by two mysterious men, who had been waiting for her in the station's operations room.[9]

These stories were put into perspective on May 19, when, in the House of Commons, Captain Faber asked the First Lord of the Admiralty if he was aware of the alleged attack on the Humberstone station. Mr McKenna replied:

> The Cleethorpes wireless telegraphic station, which is situated at Waltham, near Grimsby, was broken into by two men on the night of Sunday, March 28th. The two men are thought to have been employees of the contractor who had built the station. The station was not in working order at the time, and has only just been completed. The arrangements since made for guarding the station are considered satisfactory.[10]

No sooner had that scare been scuttled than a new one emerged. This started when three Germans visited a nautical instrument maker on Grimsby docks. One of them left a camera to be repaired, and supplied the foreman with a calling card indicating that he was a professor. Later a titled gentleman, who had been in the diplomatic service, learned of the Germans' visit, and when they returned for their camera he spied on them. He recognised them as being diplomats who had responsible positions in German Government departments. Having confirmed his suspicions he informed the police of the matter. The police shadowed them, and had to prohibit them from taking photographs of Grimsby docks. Later they disappeared, though it was found they had been to see a new deep-water dock at Immingham, where they were turned away by contractors who were still working on it. This made their activities doubly suspicious, as the navy had considered using the dock for their shipping, including vessels of the Dreadnought class.[11]

Later these Germans "diplomats" were actually identified as businessmen who had been on a commercial visit to prospect for trawlers. It was said that they had stopped at the Royal Hotel, and like any other class of respectable citizens had "actually paid their bill!".[12]

Another story told how workmen at Killingholm, near Immingham, had encountered motorists who wanted to know if there had been any local airship sightings, and whether the Humber between Immingham and Spurn had been mined. But as a newspaper columnist reported: "this story, however, ends rather tamely with the intimation that the motorists finished by enquiring the way to the nearest refreshment house".[13]

During the 1913 airship wave which struck Britain in January and February, newspapers again emphasised the vulnerability of the English East Coast. One report noted a rumor that a small

German cruiser had sailed up the Humber undetected under cover of darkness.[14]

Due to the greater range and durability of the German Zeppelins, and the acceptance of the German threat, the 1913 airship sightings were given more far more importance than the 1909 sightings. Indeed, the War Office took an interest in the many airship sightings in Yorkshire. On February 25 it was alleged that Mr Grahame White, a well known aviator, visited the Prime Minister in Downing Street. Mr Asquith had unexpectedly returned from Berkshire to attend the meeting. As a consequence of their conversation, Mr White left "indefinitely" for the north, though nothing was known of his mission. The obvious conclusion to make is that he was sent to investigate the airship sightings.[15]

The observation of an airship by Capt. Lundie and his Second Officer of the Grand Central Mail Steamer 'City of Leeds', who saw it over Spurn Point on February 22, created a lot of press publicity in early March when they reported their experience. Their sighting aroused such interest that on March 3 the Admiralty sent an official to Grimsby, who had a long interview with the two men.[16]

With these early 20th century cases there is a mixture of speculation, rumor, fantasy and real encounters with MIB-type figures. However, in our modern-day era, British UFO expert Jenny Randles also finds "the evidence persuasive" that there is "a real phenomenon in which human beings with apparent high levels of understanding about specific UFO events choose to visit certain witnesses." In the U.S. the myth of the MIB could have been deliberately started by the Government to hide their own secret projects, and/or to discover more about the UFO situation on an unofficial basis. Similarly, in 1909 and 1913 official investigators and strangers who took an interest in phantom airship sightings were also mistaken for foreign spies that we would call MIB today.

Nightmares on the Edge of Reason

So far we have regarded MIB as basically flesh and blood operatives, but the waters are muddied by Albert K. Bender's classic MIB encounters. In 1952 he set up the International Flying Saucer Bureau (IFSB) in Bridgeport, Connecticut, and it quickly gained branches throughout the United States and the world. However, Bender came unstuck in September 1953 when he wrote to a friend to say he had found the 'true' answer to the riddle of the flying saucer phenomenon. Not long afterwards he was shocked when three MIB came to his home brandishing the letter. They confirmed that his ideas about the flying saucers were correct and that if the public knew the truth there would be mass hysteria and a breakdown of civilization as we know it. He was told to close down his organization, or else; the experience was so frightening that he promptly did what he was told.

In 1962, when he felt he was safe enough from the menace of the MIB, Bender wrote *Flying Saucers and the Three Men*. This revealed that the three MIB were tall, dark-skinned and slant eyed, who turned into serpent-like creatures during his encounter. Later on they also took him on an astral journey to an underground base in Antarctica. Regarding this trip he wrote: "How much time this floating consumed I do not know, but it seemed like days."

At the underground base he saw beautiful female aliens and extraterrestrials in the form of men. The purpose of the base was to extract chemicals from seawater to send back to their home planet. They told him that they could detonate all of our atomic weapons if we attacked them. Bender's account is confused and full of the kind of gibberish found in the worst contactee stories.

His MIB are more like ghosts, and his experiences following their appearance are nightmares on the edge of reason. Some think he told these wild tales to finally put-off, or at least appease, the demands of the UFO enthusiasts who kept asking him about the MIB. Others think it proves the MIB are not human secret agents but supernatural, or as Keel called them ultraterrestrial beings who have plagued humanity since time began.

From this viewpoint MIB are the modern-day manifestation of the Devil. The MIB can be literally regarded as the manifestation of evil, and their association with aliens and UFOs proves they should be avoided at all costs. On the other hand, the MIB could symbolically represent our fears and fantasies that are fuelled by watching too many science fiction and gangster B-movies. Peter Rogerson eloquently puts the case for this viewpoint like this:

> One of the most important, powerful symbolic figures in the new ufology is the Man in Black. The wealth of possible interpretations is great. The popular descriptions of the MIB are, self-evidently, a projection of all the images of the comic-book villain; spy, foreigner, gangster, anarchist, devil. He is the universal scapegoat on to which men project their undesirable qualities. Such projections in the past, on to various minority groups, have led to the great tragedies of human history, the attempts to exorcise the Man in Black merely confirming his existence. In the European witch tradition the devil is portrayed as the man in black. Black is the colour of the night, death and the hidden side of things… the MIB is an aspect of ourselves, not an external 'thing'…

It is not inconceivable that the CIA or other organisations have played up the 'mystical' and ghostly aspects of MIB encounters to make the reporters of them look stupid, paranoid or downright insane.

The mix has been confused by people who pretend to be MIB or who have been unwittingly mistaken for MIB. As we saw in Britain during 1909 many sightings of tramps or strangers generated fears of German spying activities in combination with sightings of UFO-like objects in the sky. The situation doesn't seem dissimilar to modern-day reports.

We can conclude that MIB have operated in combination with the phantom airship scares and UFO waves since at least the 19th

century onwards. But what the MIB actually are is down to your own view, as to whether they are the product of dark forces or a trick of human imagination.

Nigel Watson is the author of *The Alien Deception* (2009), *Portraits of Alien Encounters* (1990), *Supernatural Spielberg* (with Darren Slade, 1992) and editor/writer of *The Scareship Mystery* (2000). He has written for numerous publications, including *Paranormal Magazine, Fortean Times, Beyond, Wired, History Today, Flipside, Strange Magazine, Magonia, The Unexplained, Flying Saucer Review, Alien Worlds,* and *UFO Magazine.* He produces the media website Talking Pictures (www.talkingpix.co.uk). He has a BA degree in Psychology (Open University) and a BA (Hons) degree in Film and Literature (University of Warwick). He lives in Plymouth, UK, with his wife and three children.

Credit: Chosovi (License: CCSA

Discovered a tomb, rain in the evening...

Observations regarding the mystery of Rennes-le-Chateau

by *Blair MacKenzie Blake*

On a list of the world's greatest unsolved mysteries, Rennes-le-Chateau and the legendary treasure of Berenger Sauniere certainly ranks near the top. To some it is the grandest puzzle of all, and with the phenomenal success of *The Da Vinci Code*, the tiny Pyrenean village that is the setting of fabled riches and an enduring riddle has become the focal point of an international conspiracy. To many captivated by the mystery, the place is believed to harbor an explosive secret. Whispered through the ages and encoded for posterity by its shadowy guardians, if provable, these revelations could shake the very foundations of Christianity. Still, others claim the secret involves the discovery of a material treasure, rather than something of a purely spiritual nature. If not long-hidden gold, then an object of considerable consequence and importance to someone, although what exactly this might be continues to be the subject of intense speculation.

However, with all of the attention that the controversial novel has brought to what was once a local curiosity, many of the most intriguing details of the story have come under closer scrutiny. Using only the "verifiable facts", as opposed to the more colorful elements of the tale, a new wave of researchers have attempted to demystify the entire Rennes affair. To these historical detectives there is no mystery to unravel. No cryptic parchments to decipher. No accursed treasure to unearth, and above all, no centuries-old conspiracy of staggering proportions. The whole thing is nothing more than an elaborate hoax concocted by a few shady individuals. For the deception, the perpetrators hijacked a minor scandal that had been embellished by carefully placed rumors of a fabulous treasure in hope of stimulating tourism. Whether a deliberate fabrication for political aspirations, a unique art form, or a practical joke that got way out of hand, the elusive secret society pulling the strings was a modern invention. Even the inexplicable wealth of the priest at the heart of the mystery was easily explainable once subjected to a thorough investigation. Any remaining peculiarities are merely the fevered imaginings of fortune hunters, or wishful thinking of would-be 'solvers' of historical enigmas. Though now on tourist maps around the world, Rennes-le-Chateau, it would seem, is but France's version of Roswell, Bigfoot, or the Loch Ness Monster.

But what if both camps were looking without seeing? The skeptics with their rants about modern forgeries, and those who are absolutely convinced that the *dramatis personae* involved were (are?) the custodians of a powerful secret. Suppose that there really are enigmatic hints of something that dramatically changed the course of one man's life – layer upon layer of clues that have never been properly understood except by a wonderfully privileged few?

Suppose further that the solution turned out to be so incredibly bizarre – so seemingly contrary to all of the other various possible explanations that have been put forth over the years, so as to elude the most scrupulous examination by the most persistent investigators. And yet, as far-fetched and improbable that the solution might seem, what if, as the final missing piece of an age-old puzzle, it fit perfectly... accounting for all of the unusual activities of the key players involved? This would include all the cryptic messages, recondite symbolism, archaeological and topographical oddities, mysterious deaths and historical antecedents. Before proposing such a solution, or at least sharing certain observations that have gone unnoticed despite the torrent of ink devoted to the subject by countless 'players of the game', for those who are unfamiliar with the mystery, it is necessary to give a brief account of the strange sequence of events that have sparked the imaginations of its ever-expanding audience. Although some of the details are admittedly sketchy, and accounts vary depending on who's relating the story, from the best available evidence (eye-witness testimony and surviving records), there are certain key elements of the drama that most researchers can agree on.

Essential Elements of an Enduring Enigma

In June of 1885, at the age of 33, Berenger Sauniere (1852-1917) was assigned to the remote and impoverished parish of the small hilltop village of Rennes-le-Chateau in the south of France. Although at the time of his appointment the neglected hamlet of some two hundred inhabitants seemed of little significance (in common with other half-abandoned rural communities in the area), as we shall soon see, this was not always the case. At any rate, upon his arrival, the energetic new priest found the 11th century church to be in a hopeless state of disrepair, with a leaking roof, broken windows, and crumpling masonry. Borrowing money from the village funds and receiving small donations from anyone who would contribute, he eagerly set about making some essential repairs. It was during the course of this modest restoration that he is thought to have discovered something of major significance. Exactly what this was is difficult to say, but it is widely believed that the priest's initial find consisted of several rolled-up parchments inserted into sealed wooden tubes that were hidden in a cavity inside one of the ancient columns that supported the altar-stone. Having confided his discovery to a local bishop, some contend that Sauniere was dispatched to Paris, where he was instructed to meet with scholars at the Seminary of St. Sulpice who might be able to translate or decipher them. However, it is also possible that, after realizing the importance of the documents, he eventually made contact with certain individuals that were experts in cryptology and/or knowledgeable in things of a far more esoteric nature.

At some point after returning to Rennes-le-Chateau, a further donation – this time from a wealthy benefactress – enabled the village priest to begin more ambitious renovations to the dilapidated church. Whether or not the coded parchments led him to his next discovery is unclear, but having enlisted the help of some youths to exhume a carved flagstone that had been placed face down near the altar, they reportedly uncovered a tomb. Discerning some shiny objects in the feeble glow of a lantern, he quickly had the ancient slab placed back over the hole in the floor, explaining the items as worthless artifacts before dismissing his inquisitive helpers.

While engaged in subsequent excavations that were mostly undertaken at night (when safe from watching eyes), it is believed that the priest eventually gained access to a larger mortuary chamber under the false tomb that had been arranged to conceal its entrance. Though it's uncertain whom or what might have been interred in this crypt, after the secret diggings inside the church, an even stranger series of events began to unfold. During nocturnal excavations in the church graveyard, using a stonemason's tool, Sauniere obliterated the cryptic epitaph and strange markings on the headstone of the last noble woman of Rennes, Marie de Nègre d'Ables. If this and other desecrations raised a few eyebrows from the villagers, few complained. They must have been curious, however, when he took long secretive walks through the local countryside during the day, often returning with a basket filled with something that he was careful to remove only in the privacy of a secret room accessible by a 'false wall' in the sacristy.

Again, while the motive behind these unusual, nay sacrilegious, activities is not known, the general consensus of most Rennes aficionados is that it was in 1891 that Sauniere made his fateful discovery. In his personal notes, an entry from September 21, 1891 mentions, rather cryptically: "Letter from Granes. Discovered a tomb. Rain in the evening." Later we will take a closer examination of these seemingly mundane details, but from that point on, the priest's fortunes changed spectacularly.

While relegated to an inferior backwater post, for years he had been forced to survive on his meager stipend and the gratuities of his parishioners. Now, suddenly, he was living in the lap of luxury. He built a lavish villa where he entertained growing numbers of distinguished guests with sumptuous banquets. Spending money on a grand scale, the Abbe's *domaine* would soon boast an orangery, ornamental garden, and, most audacious of all, a mock-Gothic tower that offered a postcard view of the green valley floor below. While indulging himself with the finer things in life, he was also generous to the municipality, helping to provide running water as well as funding a modern road. Along with these commendable public works, he also continued with the refurbishment of the centuries-old church, sparing no expense to redecorate it…in a most bizarre manner.

Whether for his own amusement or, perhaps, to immortalize his secret, at the insistence of the obstinate priest (or *someone*), the interior of the tiny church was crammed with a bewildering mass of garish, near blasphemous, religious imagery. A frightening plaster demon greeted visitors in the doorway, but its hideous appearance was just one of the many furnishings devised in a mischievous and eccentric manner. Among the gaudy coloration and gilded flourishes of plaster saints, the walls were hung with religious bas-reliefs imbued with an aura of sinister glory. Above the confessional, a brightly painted tableau was altered to include several puzzling details – the priest's way of confessing, perhaps, the source of his unexplained prosperity. Other decorative features included stained-glass windows with arcane symbolism and optical anomalies that continue to mystify those who endeavor to interpret them.

As was to be expected, the priest's extravagant lifestyle didn't escape the notice of certain ecclesiastical superiors. Neither did the spectacle of darkly ostentatious religious adornments, the vandalism of gravestones, and the constant stream of illustrious visitors to his grand estate. When called upon to account for his astonishing expenditure, Sauniere remained defiant, brazenly refusing to divulge any details to the bishopric. In attempts to defend his good name, he sent letters stating how he had improved the church from its deplorable state, and on a grandiose scale. Regardless, the authorities that accused him of illicitly selling masses and pardons took disciplinary action. Although suspended of his priestly duties, Sauniere chose to remain at Rennes-le-Chateau where his loyal parishioners continued to attend masses at his opulent villa, rather than celebrating them with his replacement.

In the troublesome years that followed the official inquiry, Sauniere had further projects in mind, using the capital at his disposal, perhaps, to pass on more information about his 'lucky' find. Then, on January 17, 1907, at the age of 65, he suffered a major stroke. Besides the suspicious date (January 17 being a recurrent date in the Rennes affair), a few days earlier he had ordered his own coffin – this despite appearing to be in enviable health. While on his deathbed, a priest from the neighboring parish was summoned to hear his final confessions and to administer the last rites. Whatever Sauniere had whispered to his old friend in his final hours, witnesses claim that he emerged from the sickroom visibly shaken, having refused to grant absolution. The following morning, Sauniere's dead body was placed in an armchair on the sunny terrace near his crenellated tower. In a bizarre ceremony, the significance of which has never been fully explained, as mourners solemnly passed by to pay their final respects, each paused to pluck a scarlet tassel from his priestly garment.

While we have no way of knowing what had profoundly shocked Sauniere's colleague, there is one person who it appears he had entrusted with his secret. This was a young woman from the local peasantry who became the priest's housekeeper and lifelong companion. Her name was Marie Denarnaud, and in the years that followed her master's death, she told a friend that she would one day reveal "a secret that would make one rich and powerful." On other occasions she was heard to say that "the people who live here are walking on gold without knowing it," and "with what the Monsieur le Cure has left, one could feed all of Rennes for a hundred years and there would still be some left." When asked why she didn't attempt to exploit this, herself, she replied that she "could not touch it."

If trafficking in masses fails to explain the totality of Sauniere's sudden wealth, then what was it that transformed the destiny of a humble country priest living in abject poverty to spending on the magnitude that account receipts and more tangible remains attest to? From the comments of his maid, are we to gather that he had chanced upon the tombs of ancient royalty and systematically plundered them of their precious heirlooms? Was the temptation simply too great – walking about penniless, knowing that beneath his feet lay the bejeweled dead? Might this be why he filled the interior of the church with cryptic allusions to hidden treasure? Was all the bedazzling and teasing with jeweled colors merely a masterful attempt to cover his tracks?

For those who would like to believe that the secret of the priest's 'overnight riches' involved something more palatable than being a sordid grave robber, in a region that is filled with historical traces of lost treasure, there are many possibilities yet to consider.

Visigoths, Merovingians, Cathars and Templars

Undoubtedly, one of the most fascinating aspects of the mystery is the exceptionally rich and turbulent past of its setting. When it comes to evocative legends of ancient treasure, the Languedoc province of southern France has few rivals. Its rugged beauty is also the site of one of the blackest marks in history. Though a remote backwater during Sauniere's tenure, the sleepy hamlet was once a bastion of the Visigoths – those nomadic hordes of pillaging barbarians who accumulated many spoils, including, possibly, the magnificent Treasure of the Temple of Jerusalem. The vast wilderness of the Languedoc was also the dramatic, blood-soaked stage of the Albigensian campaign. Here, in the early 13th century the Church of Rome attempted to eliminate the unorthodox doctrines of the mystically oriented Cathars with fanatical persecution. Hence the persistent tradition of a repository of esoteric writings and unlimited wealth concealed in mysterious grottoes near their mountaintop stronghold. The same craggy gorges and wooded slopes also echo

Walled city of Carcasonne, in the Languedoc (Credit: Bmsgator; CCSA)

with tales of the sacred relics of the Merovingian kings (including the Holy Grail itself!), and the missing treasure of the outlawed medieval Knights Templar. Visigoths, Merovingians, Cathars, Templars and, so as to leave no stone unturned, even the former seigneurs of Rennes buried in all their glittering finery – all strong contenders for the priest's good turn, and the solution to an enduring enigma.

Sacred Geometry Stretching for Miles

While many drawn to the mystery were searching for answers in the shadowy torch flicker of limestone caverns or in the catacombs of a jeweled bloodline, some investigators were using detailed survey maps in order to pinpoint the location of the treasure of the ages in the Corbieres. To these researchers with their theodolites, aerial mosaics, and official maps, the brooding atmosphere of the Rennes valley held yet another surprise. According to several remarkable theories, the region's unique topography explained why the place has attracted so much attention over the centuries. Amazingly, stretching for miles over the landscape in the vicinity of Rennes-le-Chateau are the massive alignments of a temple-complex formed by both natural* and artificial features that

* There is a natural pentagram of mountain peaks in the region that supposedly accords to the pentagonal geometry concealed in parchments, paintings, etc. that feature prominently in the mystery. With that being said, despite the continuous efforts of someone who would want us to believe that along with Sauniere's discovery of encrypted parchments were ancient genealogies attesting to the survival of a royal bloodline that stemmed from the union of Jesus and Mary Magdalene, even if the demonstrable terrestrial geometry suggested a gigantic effigy, for now, we need not concern ourselves with the actual identity of the person being memorialized.

appear to the map-trained eye with staggering exactitude. Although the symmetrically-spaced landmarks would make the enormous 'temple' the ideal place in which to conceal (or reveal) something of immense value, if the structured layout revealed to be based on human proportions - perhaps the funerary monument of some long dead king (or queen), things could get even more interesting.

Paranoia and Conspiracy from a Spinning Bookstand

But as to the parchments in question, there continues to be a heated debate between those who are convinced that they are outright forgeries, and those who accept them as being genuine. And then there are those who suspect that the bloodline scenario is merely an elaborate smoke screen to divert attention away from something else. The authors of *The Sion Revelation* speculate that this involves a vast global conspiracy being woven by a politico-mystical current – its aim being a form of joint rule known as synarchy. However, while it is quite possible that the parchments are of great importance to a secret elite, the mystical beliefs and motivations of those behind the scenes may, in fact, have nothing to do with the synarchic principles of a political movement.

Those who see a connection between the treasure of Berenger Sauniere and golden-age synarchic plots would do well to remember that before a series of BBC documentaries about the mystery, and the subsequent publication of the international best-seller, *Holy Blood, Holy Grail* (the book that inspired Dan Brown's blockbuster), Rennes-le-Chateau was virtually unknown (even in France). And just how did the man most responsible for RLC's now worldwide fame become entangled in the supposed grand scheme of this nebulous cabal? Well, in author Henry Lincoln's own words: "The most casual and mundane of actions sometimes changes one's life... While looking for some light and entertaining reading [at a pavement bookstand outside a shop in

France], as haphazardly as a roulette wheel, the spinning bookstand [had] presented him with a winner." The "winner" he was referring to was a little known buried treasure mystery entitled *Le Tresor Maudit* ("The Accursed Treasure"). Intrigued by some of the riddles presented in the book, as a writer for television, he eventually managed to convince the BBC into producing a short series of programs on the subject. As to why the treasure in the story was "accursed" – this wasn't evident to Lincoln, though he was aware of the disproportionate number of mysterious deaths associated with it. Nibbling at red herrings and chasing false trails, he admitted that at times while standing near Sauniere's grave, he often "felt the urge to reach down into the earth and shake those mouldering bones back to life." In a place like Rennes-le-Chateau, where nothing is as it appears, in the search for answers, Lincoln's idle 'threat' born out of frustration is, perhaps, more apropos than would appear.

Shepherdess No Tempation

If Lincoln had actually attempted to communicate with Sauniere during a séance or by other occult means, what might the recalcitrant priest have disclosed? Possibly that: while his strangely decorated church is perceived by many to be a treasure map, it's other more important function is quite the opposite (as opposite as black and white, and fire and water), and that a correct interpretation of the clues embedded in the gilded, florid ornaments indicates the precise location of where there once was a treasure that has since been removed. But why would anyone go to all the trouble and expense of creating a *reverse* treasure map? For that matter, why would someone erect a treasure map that enabled others to fill their pockets with what another had discovered? This would seem contrary to human nature, unless the treasure was inexhaustible, such as the fabled touchstone of the alchemists, or the unlimited wealth (*pecunian infinitam*) believed to have been hidden by the Cathars in their decorated grottoes (*spelunca adornato*). But of what significance would it be to someone to know precisely where a treasure had already been found? Could the apparent paradox be explained if this someone was another priest, and the treasure involved had been plundered from a tomb of which it was now unnecessary to violate again? Might this be why Sauniere had years earlier erased the coded epitaph of a woman from an aristocratic family who had been buried in the churchyard?

Let us now examine more closely certain oddities on one of the tombstones of Marie de Nègre D'Ables, Dame de' Hautpoul de Blanchforte – those which Sauniere took great pains to efface. By extracting the numerous errors and anomalies on the grave-slab's seemingly conventional inscription, we end up with the French words *mort epee* ('death sword'), a phrase suggesting cutting something (as well as a curse). However, *mort epee* is also a perfect anagram of *emportee*, which could mean: "She has been carted away." Along with the January 17 'password' (the supposed date of Marie's death in 1781), this could be a signal to others that any valuables buried with the noble woman are no longer there. As for the "Marie" tombs' cryptic message, it would appear that other individuals connected with the region's ancient nobility have been buried twice! Further compounding the mystery of the double tombs is the realization that their inscriptions contain deliberately conflicting erroneous dates. If these baffling epitaphs truly are indicators to others of prior pillaging, is it possible that, rather than the precious grave goods, the corpse, itself, was the true prize? This being the case, the message transmitted by the enigmatic inscriptions might be that the person buried is now untouchable. Which takes us back to those ancient parchments allegedly discovered by the priest. Here I'm not referring to the genealogies that some claim bear witness to a sacred bloodline. Those relating to the Merovingian survival are but a marvelous distraction – having been devised as a precautionary measure to draw our attention away from the documents that could provide the answer to the mystery.

The Strange Will of François-Pierre d'Hautpoul

A document that should be of great interest to us is the 1644 will of one of the seigneurs of Rennes, François-Pierre d' Hautpoul (and/or the testament of Henri d'Hautpoul). The authors of *The Sion Revelation* are on the right track when they state that there is something very unusual about this particular will.

Ever since its discovery by a notary in 1780, until its disappearance from the records prior to the French Revolution (when in the possession of Marie de Nègre after her marriage to François d'Hautpoul in 1732), the will was said to be of "great consequence." Interestingly enough, other papers in the Hautpoul family archives were said to be "dangerous." So much so, in fact, that one member of the aristocratic family deemed it prudent that they first be deciphered in order to determine if certain things (titles, estate and effects) were actually the property of the family. But if these interests weren't the property of the family, then to whom did they belong to? Could something of great importance connected with the Hautpoul archives be the property of a highly secret organization whose name and origins are shrouded in obscurity? If so, is the will highly unusual because of the strange nature of what's being willed?

"... And it is Death"

If we were to look for a common thread running through the Rennes tapestry, it would be decidedly dark. Inside Sauniere's refurbished church the iconography of death greets us at every turn – in paintings, statues and stained-glass. And juxtaposed with the persistent theme of death are oblique hints of a great treasure. Death and treasure. Treasure and death. For those with eyes to see, the encoded symbology ingeniously embedded in standard Christian adornments is that of alchemy, with the *memento mori* of skulls in the altar bas-relief and elsewhere representing the process of the Great Work (the entire praxis from start to finish) known as *Caput Mortuum* ('Dead Head'). It is this *Nigredo* stage – death, decay and putrefaction – that is identified with the *prima materia* (prime material or initial condition) necessary to transmute baser substances into alchemical gold.

Before proceeding into the nave to take a closer look at the eccentric furnishings, we must first cross the (cracked and broken) checkered floor, with the alternating black and white squares reminding us more of the tessellated pavement of a Masonic temple than a Catholic church. Equally as strange as the mosaic tiling is the gaudy plaster demon that welcomes us at the entrance. He has been identified as Asmodeus – custodian of secrets, guardian of hidden treasure, and the builder of Solomon's Temple. However, in this place of mirror opposites, it is not the rebuilding of the temple that is being alluded to, but, rather, its triumphal destruction. The demon's other function is that of supporting the baptismal font, with its four colorful angels whose hand gestures appear to be making the sign of the cross. It might not come as a shock then, that the angels are actually tracing a symbol that is familiar to occultists, and despised by the church – a pentagram. This, it is believed, is another clue to the vast pentagonal temple laid out on the ground in the vicinity of Rennes-le-Chateau.

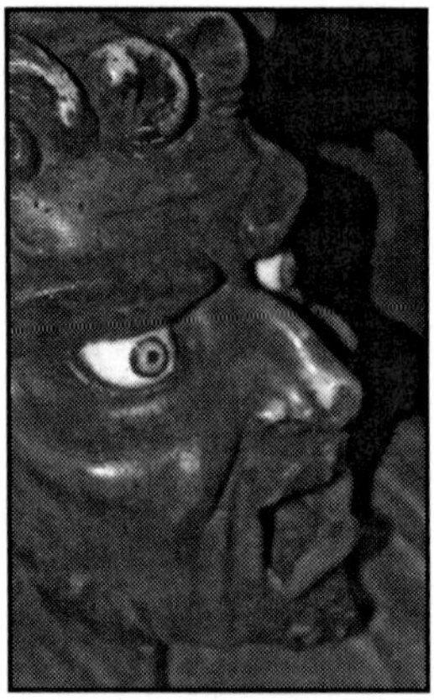

'Asmodeus' (courtesy RlC Research: www.rlcresearch.com)

Moving along in the dizzying confines of the church, we come to the striking mural above the confessional entitled "Terrain Fleury." This depicts Jesus preaching to his disciples on a hill that is reminiscent of a flower-strewn grave. For those looking for treasure, but particularly for those who don't want to despoil a tomb in which a treasure has already been taken, the glint of gold is discernable through a hole in the cloth of a drawstring moneybag.

The name of the tableau is undoubtedly a reference to the lands of the Hautpoul-Fleury dynasty. As touched upon earlier, certain members of these noble families have two tombstones, each containing cryptic epitaphs that would seem to indicate the Masonic affiliations of the deceased (or membership in another fraternal Order whose obligatory banquet was a far more macabre affair).

We can now direct our attention to the Fourteen Stations of the Cross. Erected with typical idiosyncratic flair, perhaps not surprisingly, here the plaques depicting the ordeal of the crucifixion run anti-clockwise. Although there is nothing glaringly obvious about each one, a careful examination reveals certain inconsistencies from the generally accepted scriptural accounts. However, as to these added touches, it is the first and last stations that give away the game. In Station XIV ("Jesus Is Laid In The Tomb"), the dead body of Jesus is being carried from the tomb under the cover of darkness (shades of Sauniere's nocturnal diggings). Station I ("Pilate Washes His Hands") is even more vague and ambiguous. A figure (priest?) is holding a shiny golden object to the forehead (pineal gland/third eye?) of Jesus. Whether or not this is the gold taken from the torn moneybag, the 'X marks the spot' location corresponds with the pentagonal geometry concealed in a famous painting by Nicolas Poussin that is inextricably linked with the mystery. The painting (which shows several figures contemplating the enigmatic inscription on an austere tomb) is framed in such a way that the vertical axis (the focal point, geometrically speaking) of the pentacle radiates from the forehead (again, the third eye?) of the shepherdess depicted in the painting. And while the idea of Pilate washing his hands is considered by most to be symbolic of his innocence of the crucifixion, it might

Station XIV (© Danny Carey)

have another more esoteric meaning. Traditionally, before one sits down to eat, one washes their hands.

But there is more. In a stained-glass window that shows Jesus raising Lazarus from the dead, Lazarus resembles a mummy in an Egyptian-style gold-sheathed sarcophagus. Is Sauniere trying to convey that he was one of the privileged few versed in the veiled practices of a secret resurrection ritual? With the phantasmagoric excess of ornamentation, perhaps our imagination is playing tricks on us. Are we simply conjuring pictures in a fire? Clutching at straws? Is this nonsense defended by nonsense? Perhaps it's time to leave this "theological funhouse." Stepping outside into the glaring sunlight, unable to resist glancing back, we notice the Latin inscription incised on the lintel above the church entrance: *Terribilis Est Locus Iste* ('This place is terrible'). Another inscription above the entranceway informs us: *Domus Mea Orationis Vocabitur* ('My house is called the house of prayer'). The rest of the phrase goes: "...And you have made it into a den of thieves."

The Peculiar Dilemma of a Flamboyant Priest

Sauniere's contacts with the Parisian esoteric sub-culture (in particular his possible involvement with Martinism) has been the subject of speculation by numerous researchers, but with regards to this double life, it is an entry recorded in his diary in the fateful year of 1891 that is perhaps the most telling of all.

The laconic "Letter from Granes. Discovered (or discovery of) a tomb. Rain in the evening." note hints at an unconventional form of Freemasonry that concerns itself with the ancient rite of the Egyptian funeral/coronation and related mysteries. The seemingly trivial mentioning of the "Rain in the evening" right after the news of his all-important discovery was a cryptic way of informing his confederates that the uninitiated might be 'listening', and therefore to look for further messages elsewhere.

"TERRIBILIS EST LOCUS ISTE", on the lintel above the entrance to the church at Rennes-le-Chateau (courtesy RlC Research: www.rlcresearch.com)

Though he was sworn to protect the secret at all costs, besides his housekeeper, Marie, he might have imparted certain things to the priest of the neighboring parish on his deathbed. But what could it have been that had such a traumatic effect on his friend? Did he speak of the Knights Templar with their trepanned skulls in gem-encrusted reliquaries, or of the Cathars' decorated grottoes (i.e. human brain) that contained unlimited wealth in the form of glittering deposits of a precious substance? Did he describe an enormous temple that encodes our occult biology, and confess to plundering the graves of an ancient necropolis in the area – taking not the priceless artifacts of the former lords of Rennes, but their mummified or otherwise preserved heads, which contained the infinitely more valuable "Golden Womb of the Black Virgin?" In what language could he possibly explain to his fellow priest that the alchemical fifth element – the incorruptible quintessence – is actually a residue of human post-mortem biochemistry, and that when extracted and consumed in a necromantic feast, the states of hyper-lucidity experienced are such that all of the luxuries on earth pale by comparison? Was it in the terminology of the scriptures that he described the miraculous visions and beneficent spirits encountered by partaking this mysterious death-born radiance of the grail? Finally,

Magdalene and Skull on RlC Church Altar (© Danny Carey)

was he refused Extreme Unction for divulging that – as a priest in the highest sense – "sinners" had paid him great sums of money to perform the Consolamentum ceremony of the Cathar Perfecti, of which the Jewel of Divine Anthropophagy was the true Eucharist sacrament? Perhaps he just whispered, "Deliver me out of the mire and let me not sink."

Posthumous Eccentricities

Readers will recall the strange ceremony that occurred on the morning following Sauniere's death. As 'parishioners' solemnly passed by to pay their final respects, for reasons unknown, each paused to pluck a scarlet pompom from his cloak. Although the odd souvenir mystified the residents of the tiny village, it was actually another tantalizing clue. The tassels that adorned his priestly garment represented miniature pomegranates – a favorite object for recondite symbolism. The sanctity of the pomegranate is that it was said to be the only fruit that worms don't eat. It is also associated with abundance... and cannibalism. With the recent flurry of interest in the mystery of Berenger Sauniere and Rennes-le-Chateau after the publication of Dan Brown's novel, those who are revolted by the occult significance of this ritual might want to consider Leonardo Da Vinci's other interest: that of dissecting cadavers...

Blair MacKenzie Blake has been studying, practicing, and writing about the western esoteric tradition for over twenty years. More recently, he has been focusing his attention on the neurochemical basis of successful magickal workings (and paranormal activity in general). Incorporating a magical vocabulary and nightside symbolism, his first book, *IJYNX*, a collection of occult prose-poems, attempts to convey the ritually-machined ecstatic states that allow one access to hyper-dimensions of consciousness and encounters with transmundane entities. BMB is also the writer for www.toolband.com and www.dannycarey.org.

Helicopters? In Ancient Egypt?!

EXAMINING THE INFAMOUS 'ABYDOS GLYPHS'

by *Greg McQueen*

The Egyptian city of Abydos is located about 300 miles south of Cairo and just a few miles west of the Nile. The city was an important cult centre for the worship of Osiris and Isis, and is also notable for being the place where the pharaohs of the First Dynasty were given burial. The Temple of Seti I, a ruler of the XIXth dynasty of the New Kingdom, is located in Abydos, constructed circa 1280 BC.

Since the late 1990s, an unusual set of hieroglyphs in this temple has drawn considerable attention. The hieroglyphs in question are situated beyond the forecourt of the temple, in the outer Hippostyle Hall. Sometimes referred to as the "Abydos Helicopter" or "Pharaoh's Helicopter," these hieroglyphs have drawn wildly disparate opinions from reviewers. Some researchers identify the hieroglyphs as proof that this ancient civilization possessed technologically advanced flying machines. More conservative voices argue that there is a simple and mundane explanation for this supposed anomaly.

The Discovery

The discovery (or rediscovery) of these potentially earth-shattering glyphs is in itself a mystery worth exploring in its own right. Richard Hoagland of the Enterprise Mission website has suggested that he should be credited with bringing the glyphs to the attention of the world. Certainly, Hoagland can be appreciated for having directed attention to the find in a 1998 televised broadcast on Fox, as well as through appearances on Art Bell's radio show in early 1999.

However, Ralph Greenberg, in a letter to Jeff Rense, has accused Hoagland of fraud in relation to his claims. Hoagland, in turn, has disputed these accusations of fraud. I will leave the verdict in regard to this claim and counterclaim to those of you who may be inspired to examine these letters in more detail (see the references to this article for web addresses).

Another individual, Richard Motzer, has stated that the real credit for rediscovering the unusual glyphs should be given to Ruth and Harry Hover. Motzer states that the Hovers had taken two photographs, with the second smeared through camera movement resulting in a "ghost-like shadow." Motzer goes on to explain that the Hovers had asked him to remove the flaw using a photographic manipulation program, while using the second picture as a point of reference. Motzer writes:

> Now, the next part is very important. I made several mistakes by removing icons from this photo. It was a judgment call on my part, and the ABYDOS site caught this right away. They thought I had

> created a HOAX but that was certainly not the case...it was just an 'over clean-up' of a legitimate photo.

But many people have pointed out that the anomalous glyphs were receiving coverage on various 'alternative history' websites well before the Fox television special "Opening the Lost Tombs: Live From Egypt", which aired on March 2, 1999. Hoagland himself recognises that pictures of these glyphs may have been receiving cursory attention for some years prior to that, and that these may have also caught the attention of 'alien abduction' experiencer Whitley Strieber, an influential figure in the New Age genre through his best-selling book *Communion*, 'Dreamland' radio show, and popular 'Unknown Country' website. However, given that Hoagland and Debra Gussin were the ones who brought the glyphs so readily to the mainstream public's attention, it is perhaps legitimate that they are allocated some credit.

Another individual appears to have documentary proof though that they noticed the glyphs some seven years before the Fox television special. Bruce Rawles, co-author of *The Geometry Code,* took a Hi-8 video of the hieroglyphs in November 1992. One frame of that video was used to create the individual image shown on the following page. It might well be said that if anyone should receive credit for the 'discovery' of these glyphs, that person may well be Bruce Rawles.

Alternative Theories

Alternative researcher and author Alan Alford grappled with the images and expressed a degree of dissatisfaction with the standard explanations. He noted the helicopter-like shape among the glyphs, yet was quick to refute fanciful ideas such as helicopters flying about in Egypt three thousand years ago. Intelligently, he noted, "if that was so, we would find numerous such representations all over Egypt,

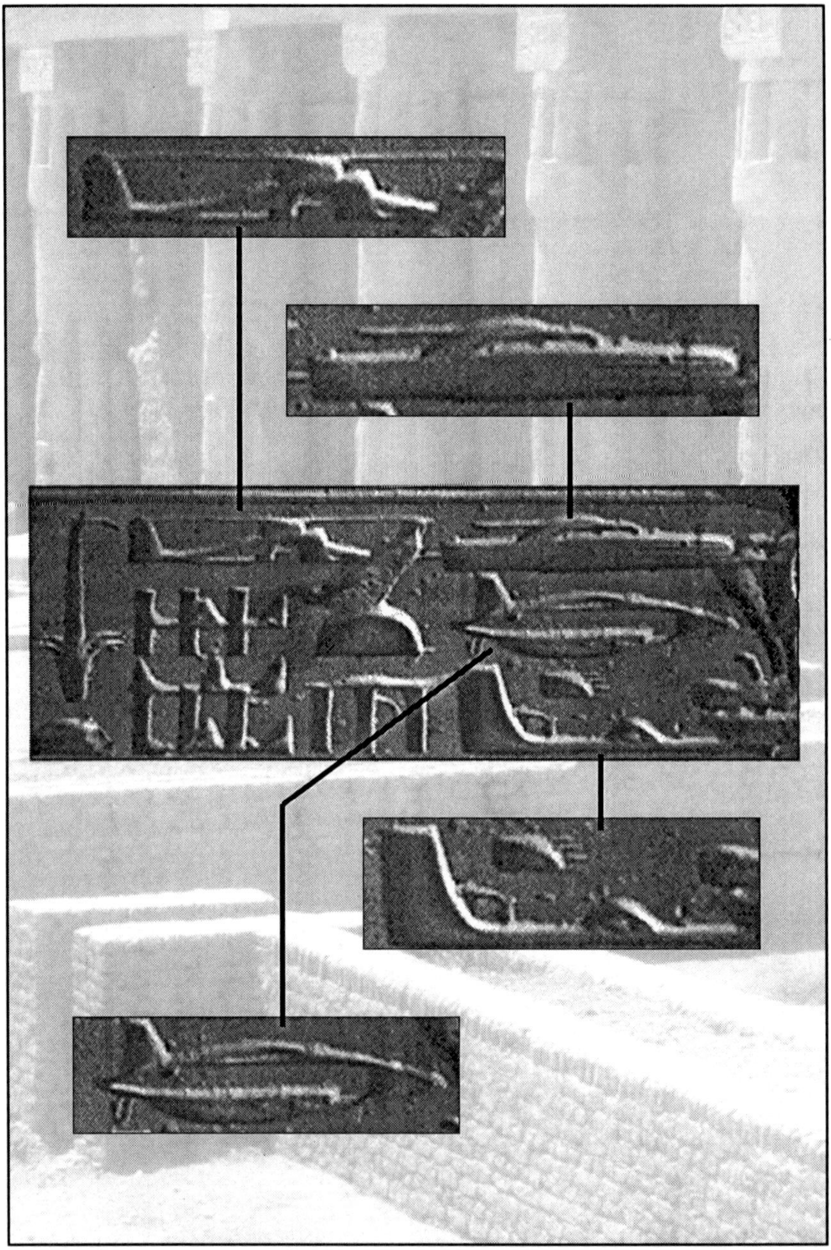

Photo ©Bruce Rawles. Image used with permission of Elysian Publishing (www.geometrycode.com) which provides educational services on Sacred Geometry

because this is a period from which a great deal of Egyptian art and architecture has survived. But there are none."

Alford then contemplates (rather laterally indeed) that the helicopter image may instead be "an archaic image of a real flying machine at the beginning of Egyptian history, which has been copied and recopied countless times." That is to say, while Alford dismisses the idea of a 3000-year-old helicopter, he appears to be comfortable presenting the case for a 5000-year-old pre-dynastic version of the same. Go figure.

Opinions vary as to the precise nature of the depicted craft. New Age writer Jan Wicherink has identified a helicopter, submarine, airplane and unidentified flying object (UFO). David Hugo Boyle ventures further to attest that two of the images are "undoubtedly war machines." Other authors in the genre identify objects as possibly 'vimanas,' described by David Hatcher Childress and Bill Clendenon (in their book *Atlantis and the Power System of the Gods*) as vehicles able to take off vertically and hover over the land. According to these authors, such vehicles are referred to in recently rediscovered Indian texts from the 4th century BC. Additionally, these authors speculate as to whether these texts might also describe potential fuel sources for these vehicles, including 'free energy' sources such as solar or gravity propulsion.

The Palimpsest Theory

The term "palimpsest" refers to the recycling of a writing surface. Throughout much of history, graphic surfaces have not been as freely available as they are today. Historically, when original texts became redundant, they were often erased or scraped away, with new writing then superimposed over the original. Palimpsests generally refer to this process on bases such as wax tablets, animal skins (parchment) or paper. In this instance, the term palimpsest is used to describe stone carvings that have been reinvigorated with a thin layer of mortar or concrete, and then overlaid with new carvings.

Supporters of this theory (in regard to the Abydos hieroglyphs) point to evidence including a thin concrete layer on the surface that appears to have partially broken away from the base. This damage or weathering has left sections where both the original and secondary layers of carved glyphs are partly visible. These dual images then appear to the untrained eye as pictographs resembling – to the modern eye – items such as a submarine, jet aircraft and helicopter.

Archaeologist Brian Haughton has looked at the evidence and drawn on the research of renowned Egyptologist Kathy Griffis-Greenberg, in order to provide tentative translations for the inscriptions. The conclusion is that the original engraving renders the common titular office of Seti I and that the overlay, most likely commissioned by his son Rameses II, translates as "The One of the Two Ladies, who suppresses the nine foreign countries." Political boasting seems to have changed little over the millennia.

There is no doubt that original hieroglyhs on the panel refer to the throne name of Seti I – the long upright glyph on the far left of Bruce Rawles' image is the sedge glyph which stands for *nsw*, the first part of the praenomen of the pharaoh (*nsw bty*, the glyphs for sedge and bee and which translate as 'King of Upper and Lower Egypt'), which usually precedes the cartouche containing the pharaoh's name (and which more recent images of the panel show to be present). You can see the same glyph at the top left of the image shown here. Similarly on the far right of Rawles' image we can just make out what is possibly the cobra element found in the 'Two Ladies'/*nebti* hieroglyph, as illustrated in the image on the following page.

Nebti hieroglyph (credit: www.nebetbastet.net / CC att. share-alike)

A knowledge of Egyptian hieroglyphs also makes it is easy to see how other elements of the panel may have been 'created'. The "submarine" at the top right of the Rawles image certainly looks

like the hand hieroglyph, squashed a little by the perspective and obscured by erosion and/or other glyphs. Indeed, author Dan Richardson draws attention to how the "murky photos" of the superimposed hieroglyphs and eroded panel have spread around the Internet, resulting in the emergence of alternative legends for this particular set of glyphs.

Direct evidence for an 'overlay' of two different sets of hieroglyphs can be found towards the bottom left of the Rawles image. There we see the desert hills hieroglyph overlaid with the vertical strokes used for representing numbers (each stroke corresponds with a single unit).

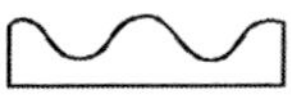

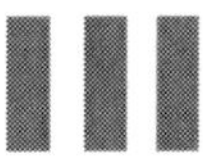

If we pursue this with a few of the common hieroglyphs, it is not difficult to create some of our own futuristic technology. The 'arm' hieroglyph comes in a variety of forms, with different meanings and phonetic sounds. But it does

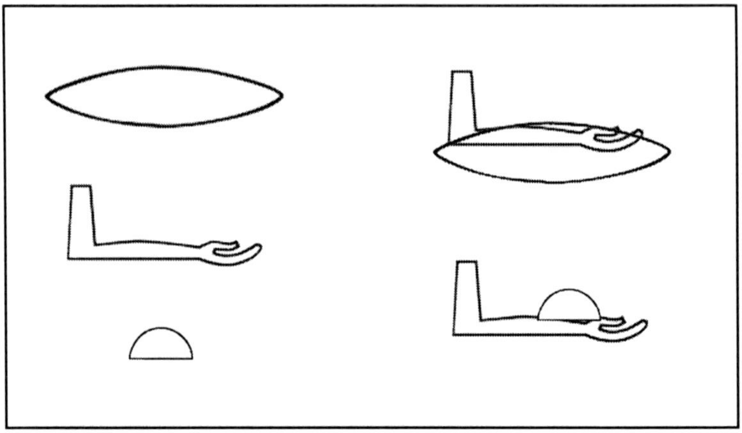

provide a wonderful 'tail fin', similar to that on the jet, the helicopter and the 'UFO' in the Abydos panel. Adding the 'mouth' hieroglyph to the 'arm' gives us a rough approximation of the 'UFO', and adding the glyph for 'bun' to the 'arm' provides a good cockpit for a Roger Ramjet-style jet. While I leave the correct identification and translation of the Abydos hieroglyphs to others, this short exercise should at least make clear the strength of the 'palimsest' explanation.

Eternal Truths?

The palimpsest position is also articulated well by Fortean writers Lionel and Patricia Fanthorpe. They explain that the processes of alteration and overlay may have resulted in "shapes and forms (that) may arise that are neither one character nor another, and which can look remarkably like some exciting anachronism such as a plane or helicopter." However, after laying out this common understanding, the Fanthorpes comment that this conservative view is "not necessarily" the correct one. They have elaborated further on their position, which includes the possibility of early masonic mystery school influences on the drawings contained in these hieroglyphs.

Whether you, the reader, agree with the palimpsest theory, or instead lean toward more novel (and sometimes absurd) theories is somewhat immaterial. For whatever you choose to accept or believe, the mystery of the Pharaoh's helicopter at Abydos may still serve to inspire a passion for study. I hope you will become (or are already) enticed by the allure of history, mystery, archeology, ancient languages or some other field of interest. If you have a passing or dedicated interest in Egyptology, you may like to try your hand at translating the text yourself.

I would like to conclude this essay with a quote from Bruce Rawles, contained in an email exchange with this Author dated June 23, 2009. Mr Rawles, whose photograph seems to have have ignited the controversy of the Pharaoh's helicopter, believes it is largely immaterial as to whether or not the hieroglyphs represent advanced forms of traveling machines. He states:

> In summary, I would say that linear time is something we made up, and that regardless of whether the technology that APPEARS to be shown in the lintel photo of the…temple in Abydos was actually a historical record at the time the temple was built, the fact that all ideas are present throughout time as we (incompletely) understand it suggests the more important idea that we have access to [is] what is eternally true for all of us regardless of our space/ time circumstances!

Greg McQueen is a psychologist from Brisbane, Australia, who is interested in Egyptian hieroglyphs, Fortean mysteries and cults. He has three amazing children, Sarah, Emily and William.

The Goatsucker Family Tree

They are saying that this is the work of a vardoulacha. See how white he is, drained of blood...
– Tom Holland, 'The Vampyre'

by *Neil Arnold*

Long before researchers, cryptozoologists, authorities, hunters and the press were trudging through the rainforests of Puerto Rico looking for the elusive 'vampire' of Moca (an elusive local bogeyman said to prey on livestock), *el Chupacabra* (pronounced Chew-pah-cahb-rha) – which means 'goatsucker' in Spanish – local beliefs and cultures from across the world had already given birth to similar beasts that would form the much-ignored family tree of this vampyric predator.

Many cryptozoologists believe to this day that the monster of Puerto Rico (a self-governing unincorporated territory of the United States, located in the north-eastern Caribbean, east of the Dominican Republic and west of the Virgin Islands[1]) is a flesh and blood creature.

To them, being adorned in back-pack, Indiana Jones-style hat, and camouflage gear, is what is needed to uncover the secret lair of a creature that is – in my opinion – a sum of many facets of cultural belief instead of strange mammal or bird awaiting discovery. To me, the vampire of Puerto Rico's rainforests and dark caverns is nothing more than a projection put there by fear. And I will stand by this even as this creature continues to allegedly leave a trail of exsanguinated carcasses in its wake, and local folk petrified as its scrawny shadow passes by their window. To the hardened cryptozoologist, these creatures *must* be real, because there's no way that they are going to trek through the mountains, backyards and remote woods in search of a mythical animal. But they do.

The goatsucker was due to come along. It's the same cycle that concerns many other beasts of this ilk. Some just happen to stick around longer than others and leave more of a lasting impression, similar in type to Mothman (red-eyed winged humanoid which haunted West Virginia, USA in the 1960s), Monkey Man (hairy, helmeted night prowler of Asian lore which haunted Delhi in India just after the dawn of the millennium) and the Jersey Devil (winged, dragon-like form which has loitered in the Pine Barren region of the United States for several centuries, and resembles some reports of the goatsucker). But it all comes with the territory. Somewhere, many thousands of years ago, there were Mothmen and Devils. There were werewolves, harpies, banshees, omens of death, screaming vampires and zombies. And there has always been a goatsucker. Of course, these things allegedly shape-shift. Well, they don't really, it's just that mankind alters with evolution and these monsters are moulded each time they are spewed into our psyche, so that our society can understand them more. In certain parts of this absurd globe, these monsters have wings. Some are satyrs, or centaurs, whilst others are blood-drinking vampires of many forms, far more horrifying than the cloaked, fanged human spectres portrayed in films. They've always been here. They don't just emerge from spacecraft alleged to hover over the forests of Puerto Rico. They aren't just born into the woods, as many claim the Jersey Devil was, and they aren't created by clandestine government operations or mad scientists. They exist in the mind, all of them, because they are cultural phenomena, despite how much the idea might make any budding or professional cryptozoologist cringe. These beasts roll from the tongue, and not the ramp of some abandoned surreal Ark.

The Coming of the Vampires

Vampire mythology is strong. Myths literally concern every animal on the planet, from dogs, to bulls, to lizards, snakes, wolves, owls, and so on. Some of these myths have transformed into dark and sometimes grisly offspring, whilst other animals just aren't cut out for the sinister side of mythology (rampant chickens and satanic sheep just don't work). Black phantom dogs, giant owls, goat-like demons, humanoid bats…now we're talking. True ethereal scavengers and energy eaters.

In the Ajuela Province of Costa Rica, in March 2004, a male witness had a close encounter one night with a vampire. The man, with his son, woke after hearing a commotion in the henhouse and with a torch went to investigate. As they reached the back yard they disturbed a black animal, resembling a dog, which stood on its hind legs. The critter, stunned by the torch beam, fled the area, leaving behind over twenty dead hens which all bore the same mark, two holes in the back and no sign of blood.[2]

The Devil himself often appears connected to many of the more macabre monsters that litter mythology. If some clandestine creature puts in an appearance, it is often considered the work of the Devil, or perhaps even that Lucifer himself has just walked into the village. The Devil preys upon our fears.

Two thousand years ago in Persia, locals believed in what could well be the original goatsucker. A mysterious creature named the

Mardkhora,[3] or 'man-eater'. This frightening critter was said to have the body of a lion, but was covered in quills like those of the porcupine. It had the head of a man but the tail of a scorpion, only longer. This beast was described by early scientists writing about the world in which they lived; we find it described in Ctesias' *Persica* and in Aristotle's *Natural History*. Unfortunately, like so many creatures from this time, any evidence or 'attacks' were not documented as they are today.

The legend of the fabulous European Manticore[4] stems from the Mardkhora. The Manticore was described as having the face of a man but a lion's body, and having several rows of sharp teeth, however this creature was said to be harmless. Like the Harpies, and the Cockatrice, they aren't in fashion anymore – today's creatures are more slim-lined now, altered to fit into today's nightmares – but in mythology and history these strange monsters are dominant and exist beyond the realms of fantasy films such as *Sinbad* or *Jason & The Argonauts*, although it's in these films they were exposed to audiences.

The legend of the fearsome Mardkhora went into the mountainous regions of Spain with the Muslim invaders around 711 AD. The Muslims, from Arabia and north Africa, brought with them many cultures and beliefs, until 1492 when they were ejected from southern Spain, their mosques converted into churches. But what they left behind was another nightmarish fear, an offspring of the manticore known as the Mantequero. Even at the beginning of the twentieth century, in parts of southern Spain this fearsome entity was believed in as a literal monster. To some it was known as Sacamantecas, a humanoid creature that devoured humans and indulged in their body fat. Before this creature gorged on its victim's fat, it appeared as nothing more than a scrawny, almost pitiful animal said to give off a shrill cry. However, once this creature had fed upon its prey, its body would swell, like that of a mosquito.

Vampirism in the south of Spain could well have been born around the same time as these legendary creatures, when some Spanish peasant populations strongly believed that by drinking blood – said to be scraped from babies which they hung in trees – could make them eternally young. Other peasants stole babies and transfused blood into themselves, becoming known as Mantequeros also, as their acts were actually recorded at the time. The herbal healing curanderos of southern Spain were known for the trafficking of blood in order to cure disease during the early 1900s also, so vampyrism existed in one form or another for many centuries in Spain.

The folklore of the Mardkhora went anywhere that Muslims travelled. In the age before the Prophet, in Persia, there was the religion of Zoroastrianism. After the Muslim conquest this was displaced with some of the Zoroastrians fleeing to Armenia where they became Christians, others fled to the Himalayas to create Tibetan Buddhism, others to India, each of these taking with them the legend of the Mardkhora.[5]

In parts of Persia lives another goatsucker, a real, living, flesh and blood lizard. Its local name is *buz majjeh*, meaning 'goat-sucker', and it is a three-feet long reptile with a flat head and forked tongue, said to creep up on sheep in the dark of night and suck the udders of the ewes. Unlike many goatsucker legends, this one has evidence in natural history. And so does the next 'thing'.

In Puerto Rico we find the Chotacabras.[6] In 1989 such a creature, a bizarre looking bird in fact, was blamed for several attacks on small animals. One of these vampire birds was captured in Gurabo in 1989 by Jose Gonzalez, and another was caught and examined by a Maria Ortiz. These birds had two fangs, a serpent-like head, talons of an eagle and a fearsome appearance...despite being smaller than a hen.

At the time of the coming of the birds, religious leaders, during the UFO wave at the time, called these flying serpents 'the antichrist' – shrieking, flying things that leapt onto raw meat to feed ravenously. It was claimed that the birds were mutants, with one biologist stating that the creatures showed little in the way of avian tissue, but to some extent did have human tissue! Skeptics simply argued that the birds were wrongly identified, or 'man-made' hoaxes – but whatever their origin, they certainly contributed to the Chupacabras scare that was to really hit the media headlines around six years later. However, there had been myths and lore of unusual vampire creatures for several decades previous in the Puerto Rico rainforests, though these critters took on many forms, whether bird-, human- or cat-like...just like the Mardkhora.

Ethiopia, just before the Italian invasion during World War II, had its own wave of 'death birds',[7] said to live among the high rocky pinnacles and foliage near the area of Devil's Cave. These birds, originally dismissed by scientists, were proven to feed off human blood by way of puncturing the skin. At the time the only recognised species of 'vampire' was the New World vampire bat. According to sources, there isn't one single species of sanguinivorous bat on record from the Old World. Is this flapping oddity similar to the Chotacabras? Is the Chotacabras the Chupacabras? Or are these vampires part of some seemingly more widespread and complex puzzle?

The Wave of Weirdness Begins

A lot of UFO activity over Puerto Rico during the early 1990s, particularly the mountainous region known as the Adjuntas, has been attributed to strange covert government operations. At Laguna Cartegena, there were numerous sightings of strange aerial craft disappearing into a secret tunnel beneath a lake, several cases of alien abduction and also the bizarre mutilation of deer at Mayaguez Zoo. When researchers study the goatsucker reports from the mid-90s, and look back at the previous decade, they tend to connect such bouts of high strangeness to the coming of the Chupacabra, but there's no real evidence to tie these phenomena together.

In the Spring of 1995, Reynaldo Ortega from Naranjito saw a huge, dark-coloured bird on the roof of his property whilst he was searching for his missing goat in his yard. The flapping intruder stood more than four-feet in height, had the black plumage of an eagle, a thick neck and big, glaring eyes. The most unusual aspect of this 'bird' though was that it had a muzzle…not a beak! Around the same time a flock of sheep had been found slaughtered in the region of Orocovis and a police officer claimed to have seen a vaguely humanoid creature of orange colouration. A man named Jamie Torres observed a strange beast which was perched on a branch not far from the area of the previous sighting. Mr Torres stated that what he saw had a hairless head, large claws, slanted black eyes and dark grey skin. The witness also claimed that the creature seemed to make him feel sleepy as it hissed aggressively, and then it sprang from the tree out of sight. In the April of 1995 more than fifteen witnesses saw a three-foot tall, grey-coloured being, but over the next few months more than fifty reports would emerge with regards to a similar humanoid.[8]

A majority of the eye-witness testimony came from the region of the El Yunque rainforest and the villages at its base. Many animals were found bereft of blood, drained by an unseen predator which, in the dead of night, broke into yards. The predator's calling card was a set of puncture wounds, or one hole, left in the body of the prey. Sheep, goats, cats, dogs and chickens began to fall foul of this mysterious killer, and all exhibited the same grisly marks. The slaughter was so persistent that the Mayor of Canovanas, Jose Soto, assembled a team of more than thirty volunteers and patrolled the dense foliage and shadowy caves but did not flush out any apparition.

Two fishermen angling for sunfish on November 6th were distracted by a form moving about in the nearby undergrowth. Luis Angel Guadalipe observed a devilish critter with large, glowing eyes, huge ears and a set of wings upon its back. He estimated the creature to stand around four to five feet tall, before it flew away.[9] Other witnesses came forward to speak of unusual flying creatures. However, one witness when describing their encounter spoke not of a hideous creature, but something "cute", which seemed to levitate because wings were not evident.

A Hazy Legend

It is clear that descriptions of the phantom were not clear at all! Although a majority of sightings mentioned a grey-coloured being, when analysing the hundreds of cases on record I find it strange just how many descriptions did not match but which overall seem to describe a creature that is 1) able to fly by the use of leathery wings or 2) levitates but has no wings, 3) omits a sulphuric odour or 4) leaves no trace of smell, 5) stands around three-feet in height or 6) stands five-feet in height, 7) has spines running down its back which, when the creature becomes agitated, alternate in colour, or 8) no mention of spines, 9) makes a hissing noise or 10) is accompanied by a buzzing noise or 11) makes no sound at all, 12) resembles a bipedal humanoid or 13) resembles a bird, 14) the creature is a servant of the Devil or 15) the creature is a product of a government experiment or 16) the creature is extraterrestrial, 17) the creature resembles a cat or 18) the creature resembles a baboon, and so on and so on. And these descriptions, however inconsistent, match the legends of so many other similar creatures sighted around the globe.

The goatsucker only really took on some kind of substantial form when a Puerto Rican magazine published an illustration of what the monster 'probably' looked like. From that point on, eye-witness testimony seemed to greatly alter and most descriptions seemed to speak of the beast as the creature whose image soon became plastered across the internet. The sketch depicted a creature, greyish in colour, standing around three-feet tall. It was bipedal with a human-shaped head which bore large, black bug eyes, a small nose and a slit for a mouth. Down the creatures back ran a series of spines, and the beast had two small arms with clawed hands, and clawed feet. And so, the legend was born, pushed out there into the world for all to see...and fear.

A Menagerie of Monsters

The ever-changing form of the Chupacabra in Puerto Rico mirrors the evolution and distribution of vampire myths across the globe. For example, the legend of the Mardkhora went from Persia to Arabia to Spain, and to Greece, and from Persia to India via the Parsees; it exists in mythology everywhere. And if we search across the globe, we find an almost endless pageant of blood-sucking, flesh-eating ghouls.

For example, there is another Persian cryptid known as the Al – a peculiar name for a legendary swamp-dwelling, shaggy-haired monster said to have glowing eyes and which feasted on children. Armenian legend speaks of the creature as one-eyed, half man-half beast and a devourer of pregnant women. In parts of Arabia flying vampires with Chupacabra parallels also exist, as they do the world over. The Jaculus is a serpent-bird said to live in trees and wait in the darkness for victims, whilst the 'foot licker' – also known as the Palis – is another vampyric entity found in the hot sands of the Arabian desert. Such phantoms may well be considered as nothing more than local nightmare, but this latter soul drainer, which sucks blood from the feet of its victims, remains very much feared.

In India, the Kali are vampires said to mainly appear on battlefields during long and bloody wars. Their goatsucker connection comes from their straw-like tongue which is used to drain prey of blood. These creatures are black-charred in appearance and have fiery eyes, whereas the corpse-scavenging Bhuta is a spindly, white spirit. The Brahmaparush is more akin to the goatsucker in that in order to lap its victims blood it makes a hole in the skull and sucks the crimson through a straw-like protrusion from its mouth. The Rakshasas are also similar blood-drinkers, predominant in Hindu lore as fanged vampires which feed on horses and inhabit the vast forests of Lanka.

In Mexico, another haunt of the Chupacabra, the 'Mochis monster' had been terrifying pets and livestock for years before the goatsucker. The beast was often described as looking like a small dragon with large fangs, and was blamed for several animal deaths in the Sinaloa region. In Guatemala, the Chupagente is often compared to the Puerto Rican legend and certainly bears a striking resemblance.

So, we seem to be dealing with recurring themes here regarding the creature's appearance. One version of the goatsucker describes something reptilian, with dog-like features, sometimes winged, whilst some of the older legends speak of a creature cat-like and ground-dwelling. This either means that folktales travel well or there are indeed several sorts of mysterious, unidentified creatures at large. Perhaps stories are becoming exaggerated, or disfigured through time, hence the variation in reports from different parts of the globe. Are there many differing species of goatsuckers across the globe, or simply different beliefs in the same legend? Let's look at more.

In Brazil the O Bicho is a reptilian critter, spindly in appearance, blamed for many attacks on livestock whilst the Kiru Pira is more of a large man-beast with glowing eyes and sharp fangs which are used to puncture the skulls of its prey. This creature seems more related to the other South American man-beasts in that it is said to walk with backward turned feet and be covered in long hair. Some say the monster is a werewolf or something akin to Bigfoot.

The Arrancalengus, or 'tongue ripper', is a ferocious entity from the remote forests of Brazil. These creatures resemble winged dogs and have long tails. They remove the tongues of their victims and were said to be heavy in population around the 1960s.

In Chile, the Arrancalengus may still exist. On July 11, 2004, the *Journal Of Hispanic Ufology* reported that peasant Juan Acuna Periera was attacked by 'winged dogs' near the vicinity of Las Cabras farm in the rural vicinity of Paso Hondo, the same area where many hens had been killed in 2003 by a mysterious predator. The Chonchon is also another known Chilean, and Peruvian nightmare said to take the form of a flying head in order to suck the blood from prey. One of the oldest monster tales of Chilean folklore pertains to the Chivato. In 1880 a magician, whilst on trial for relations to a sect, told judges a remarkable story of how he had visited a Royal cave in Quicavi, via a secret passage which began in the house of one Jose Merriman. The cave was guarded by shaggy-haired animals called the Chivato. Such critters, alongside phantom black dogs, are also feared in Panamanian folklore.

Monsters resembling the goatsucker are abundant in the colourful lore of China and Japan. The Bakeneko take on feline form to devour their victims flesh, often appearing as white or black cat-like entities whose bodies swell up after a veritable feast of blood and gore. The Hsigo are more like flying monkeys, and inhabit the dense regions of China whilst the more popular Tengu are rampaging birdmen said to feed off the blood of priests. They wait in cedar trees, which grow in abundance in mountainous regions, and they are equipped with sharp claws and small wings. They look like dogs but hover in the air when about to pounce on their prey, and have become local bogeymen to children and adults alike. There are also an abundance of flying, blood-sucking limbs said to represent vampire-like monsters and crimson-seeking demons. In Japanese and Chinese lore these are often colourful and almost ridiculous beasts, twisted and contorted by the imaginations and tongues which speak of them over time. No country is safe from the blood-drinking Chupacabra relatives.

In Africa the feared beasts are the Asanbosam and the Luucrota. The former being a tree-dwelling beast with iron-like teeth which puncture the victims flesh after it has seized them with its hook-like talons. The Luucrota takes on the form of something more akin to some of the South American goatsuckers in that it is hyena-like, whilst some argue that it's a cat-like animal with a canine head. In Egypt mythology dog-like vampire figures appear in great number, some as highly regarded beasts, but others, such as the Salaawa, are considered creatures of dread and menace to the locals. The Salaawa, said to roam parts of Cairo, has been blamed for several attacks on small children, especially around 1996 when many victims were bitten during nightly raids by the roaming terror. Some witnesses said the beasts were giant hyenas, monster dogs even, but something the press preferred to call it 'the Egyptian goatsucker'. Salaawa means 'female ghoul' and 'she wolf', and is a very real nocturnal fear in the Nile Valley, and city areas inhabited by rare foxes, wild dogs and other strange canids. Many believe the beast to be a modern form of Anubis, a jackal-headed god associated with the afterlife and mummification.

In the U.S.A. the Devil Monkeys may well be a relative. These elusive creatures appear as kangaroo-like animals capable of giant leaps, and which emit piercing screams. Some reports have suggested baboon-like creatures which, in Native American folklore, are also known as Nalusa Falaya, meaning 'long evil being'. They stand between four and six-feet tall on two powerful legs, and are said to be greyish in colour with pointed ears. Three-toed tracks appear to be the only traces left by these weird beings which are said to roam far and wide from Wisconsin to British Columbia. The United States harbours many a vampiric monster legend, the most popular being the Jersey Devil. This small, dragon-like beast has roamed the dense forest area known as the Pine Barrens for centuries, but in description is resembles some of the original goatsucker stories. This terrifying creature of the night is said to omit piercing shrieks, flap leathery wings, and prey on livestock. No human attacks have been

recorded, but the creature has been observed by thousands, and in one incident, even shot at. Researchers suggest the origin of the Jersey Devil legend can be found in the 1700s, when a Mother Leeds, awaiting the birth of her thirteenth child, screamed to the heavens, "Let this one be a Devil...", and so it was. It is alleged that the tormented woman dabbled in the dark arts, and her abomination of a child was the product of such sorcery. This deformed offspring grew quickly into a ghastly manifestation and took to the woods.[10] Beyond the Jersey Devil mythos though, various livestock attacks in the U.S. have also been blamed on large cats such as the endangered Florida Panther (critically endangered felid of the genus *puma*), whilst in the river bottoms of Texas the elusive Skunk Ape, a hairy humanoid, is sometimes blamed for attacks on pens and pets in backyards.

In Canada similar creatures are said to appear as black, cat-like animals with smallish wings, which enable these blood-drinkers to pounce upon unsuspecting cattle in the Ontario region. With cattle mutilations in abundance across the world, UFOs and government operations appear to have competition for any finger-pointing. Canada also has the hilariously named Gwagwakhwalanooksiwey. It is a monstrous bird told of by the Kwakiutl people, which pierces the skull of its victims with its giant beak.

Meanwhile in Nicaragua's remote regions the Comeleguas – also known as the 'tongue eater' – is said to feast on cattle and pets, whilst the Mayan people often spoke of a dreaded winged dog known as Zotz which was said to pluck prey from the ground in one swift, silent movement. The Utukku of Sumeria is also a greatly feared winged humanoid said to be reptilian in appearance, whilst in Malaysia the Langsuir is a flying, female vampire said to drink the blood from its victims after piercing the neck. Lore claims that these monsters are shape-shifters which, in order to obtain prey, have to take on the form of large birds. In other parts of Malaysia we find the polecat-like Bajang, a silent, agile and elusive creature said to drink the blood of animals and small children. In the Philippines their version of the goatsucker is the Aswang, a female mutation which perches on the rooftops and with a straw-like tongue accesses the veins of its victims by inserting it through the cracks of the building (or pen, depending on which prey it is hunting). Once the Aswang has had its feast, it will remain in the vicinity, bloated by the crimson it has lapped up. The strangely named Alan are more like birdmen and inhabit the more remote areas of the Philippines. They hang upside down in trees like bats and wait to pounce on their targets.

In Germany, where werewolf lore was once rife, there is the Alp, a vampire-like beast that drinks blood from its victims nipples. In Portugal there is the Bruscas, a drinker of children's blood (in 1996 near a village west of Castelo Branco, twenty-eight sheep were found with a single puncture mark in the right side of their neck) and in Jewish lore there is the Bruxa, a phantom bird said to feast of the milk and blood of cows and goats.

Not even Australia escapes the vampire grip. The Yaya-Ma-Yha-Who from Aboriginal culture is a four-feet tall, red-skinned humanoid with a large head and big mouth said to drain its victims by the use of suckers on its fingers and toes. This spectre lives in fig trees where it remains until dark then begins to hunt. The Bagim and Bagini are also Aboriginal vampires, the former being something of a winged Harpy-like manifestation, while the latter are clawed creatures said to rape men.

In Haiti lore their goatsucker is the Loogaroo, a skin-shedding night-flier that lives in its own 'Devil Tree' before taking to the night as a sulphurous ball-like mass. In the Dominican Republic their version of the Chupacabra is a water-dwelling beast known as the Ciguapa, known for its horrendous, shrill cry. This creature is described as having backward turned feet, although this may only be the case when it swims.

Even the rolling fields and rural lanes of Great Britain have sinister legends of vampires. During the lambing season of 1991 in the small Scottish village of Kinlockewe several sheep were found dead and talk of vampires was rife in the area.[11]

The *Sunday Mail* at the time reported…

> …a killer beast which is terrorising a remote highland village has baffled experts. The beast, which attacks at night has killed nine sheep leaving a puncture wound under the ear. When the bodies were found the crofters called in a vet from fifty-miles away. He stated, "I have never seen anything like this before, there was a puncture wound under each ear. The wounds were so definite that we thought the sheep had been shot at first, but this was not the case.

It was suggested, after the find of a large paw-print impression, that a cat-like predator had been responsible but the dead sheep were not eaten and there was even talk of a 'vampire fox'! However the vet concluded that, "…we cannot suggest any animal which could have been responsible for the wounds of this nature, and the total blood loss."

In the summer of the same year forty-five sheep were found one morning in Kettlewell, North Yorkshire. The victims had been piled upon one another to form a large stack, although it's possible they had been terrorised by something and in panic suffocated one another as they scrambled to escape.

In 1929 many mink (small, ferret-like animals) were brought to the United Kingdom and farmed for their fur, and it is rumored that several escaped into the wilds. Farmers blamed these ferocious animals for the deaths of many lambs which were found with a single puncture mark to the skull, and the decapitations of almost two-hundred seagulls were also blamed on the animal. However, the mink is not large enough to take down a sheep and certainly unable to terrorise an entire flock. Attacks have also been reported on horses, seals, domestic cats and dogs across the country, and continue to this day. However, in the UK there is no talk of the goatsucker, but instead phantom slashers, large elusive cats such as the puma, lynx and black leopard, and ghostly rippers. Maybe such Latin monsters cannot fit into our folklore, and so we create further bogeymen.

During the 1960s in the village of Highgate, London, a vampire was said to roam the crumbling confines of the local cemetery on Swains Lane. A tall, dark figure was often seen floating by the North Gate of the Western section. The fiend had red-eyes and was said to drain the energy from anyone who walked by of a night. The legend of the 'Highgate vampire' was born, but the mania it caused unfortunately clouded a lot of the truth as thousands flocked to the burial ground over the months in the hope of catching a glimpse of the terror. Some argued that the presence was simply a malevolent spirit which drifted across the foggy lanes, but others argued that the spectre was a real, blood-sucking vampire responsible for several attacks on local women who lived nearby. The hysteria reached a confusing climax after the discovery of several dead foxes in the cemetery, a skeleton in a vehicle, bouts of grave desecration, acts of Satanism, petty feuds, witchcraft, arrests, newspaper headlines, television exposure and exorcisms. Today, the cemetery is managed, and guided tours will only allow a brief peek into the wonderful Gothic façade and interior of this once allegedly vampire-infested place.[12]

So, there you have it. The goatsucker and all its relatives, and probably not one of them will ever be caught because, whilst they may cause great alarm and panic among locals, and create such excitement amongst cryptozoologists and news reporters alike, there is not a hope in Hell, or any other remote place of uncovering one of these blood-drinking entities. For whether they be cat-like, dragon-like, dog-muzzled, winged, bat-like or even reptilian, they only exist on the tips of our tongues and in the dark unknown valleys of the mind. It doesn't matter how much carnage they leave in their wake, they will continue to leave more. It doesn't matter what set of footprints or toxic goo they leave, their victims will always bear the same grisly mark, one or two clean holes leaving the carcass bereft of blood, which at times will actually be the work of natural predators or in turn blamed upon natural predators. They will continue to raid the backyards of many a farmer, hang in wait in many a dense tree, or, as the Cockatrice did in 1733 over Cumbria, England, simply hover with arrogance in the sky, even into the pages of the King James Bible. If enough people fear these creatures then they will always be there. Some as fleeting and obscure nightmares, others with staying power.

Return of the Vampire

The Puerto Rican wave of 'vampire' attacks has refused to cease. In January 2008 at Barrio Cortes, Manati, a man named Hector saw a huge hulking creature in the jungle whilst on his cell phone. The witness ran back indoors to fetch a flashlight which illuminated two glowing green eyes belonging to a tall creature. Hector then called for his grandfather who came outside wielding an iron bar which he attempted to strike the beast with. The monster ran off into the undergrowth. One month later at Caguas, a Mr Gonzalez was leaving the Caguas Centro shopping mall at around 5:30 pm, when something in the sky caught his eye. It looked like something large and dark was about to land behind the Pep Boys Store. As the witness got a closer look he realised it was a flying creature, black in colour with a long neck and a relatively small head. Strangely, on February 20 another giant bird-like creature was observed, this time at Aguas Buenas. Two witnesses watched in horror as a winged terror swooped through the sky and made shrieking noises. When it perched on the roof of a building it stood almost four-feet high. The following morning a pet dog, chained up in a backyard, was found severely mutilated, its flesh showing huge claw marks.

In Mexico on April 11, 2008, there was much talk of a goatsucker visitation at Pustunich, Ticul, when four sheep deaths just after midnight were attributed to the Chupacabra. Locals claimed that dogs had begun to bark for no reason, and a lady was taken ill in the vicinity of the sheep deaths, but the creature that was observed by one witness through a window, was said to have resembled a bear, but bipedal.

In July 2008 Holly, in Michigan, USA, had a brief bout of high strangeness, including several UFO sightings and Chupacabra sightings. On the 24th a bizarre entity was seen in a ditch at Holly Road. It was grey in colour, appeared to be hopping and had big eyes. Of course, such a vague sighting could simply have been a hoax or misinterpretation, but the area gave way to a cluster of similar sightings. The following day in the El Yunque rainforest of Puerto Rico, William Cruz was busy taking scenic photographs but noticed that on one frame there appeared to be a strange figure. When the print was analysed he was startled to se a disfigured entity leering from the waterfall area.[13]

On August 14, 2008, numerous press releases across the world, including *The Sun* in England, asked, "Is This Count Dogula?", after two policeman had filmed a strange looking animal in Cuero, Texas. Sheriff Brandon Riedel and officer Ellie Carter said they had never seen an animal like it, and were convinced the creature was the Chupacabra, or 'vampire dog', despite the fact the animal looked nothing like the alleged 'goatsucker' of Puerto Rico.

Carter told the press, "We were checking fences when this thing just jumped out at us. I shouted, 'It's a Chupacabra, I recognised it instantly from TV. It had big teeth, a big head, short legs in front and long legs in back." The rest of the report from the English newspaper stated that "tests on the mystery creature's corpse proved inconclusive, but many scientists believe the Texas Chupacabra are a hybrid created after coyotes bred with Mexican grey wolves."[14]

Of course, such hybridisation is hardly monster-making, but what this case does prove is that throughout the world communities and cultures have their own dreads, their own monsters and their own superstitions. One witness's 'goatsucker' may be another woman's Jersey Devil, and despite the confusion one thing is for sure: we all need monsters, even if some of them turn out to be nothing more than mangy dogs.

In Ceara, Brazil, on November 2, a child claimed to have been attacked by a man with big ears and claws. The six-year-old had a deep wound under his armpit which he showed to his grandfather, whilst on the 12th in Victoria, Argentina, a black-skinned, clawed entity was blamed for the mutilation of several chickens and rabbits. In the area the creature was sighted a strange black fungus began to grow and samples of this were sent to the School of Agronomy and Veterinary Science of the University of Buenos Aires. Argentina is rife with monster lore. El Petizo is the local bogeyman of El Duraznito, a small city located in Argentina's northern Salta province. The Lobizon, also popular in Brazil, Uruguay and Paraguay, is a hairy manimal, and the Dientudo, also known as 'big teeth', resembles a Bigfoot-like humanoid.

On November 23 at 6:45 am, at a Navajo Reservation in north-eastern Arizona, Jeremy Spokane encountered a creature which was grey in colouration, and weighing about forty-pounds. The entity looked like a kangaroo, but had a pronounced spine and muscular hind legs. Despite pursuing the beast with dogs, the creature moved too quickly and soon sped off into the darkness.

2009 began with a bang, when a bizarre winged creature was seen taking to the sky at Rocklin, California, on January 10, and just over two weeks later on the 28th a bipedal dog-like creature was blamed for attacking and causing several cuts to 20-year-old Kelly Martins Becker at Sao Sepe, Rio Grande do Sul, Brazil.[15]

As these reports continue from around the world, it is clear that some 'thing' does indeed haunt the forests, skies, rooftops and dark roads, but is unlikely to be flesh and blood. It is a being which preys on our fears and litters our lore. It always has done. Morphing with age, transforming over time. It is a great mystery...a cauldron of misinterpretation, hoax, hysteria and dread.

In his fantastic 2008 book *Island Of Paradise*,[16] researcher and founder of The Centre For Fortean Zoology[17] Jonathan Downes, whilst chronicling his adventures in search of the Chupacabra, concluded, that after several sightings of a strange, spiky creature stripping bark from banana trees on the island, that some of the goatsucker reports could well be explained by an escaped/released or unknown species of porcupine. He also states that some of the animal deaths could well be attributed to the Indian mongoose,[18] which leaves a triangular shaped hole in the skull of its victims. As for vampires...well, Jon's 263-page book explores the whole history of the island, but – like all monster mysteries – the mystery remains. We need these horror stories, in fact we crave them. And the more we believe in them, the more things start to happen. And then once we fear them, then they feed on us – and so become manifest within our culture, just like every bogeyman we've ever known, loved and dreaded.

Neil Arnold was born in Kent, England in 1974 and has, since the age of 9-years-old, been interested in monsters after seeing the movie *The Legend of Boggy Creek*. He is the author of *Monster! The A-Z of Zooform Phenomena* (http://zooform.blogspot.com), which Loren Coleman voted the 2007 Fortean Zoology Book of the Year, and also *Mystery Animals of Kent*. He writes for magazines, has appeared on television and radio, is a full-time monster-hunter and runs Kent Big Cat Research (http://kentbigcats.blogspot.com).

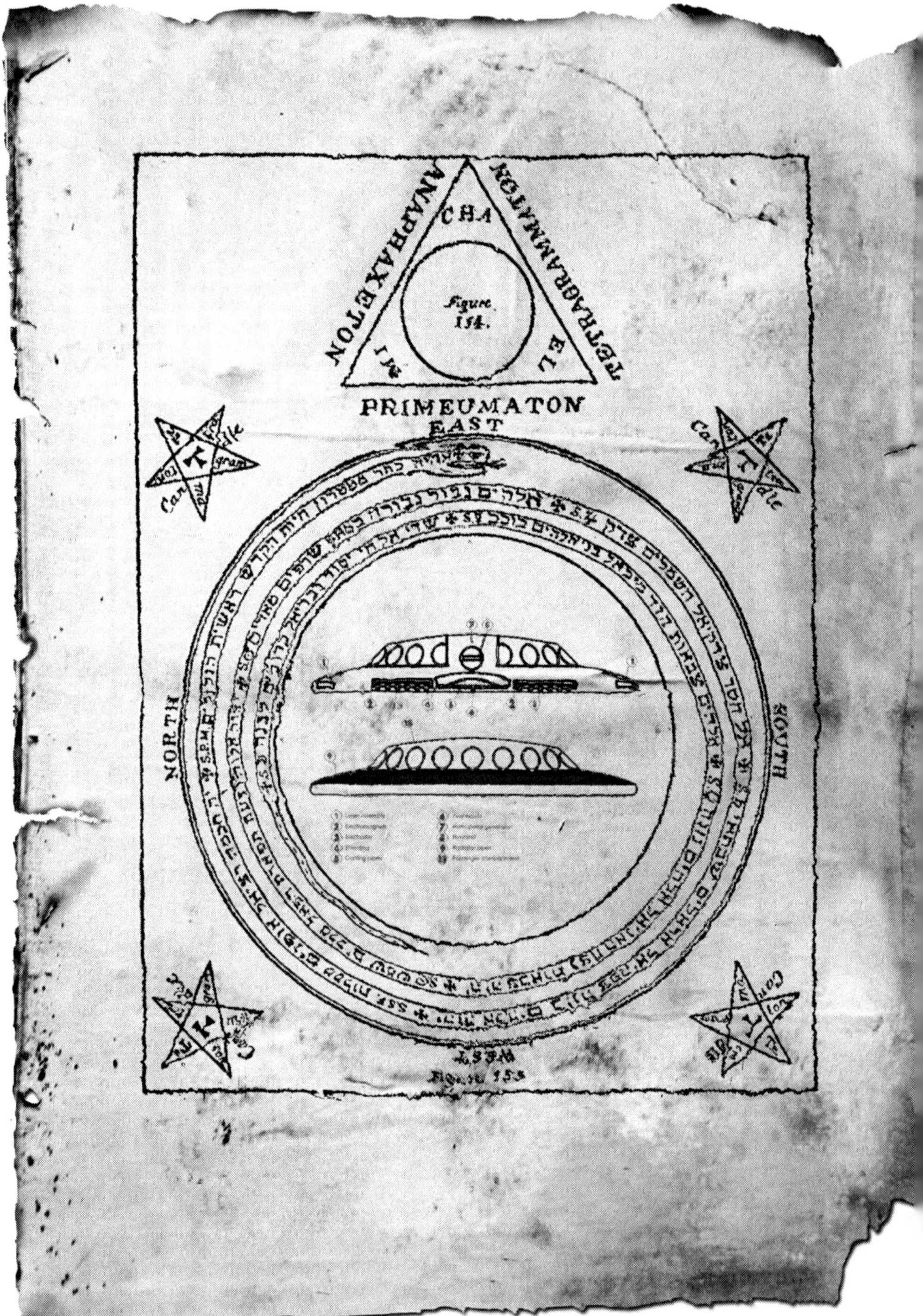
ANAPHAXETON
TETRAGRAMMATON
CHA
Figure 154.
EL
PRIMEUMATON
EAST
NORTH
SOUTH
Figure 155

Flying SAUCERERS

Re-examining the dawn of the modern era of UFOs

by *The Emperor*

In my previous piece[1] for *Darklore* (Volume 3) I looked at the odd connections between occultists and science fiction writers, at the core of which lay the strange duo of rocket scientist and occultist Jack Parsons, and science fiction author-come-religious guru L. Ron Hubbard. The overarching themes were: the influence of science fiction on Parsons' occult (and rocketry) ideas, the possibly that some things were essentially fiction presented as fact (the Philadelphia Experiment, and perhaps even the Strategic Defense Initiative) and that some events in the their story were forms of the 'Big Con'.[2]

Here we will be looking at 'the Saucerers': an oddly closely-knit group of men from the science fiction and occult communities who, through accident or design, managed to conjure the flying saucers into existence. Specifically we'll be examining the Extraterrestrial Hypothesis (ETH) that grew from this. For clarity's sake: this is the idea that aliens are visiting us in flying saucers and taking an interest in human affairs. There are, clearly, numerous theories that might involve aliens or visitors from… elsewhere (perhaps in time, possibly from another dimension) but this seems to be the general idea the man in the street has. Other more exotic variations on the theme require examinations of different individuals and their theories.

However, before we look at these characters at the Dawn of the Modern Era of UFOs, we need to peek back into those strange pre-dawn years when the foundations were put into place for the bizarre edifice that would later be built.

Before the Dawn

Although Emanuel Swedenborg was reporting journeys to other planets back in the 18th century,[3] the origins of the ETH lie at the end of the 19th century and the start of the 20th. Here we see H.G. Wells' Martians visiting in fiction and Helene Smith making the return journey in…'fact'.[4] Despite some suggestions that the craft seen in the 1896–1897 airship flap were from Mars,[5] the first significant linking of strange lights in the sky with alien visitors was in the proto-ufology of Charles Fort. However, other people were also reporting contact with aliens a number of years before Fort started publishing his findings.

In my previous article I raised the possibility that science fiction was being passed off as factual accounts of real events, and when we go back to the late 19th century we find Theosophy, which did this blatantly. And, in doing so, laid the foundations for the ETH.

The movement's hugely influential founder, Helena Blavatsky, produced two key volumes, *Isis Unveiled* (1877)[6] and *The Secret*

Doctrine (1888),[7] which claimed to synthesise the wisdom of the ancients. However, William Coleman looked at the sources and found a lot to be concerned about: rather than drawing on vast numbers of ancient texts, Blavatsky had copied large sections from a limited number of relatively recent books.[8]

H.P. Blavatsky

For our purposes, what is relevant is that she also drew heavily on speculative fiction, in particular the work of Sir Edward Bulwer-Lytton, best known these days for the opening line "it was a dark and stormy night." It is his hollow earth novel *The Coming Race* (1871) which provided Theosophy with the concept of the 'Vril' power, but Blavatsky also drew on a range of his books. According to Prof. Nicholas Goodrick-Clarke, an expert on Western Esotericism:

> Her fascination with Egypt as the fount of all wisdom arose from her enthusiastic reading of the English author Sir Edward Bulwer-Lytton. His novel *The Last Days of Pompeii* (1834) had been conceived of as a narrative of the impact of the Isis cult in Rome during the first century AD. His later works, *Zanoni* (1842), *A Strange Story* (1862), and *The Coming Race* (1871), also dwelt on esoteric initiation and secret fraternities dedicated to occult knowledge in a way which exercised an extraordinary fascination on the romantic mind of the nineteenth century. It is ironical that early theosophy should have been principally inspired by English occult fiction.[9]

This didn't end with Blavatsky's books, though. This information was passed on and the provenance obfuscated with each iteration:

> An entire procession of cults and obscure religious sects has followed Blavatsky's lead, copying their doctrines from her and

> from one another while simultaneously denying their true sources and instead attributing their second- and third-hand revelations to further contact with the Hidden Masters of the Great White Brotherhood. This process has been called "genealogical dissociation" (Johnson 1995; 158) and has continued through groups more-or-less in the classical Theosophical mold, such as Guy Ballard's I AM or Elizabeth Clare Prophet's Church Universal and Triumphant, and also into more up-to-date models in the form of the flying saucer contactee cults that replace the Hidden Masters in their Himalayan hideaways with Space Brothers winging in their cosmic wisdom from Venus or the Pleiades. J. Gordon Melton has noted that the flying saucer is practically the only new element of the story -- many of the older tales had the element of interplanetary travel already, such as Blavatsky's Hidden Masters originating in the distant past when the Lords of Flame traveled to earth from Venus -- and that even this element is often absent from current contact accounts, leaving them almost indistinguishable from nineteenth-century accounts.[10]

For example, Guy Ballard, and other Theosophists, gravitated towards Mount Shasta in California. The interest in this location was sparked by Frederick Spencer Oliver's 1905 book *A Dweller on Two Planets*,[11] which tells of Lemurians escaping the destruction of their home and taking up residence under the mountain. The book, written between 1883/1884 and 1886, but only published after Oliver's death, was allegedly channelled through automatic writing. However, it is essentially science fiction, or according to L. Sprague de Camp (who we met in the last *Darklore* piece) "a tiresome occult novel."[12] According to the 2002 introduction by John B. Hare, who also considers it "a work of speculative fiction":

> This book is openly acknowledged as source material for many new age belief systems, including the once-popular "I AM" movement

(whose founder, Guy Ballard, plagiarized extensively from this book), the Lemurian Fellowship, and Elizabeth Claire Prophet. According to Shirley MacLaine, *A Dweller on Two Planets* jumped out of a bookshelf into her hands in a New Age bookstore in Hong Kong (and obviously had a big influence on her subsequently).

Although Blavatsky included Ascended Masters from Venus, it was never a core of her teachings – it was Ballard who would "become the first to actually build a religion on contact with extraterrestrials."[13] He claimed that he was in frequent contact with them, being visited by Venusians while at Mount Shasta. The important distinction, as noted above, is that these interplanetary journeys (usually within the Solar System, as understood by science at the time) were done through more mystical means.

Contact was often made through channelling and automatic writing and "following the lead of the fantastic voyage novels, contactees either travelled astrally, woke up from a sleep to find themselves mysteriously transported to their destination, or experience some form of what might be called dematerialization" – a mode of transport best known through fiction, like John Carter's voyages to Mars, first written about by Edgar Rice Burroughs in 1919.[14] What is missing is the idea of the flying saucer itself – for that we have to look to another source, which has its roots in the work of Charles Fort.

While Fort's ideas were carried on in their original form by the Fortean Society, it was another group altogether that would expose his work to a wider audience – science fiction authors. Jerome Clark has said that the *Books of Charles Fort* (1941) were "a classic only in the cult sense, functioning mostly as a source of ideas for science fiction writers."[15] In particular this included a serialisation of *Lo!*, starting in the April 1934 edition of *Astounding Science Fiction*, the leading magazine to spearhead the 'Golden Age of Science Fiction' (publishing a large number of the key players in my last *Darklore* article). Arthur C. Clarke has said, "No choice could have been more appropriate for a science fiction magazine, and Fort's writing was to have an immense influence on the field," in particular on the young Clarke. "I found his eccentric – even explosive – style stimulating and even mind-expanding," Clare would later write, and it is evident in his various television series on strange phenomena.[16] We also know others read his work: Lovecraft checked out a number of his books from the library and even name-checked him a few times in his books.[17] The dark theme behind the phrase "we are property" proved especially influential, as were the early glimmerings of the ancient astronaut idea,[18] with some of the related ideas having Theosophical overtones.[19] It would even be science fiction writer Damon Knight who helped with the rediscovery of Fort in the later parts of the 20th century, writing the biography *Charles Fort: Prophet of the Unexplained* (1970) and overseeing the release of the *Complete Works of Charles Fort* (1974).[20]

With these ideas simmering away in the background during the first half of the 20th century, we now turn to look at how they emerged fully-formed as the ETH in the very early hours of the Dawn of the Modern Era of UFOs.

Ray Palmer

The late John Keel, the famous Fortean investigator best known for his *Mothman Prophecies*, has described Ray Palmer as "The Man Who Invented Flying Saucers," and this wouldn't be far wrong.[21] In 1938, Palmer took over as the editor of an ailing science fiction magazine, *Amazing Stories*, that would have sunk without trace except for a chance discovery in the, normally rejected, crank pile. The letter was from one Richard Shaver, and was published in the December 1943 issue. The reader response to Shaver's description of an ancient alphabet prompted Palmer to ask for more material. He received "A Warning for Man," a 10,000-word piece which Palmer then reworked into a 31,000-word story with the more impressive (and Theosophically-influenced) name "I Remember Lemuria!" Published in March 1945,[22] this wild 'true story' told of "death rays, tunnelling machines, high-tech ancient civilizations and even flying disks!"[23] These stories, and subsequent tales – mainly revolving around the underground-dwelling race of 'Deros', with evil plans for us surface dwellers – proved an instant hit. Letters flew in and the circulation would grow by an order of magnitude until it was one of the most successful sci-fi magazines, selling a quarter of a million copies and moving from being a quarterly to a monthly.[24] Although it could be dismissed as the ramblings of a paranoid schizophrenic, there was a degree of effort put into making these stories readable and engaging:

> Shaver's stories were heavily rewritten by Ray Palmer originally, and then later by other writers who were assigned to The Shaver Mystery job by Palmer…
>
> …Palmer was the publishing genius behind Shaver, and it was no doubt Palmer's sophisticated knowledge of literature, science fiction and contemporary science, myth and legend that propelled The Shaver Mystery into the public eye so successfully.[25]

Another key story at this time was Harold Sherman's Green Man tales, "The Green Man" (October 1946) and "The Green Man Returns" (December 1947), which also appeared in Palmer's *Amazing Stories*. The tales – featuring Numar, the green-hued main character – were apparently inspired by Sherman's own odd experience:

> Sometime in the year 1945, when Martha and I were living in Chicago, I had a series of visions wherein I saw Space Beings, possessed of high intelligence, visiting our Earth in space ships of different shapes and sizes, for the purpose of exploration and

> eventually to fill our skies with large space vehicles, coming in force, hopefully on a friendly mission to help Mankind save itself from self-destruction.[26]

So, by 1947, large numbers of readers were following the advice/warning that would become enshrined in the end of the 1951 film *The Thing From Another World*: "Watch the skies!"[27] They didn't have long to wait.

While flying near Mount Rainier, Washington, pilot Kenneth Arnold famously sighted a number of UFOs on June 24, 1947, which now officially marks the start of the Modern Era of UFOs. However, although the press coverage spawned the term 'flying saucer', the objects weren't classic flying saucers, being described as something more like a flying wing (half-moon or bat-wing). In addition there was no claim that they were alien vehicles. However, Palmer spotted the parallels with the stories he'd been publishing, and quickly moved to jump on that particular bandwagon – a letter from Ray Palmer to Kenneth Arnold arrived on July 15.[28] Palmer would send Arnold

Kenneth Arnold with diagram of 'flying saucer'

off to investigate the Maury Island Incident, which 'happened' three days before Arnold's sightings. It would prove to be a strange conspiracy quagmire: suggestions of bugging emerged, and the main figure, Fred Crisman – who was known to Palmer[29] – would go on to be linked with the JFK assassination.[30]

Palmer, with a keen eye on the *zeitgeist*, launched a factual magazine in 1948 called *Fate*, and the first issue included Arnold's account of his encounter. The two would then collaborate on a book that expanded on this, *The Coming of the Saucers* (1952), published by Palmer's Amherst Press.

Despite the fact that whatever Arnold saw wasn't actually shaped like the classic flying saucer, the term proved suitably evocative and it was up to science fiction again to provide the image. The back cover of the November 1947 edition of Palmer's *Fantastic Adventures* featured "a flotilla of golden saucers above the New York skyline, and the words: 'Will the ancient gods of Egypt and other lost civilisations come back to Earth in time to avert an atom war?'"[31]

As the UFO phenomena evolved, we find Palmer's fingerprints all over the work of the early contactees. For example, Orfeo Angelucci worked at the Lockheed aircraft plant in California, not long after one of the giants of the early Contactee movement, George van Tassel, had left.[32] In his 1955 book *The Secret of the Saucers* Angelucci describes how, on his way home from work, he would occasionally bump into aliens and their flying saucers. However, the origin of this seems to go back to the job he had before joining Lockheed, as he describes himself in his book:

> For several months I worked as manager of the Los Feliz Club House. In my spare time I endeavored to write a motion picture script. It was more of a hobby than anything else. I didn't really expect the script to be accepted as I'd had no writing experience. As the idea of space travel was quite popular in the films then, I concentrated on a story about an imaginary trip to the moon.

> Several studios were interested in the finished manuscript, but it was never made into a motion picture.[33]

This has led one commentator to note…

> Orfeo Angelucci's contactee story began as a movie script titled *Worlds are Mad Tonight*. He came to realize it had little financial potential and "lay gathering dust and forgotten" before the aliens came forward to tell him it was true.[34]

It gets even more interesting though, because this book was published by Ray Palmer's Amherst Press, and it appears Palmer was involved at every stage. Of course, Palmer was the editor and publisher, but there is something odd about the book's credits, as described in the 2007 introduction:

> Angelucci's name doesn't appear on the title page, simply Palmer as editor. Angelucci is, strangely, only listed as a copyright holder. … The book makes a brisk read (again, a hallmark of Palmer), and if you suspend disbelief, it works as science fiction as well.

As we've seen with Shaver, Palmer took a very 'hands on' approach to his 'editing' and this seems to be no exception.

It was also Palmer's *Fate* that gave an early venue to the man who would take the flying saucer story up to a new level. In *Fate's* July 1951 edition was an article entitled "I Photographed Space Ships" – by one 'Prof.' George Adamski.[35]

George Adamski

Adamski's story is a strange and complex one.[36] He had established the Royal Order of Tibet during the late 1920s, which preached a

Theosophical-based philosophy, although Adamski claimed it was really a front for bootleg liquor during the Prohibition.[37] However, the group continued on after the end of Prohibition in 1933 and started publishing books and pamphlets in 1936. They also moved on from their initial base at Laguna Beach, California and, after a time on a nearby ranch, he and his followers ended up at Mount Palomar in 1944.[38] There they lived in a commune with Adamski working in a restaurant catering to people visiting the Mount Palomar Observatory, further up the mountain.[39] His involvement with UFOs started with a series of sightings, one in October 1946 and another only weeks after Arnold's had hit the news.[40] This all seemed par for the course in the late forties, but things got interesting toward the end of 1949 when four military men dropped by – including two scientists from the Point Loma Naval Electronics Laboratory who asked Adamski if he could provide any photographs.[41] He soon obliged, and it was these sensational images which garnered Adamski a lot of interest at the time...and a huge amount of scorn later, as they were obviously rather bad fakes.

Although stuck up the side of a mountain, Adamski seems to have had strong connections with other contactees and esoteric groups of the period. According to Jacques Vallee, Adamski had connections with the occult fascist William Dudley Pelley.[42] Pelley had mystical experiences before WWII and become a supporter of Hitler during the war, which led to him being jailed for treason. He was only released on the understanding that he avoided politics, leading him to return to his more esoteric interests. Although there was strong crossover between his followers and Guy Ballard's group, it was in the post-war period, around 1950, that another important individual, George Hunt Williamson worked for Pelley. The latter may have even introduced Williamson to Adamski.[43]

Together Adamski and Williamson would be part of one of the most important events in the early years of the Modern Era of UFOs, when they travelled into the Mojave Desert on November 20,

1952. Leaving the rest of the party, Adamski met Orthon, a Nordic Venusian. After the alien had departed Williamson took plaster casts of some footprints, that are said to have included a reversed swastika in the pattern.[44]

The first of Adamski's books on his encounters with flying saucers and their occupants, *Flying Saucers Have Landed*, was released in 1953. Surprisingly, he did not write the bulk of it; instead, large portions were penned by British Theosophist Desmond Leslie. In keeping with the broader themes of this piece, Leslie's journey started when his publisher asked him to research UFOs for a science fiction story and he ended up concluding they were real.[45] Leslie's contribution would also be significant because it was very Fortean in tone with a distinctly Theosophical spin to it, putting forward the case for ancient visitations by aliens.[46]

Williamson would go on to write *Other Tongues – Other Flesh*, published in 1953 by… yes you guessed it, Ray Palmer's Amherst Press. According to Donna Kossy, "Williamson's version of the origin of humanity draws heavily on Pelley's *Star Guests*, which itself draws from 'I AM' (Guy and Edna Ballard's 'Ascended Master' cult which flourished in the 1930s), Theosophy, the Bible and possibly other sources."[47] Mankind's ultimate origin was said to be Sirius, but the Earth was, he claimed, also populated by other sinister races from places like Orion. This leads Kossy to conclude "Many of the space brothers' messages, as received by contactees such as Williamson and Adamski, are transparent right-wing political statements whose authority is legitimised because they come from a 'higher intelligence.'"[48]

The Theosophy link here is also important as it not only plugs Adamski firmly into the broader occult scene in California, but also seems to be a continuation of the long 'tradition' of basing your teachings on science fiction. The main difference here is that the science fiction he lifted and presented as fact, was his own. Adamski's earlier science fiction novel was little known, until it was reprinted recently, and Marc Hallet had to order a copy from the

Library of Congress. His findings, when he got to read the book, were quite startling – almost all of Adamski's space adventures were actually already all there in the earlier, fictional, work, something Palmer knew well:[49]

> *Inside The Space Ships* is nothing more than a science fiction book. The best proof we have of this is that it is a "remake" of a science-fiction book entitled *Pioneers of Space* which Adamski wrote in 1949.
>
> ...To your surprise you will discover that these two books give exactly the same descriptions of space (with the fireflies), the Moon (with snow on mountains, forests, lakes, artificial hangers and even small running animals), the scout ship (with the great lens in the middle of the cabin and the graphs on the walls), the mother ship (with its two "skins"), and even little details such as the portrait of the Great One in the mother ship, the famous Saturnian badge with the balance, etc... You will also be pleased also to see that the Masters' pompous statements are exactly the same, something that demonstrates that Adamski had a poor imagination and was unable to create new or original philosophical concepts. His lack of imagination was so great that his book *Cosmic Philosophy* published in 1961 was mainly based on texts he had written in the '30s.[50]

However, there is one element that is not from his books which helped make his story one of the most compelling from the early Contactee era – the meeting of a Venusian in the Mojave Desert.

Given Adamski's fondness for 'recycling', and apparent problems with coming up with new material, the question arises: where did he get this idea from? The answer may come from an examination of the wider occult vortex in California, and it brings us back to the focus of my previous piece in *Darklore:* Jack Parsons and L. Ron

Hubbard. In 1946, while the two were engaged in occult rituals in Pasadena, Jack Parsons claims to have met a Venusian in the Mojave Desert.[51] The exact timing and context are unclear, but as he was apparently alone, this appears to be the time when his magickal partners L. Ron Hubbard and Marjorie Cameron were both away. During this time, on February 28, 1946, Parsons went into the Mojave Desert and 'received' *Liber 49, The Book of Babalon*. He said of the experience "[t]he presence of the Goddess came upon me and I was commanded to write the following communications."[52] According to biographer John Carter, "[t]he Venusian apparently was the implied source of *Liber 49*."[53]

Both Adamski and Parsons were part of the occult scene in California, although the latter seems more central, with authors and adepts dropping by his house when they were in town. However, there are more explicit links. According to one of Parsons' biographers: "[Max] Schneider and his wife had a small cabin on Mount Palomar that members of the lodge often used for short retreats."[54] Paul Rydeen provides more details of the Palomar link:

> In "Alchemical Conspiracy and the Death of the West" Michael Hoffman writes of Parsons. Hoffman tells us that the Ordo Templi Orientis (OTO) had a temple on nearby Mount Palomar. The local Indians regarded the mountain as holy. Hoffman says, "The OTO believed that Palomar was the sexual chakra of the Earth." Parsons commuted regularly between Palomar and Pasadena. The Mount Palomar Observatory opened in 1949. Smith probably consecrated his temple on Palomar soon after his move to California in 1930, before the Observatory was planned.[55]

There is one final potential link, which, if proved, would show the direct line of transmission of this last piece of the jigsaw. It has been suggested that Hubbard and Adamski met in 1951 (i.e. after Hubbard and Parsons' relationship had soured, but a year before

Adamski said he met the aliens in the Mojave), and discussed science fiction and UFOs.[56]

Beyond Adamski

Charles Laughead is one of the best examples of the way people would rattle around the occult/contactee scene in the early days of the Modern Era of UFOs. He and his wife seem to have had a crisis of faith in the late 1940s and gone on the search for enlightenment, which brought them into contact with the group coalescing around Marion Keech (real name Dorothy Martin) in 1949–1950.[57] This group started channelling contacts with aliens (which, as we've seen, continued seamlessly from the Theosophical groups into the contactees) and started producing messages about a coming apocalypse in December 1954. This caught the attention of the media and, through them, a group of sociologists and psychologists who infiltrated the group and were able to monitor the dynamics as the deadline of doom came and went – resulting in one of the best books on the topic, *When Prophecy Fails* (1956). Although they put it all down to a simple group state, there were certainly strange events swirling around the group, including a number of odd visitors, some of whom might later have been described as Men in Black. Following the collapse of the group, Keech returned to Hubbard's Dianetics movement, which she had earlier been involved with, and would later journey to Peru where she and George Hunt Williamson established the Abbey of the Seven Rays in 1957. The Laugheads were also in Williamson's orbit – but they also, importantly, met Dr. Andrija Puharich.

Puharich is perhaps best known for being Uri Geller's mentor, but he had been researching parapsychology since the late 1940s. In December 1952 he was working with Dr D.G. Vinod, who started channelling communications from a group calling themselves 'The

Nine'. These communications continued on and off until 1953, when, in front of a group of nine (including people like Arthur M. Young[58]), they revealed themselves as the various aspects of God. Laughead and his wife would come into contact with Puharich and Young three years later in a Mexican hotel. While Puharich was not initially impressed by the information passed on to him (apparently channelled by Williamson), a follow-up letter from Laughead made him pay attention because the communications it contained paralleled what he had received via Vinod, adding an extraterrestrial spin to proceedings. This seemed to be independent confirmation of the information, and the Nine would simmer away in the background until he met Uri Geller in the seventies when, after asking Geller leading questions under hypnotism, he seems to have got in contact with similar entities. Those who have read the previous article may start to spot a similar situation to the ones we saw with Parsons, Jessup and Bennewitz, in which an individual is an unknowing 'actor' in a 'play' where the other 'actors' have access to the 'script'. Basically, it looks like Puharich is the focus of a Big Con – the information would only be convincing if the sources were really independent. Given Laughead's links throughout the occult/contactee groups, and the way he kept popping up like a Joker in the pack, there must be the suspicion that he was able to access enough information to fool Puharich. Why anyone would do this is unclear, as he ran CIA-sponsored remote viewing experiments and is considered to be very much an insider. However, it could be read a different way. Could Puharich's beliefs have been deliberately altered early on? This would then result in him being an unwitting actor in later events, which included widespread use of hypnosis to recover further information from Geller, which we know tends to generate a fiction based on a mix of the therapist's and the patient's beliefs.[59] If so, this would mean the idea of the Nine originated elsewhere, and Puharich was manipulated into believing it was true.

N. Meade Layne was also in Southern California, had links with the OTO and was member of the Hermetic Order of the Golden Dawn. Layne's contacts spanned the occult/contactee world, and he established Borderlands Science Research Associates (now Foundation) in 1945, which was discussing UFOs before even Arnold's sightings. One key role was in publicising information emerging from other sources. These included the channelling of 'E Yada Da Shi'ite' from the 'Interplanetary High Council' by Mark Probert, which "in early 1946…swerved into the same new theme Harold Sherman caught in his story 'The Green Man' – the imminent arrival of extraterrestrial craft in Earth's skies."[60] So it wasn't just the science fiction fans who were watching the skies in 1946/1947.

Conclusion

I must admit when I was younger and knew less about UFOs I had assumed the Extraterrestrial Hypothesis stemmed from…you know, aliens visiting us. However, the true origins appear to lie in the occultists and science fiction writers (and some science fiction-writing occultists) who jumped on Arnold's sighting of…something, and promoted the idea that these were the alien visitors they'd been writing about/talking to for the decades running up to 1947. Some would even go on to 'meet' these visitors from the stars. These individuals tend to fall into two groups. On the east coast we have the Chicago group associated with Raymond Palmer, "the man who invented flying saucers," which also included Harold Sherman. They had effectively primed the pump and moved hard and fast to dominate the very earliest sightings and publications. On the west coast there is the giant cauldron of California containing the powerful mix of the occult, sci-fi and UFOs. It is here that the ball Palmer put into play was picked up and run with. However, we also see his direct influence, working on and publishing books and articles from this group.

There is also another organization which certainly moved quickly in the wake of Kenneth Arnold's sighting (even if it was not overly successful in anticipating it). In light of the details covered earlier, the July 8, 1947 announcement by the Air Force that a flying saucer had crashed at Roswell – coming so soon after Arnold's (during the initial wave of excitement it generated) – seems suspicious, as it was perfectly timed to keep the momentum going with an official acknowledgement of the phenomena (even if it was rapidly withdrawn). We also have the active involvement of the Navy in Adamski's story. While we might expect to find them in connection with the Philadelphia Experiment (as it was allegedly a Navy project) and Parsons (who had contracts with the Navy), it is definitely odd in this context – and a wider examination of the field shows them popping up in strange places.[61]

On analysing the Modern Era of UFOs we see it less as a new phenomena and more an evolution of existing ideas. Theosophy's Ascended Masters became increasingly extraterrestrial, and contact with them moved from channelling, to their arriving in space ships (although, as we've seen, channelling was still important long after flying saucers appeared in the skies). The home of the 'aliens' has also changed – moving further away from the Earth as science brought us more information about the planets, forcing them to 'abandon' Mars, with its canals, for Venus and then the outer planets in the Solar System, before heading out into deep space. We can also see the abduction phenomena as a further evolution, one which shed a lot of the mystical trappings and made it a lot more personal and more modern – emphasising technology, and ditching uplifting messages for darker medical interventions.

What I do want to emphasize though is that I am not dismissing the majority of UFO reports as science fiction. My concern is that the peculiar mix of individuals had already defined the 'story' long before the Dawn of the Modern Era of UFOs, and they moved quickly to put their version of this story into place within days. A few years later this mythos was firmly in place and a number of the leading flying saucer proponents were perfectly happy to rebrand their science fiction as *bona fide* science fact. This established a framework that other people used to interpret their strange experiences, creating a positive feedback loop that reinforced the prevailing paradigm. The introduction of hypnotically-recovered memories made this even more problematic because – as has been ably described elsewhere[62] – the hypnotist and/or the subject's worldview can shape the memories. This can result in apparently consistent accounts that also help convince people of the reality of this idea.

There is another issue too. Ufology, which should be a broad and flexible discipline, is largely focused on flying saucers and their alien pilots. This serves to limit the scope of inquiry and pretty much guarantees that the broad consensus (especially amongst the general public) remains that they are in fact visitors from other worlds making a bit of a nuisance of themselves. As I showed in my first two articles for *Darklore*, there is an odd crossover between ufology and the wilder fringes of cryptozoology, with similar reports of strange clouds in connection with UFOs, religion and other Fortean phenomena. Greg Taylor also discussed this in relation to sounds in *Darklore Volume 1,* and there are many more such examples which suggest ufology isn't a discretely defined field.

The idea that the ETH (as described) is essentially artificial slots into a number of other ideas that are out there. Operation Bluelight is a pretty wild conspiracy theory that suggests some shadowy group are going to undermine the world's faiths, and then engineer a vast faked alien armada that would help them impose a new global UFO religion.[63] We could say that this fits into a class of ideas we'll call the 'Strong Watchmen Plan' – after Alan Moore's classic comic book series, in which one of the superheroes launches a vast scheme to create such an overwhelming external threat that the people of Earth would have to back away from the brink of Mutually Assured Destruction.

A more general idea for faking 'the Voice of God' (and possibly also using some kind of aerial hologram) goes back to the ideas put forward to get rid of Fidel Castro (which seem to have originated with Ian Fleming, who I mentioned in the last *Darklore*[64]), and came up again with the invasion of Iraq in 1991.[65] Ufologist Jacques Vallee also stumbled across the infamous 'Pentacle Memorandum', which advocated that the military monitor specific places that had a lot of reported UFO activity, while further suggesting that "many different types of aerial activity should be secretly and purposefully scheduled within the area."[66] As should be obvious, it might be possible to fake this in a limited way, for a handful of people – however, increasing it up to a planetary scale is almost impossible to do convincingly (and let us not forget that belief is a difficult thing to shift, even when presented with actual facts). The beauty of the concept put forward here is that you don't need to go to all that trouble. Having the idea in place early means you don't need to micromanage proceedings – people have been seeing lights in the sky, and meeting strange entities, throughout history; all you need to do is update the model they use to interpret their unusual experiences.

Lynn Picknett and Clive Prince have also looked at the interconnections between people in the occult/contactee groups and suggested that there was some kind of conspiracy at work. The main axis for this seems to be Andrija Puharich and the group channelling the Nine, but it also connects with Hubbard/Parsons and the CIA.[67] However, it would require Puharich to be some kind of *eminence gris,*[68] pulling a lot of the strings behind the scenes. But, as I noted earlier, at some points in his story he seems to have been the victim of at least one Big Con. Nevertheless, the connections they uncover are significant no matter what the underlying driving force is.[69]

While researching this piece I came across John Michael Greer's new book, *The UFO Phenomenon: Fact, Fantasy and Disinformation*, which parallels a lot of my thinking on the subject and helped fill in some gaps. Greer suggests what might be going on is what we could consider the 'Weak Watchmen Plan':

> Attempts to shape the consciousness of a culture or an age using powerful symbolic patterns, in other words, are among the things occultists do. The possibility exists that something of the sort lies behind the remarkable involvement of the American occult community in the first days of the UFO phenomena. While it is certainly possible that figures such as Meade Layne and Harold Sherman, who predicted the arrival of the flying saucers in advance were simply reporting visions and dreams that would shortly burst out in a flurry of apparitions across America's skies, the possibility has to be considered that these highly publicised reports were meant to cause such an event.
>
> ...it is at least possible that somewhere in the broad overlap between the American occult community and the science fiction scene, a group of occultists driven by the same sense of desperation set out to deliberately create the belief that extraterrestrial beings were about to intervene on Earth.
>
> They may have hoped simply to inject just that moment of hesitation into the minds of politicians and generals that could keep them from plunging into a nuclear abyss.[70]

In essence this was a magickal working on a grand scale – perhaps not designed to directly effect change, but to create a viral meme that aliens were concerned about our onward march to nuclear Armageddon. Science fiction gave them a ready-made audience, and also a means to present various scenarios in fictional form. One of the key works in that regard is the 1951 film *The Day the Earth Stood Still.* Predating the rise of the high-profile Contactees, like Adamski, by a year, it showed a classic flying saucer landing in Washington so the pilot can deliver a message expressing the concern of the aliens about mankind's development of nuclear weapons. It is believed to be the inspiration behind the off-script comments made by Ronald

Reagan during his 1985 meetings with Mikhail Gorbachev that helped end the Cold War.[71] It is also worth noting that, in essence (and without the occult overtones) this Weak Watchmen Plan is very much along the lines of the possibility I raised in the last essay: that the concept of the Star Wars program (conceived by an odd mix of space scientists, military men, aerospace executives and science fiction writers, including Heinlein) had a similar effect in the last days of the Cold War, and may have brought the world back from the brink at that time.

Another idea comes from occultist/ufologist Allen Greenfield, who is also a bishop in the Gnostic Catholic Church, the ecclesiastical arm of the OTO. Greenfield knew a lot of the players in this story, which might qualify him to speak on these topics; he has more doomladen claims to make about a lot of individuals we have looked at:

> UFO buffs have of late been touting a theory that Hubbard came to Parsons with a purpose more grandiose than "the ordinary confidence game." In pulp magazine circles, he had encountered any number of occultists and border occultists (Talbot Mundy, Col. Arthur Burks, Major Donald Keyhoe, Ray Palmer and Richard S. Shaver come to mind), and had already formulated the core of the "inner Scientology teaching" outlined above. He wished to bring this other world into Manifestation, but lacked the technical knowledge to do so. So, he came to the innocent sex magician Jack Parsons. In this version, the Babalon Working, guided by Hubbard, had little to do with "Babalon" and more to do with the hideous Old Ones of the H.P. Lovecraft Cthulhu Mythos.[72]

Speaking of Lovecraft, one particular quote from the great man of horror and science fiction springs to mind when discussing these issues. In a letter to Clark Ashton Smith, dated October 17, 1930, Lovecraft wrote:

> My own rule is that no weird story can truly produce terror unless it is devised with all the care & verisimilitude of an actual hoax. The author must forget all about 'short story technique', and build up a stark, simple account, full of homely corroborative details, just as if he were actually trying to 'put across' a deception in real life – a deception clever enough to make adults believe it.[73]

Personally, I don't really see a grand conspiracy at work. It would require a number of people to have had an important role in stage-managing a large performance. A key figure would have to be Ray Palmer who doesn't come across as some cunning mastermind. Unfortunately, he seems more driven by Fun and Profit; most of his influence on the field seems to be more opportunistic, spotting trends and exploiting them with little concern about the line between fact and fiction.[74]

There are just too many separate groups with different (often murky) agendas pushing in often opposing directions. What seems to have emerged accidentally from the collision of these ideas was a modern mythology that provided a lens for interpreting strange events. A mythology which appears to be no more of an approximation to the underlying 'truth' than ideas of fairies and angels/demons were in earlier ages.

The Emperor was baptised in the diocese of Jerusalem and the morning after friends "proved" he was the Antichrist, he was nearly killed by two nuns. These facts may not be connected, but what if they are? He has written for *Fortean Times* and a number of British small press magazines and comics. He also blogs at the Cabinet of Wonders (www.wunderkabinett.co.uk) and elsewhere. In addition his "Black Hitler" won the Nazisploitation Nanofiction contest.

Reflections at Tinkinswood

A New Theory on the Origins of Megalithic Rock Art

by *John Higgs*

On Oct 7, 2008, I visited Tinkinswood chambered cairn, also known as Castell Careg, which is a short drive from Cardiff in South Wales. Tinkinswood is unimaginably ancient, being around 6000 years old. It consists of a stone chamber which has been covered in earth and grass. Its main claim to fame is that the capstone is the largest in Europe, a monumental slab of rock that weighs 36 tonnes and which I can only surmise was raised up by trolls. It is a lovely spot in beautiful countryside, marred only by a huge electricity pylon which has been placed alongside. It is said that those who spend the night at Tinkinswood on certain dates will either die, go mad or become a poet.

Rock art is rare in Wales and I had no expectation of finding any. It was a surprise, therefore, to approach the monument and suddenly see the back wall covered in imagery identical to that which is more usually associated with the chambered cairns of Ireland or Brittany, abstract swirls and intricate curvilinear patterns. When I realised that the imagery was luminous, and animated, I stopped dead in my tracks. For a silent moment I stood dumbfounded, but sadly my rational mind stepped up and worked out exactly what it was I was seeing. A perfectly good visionary moment came crashing down to earth.

It had been raining heavily during the night and the floor of the chamber was covered by an inch or two of water. The famous capstone, over 7 metres long and 4 metres wide, shielded the far wall of the chamber from direct sunlight. The sunlight did hit the water on the floor, however, and was reflected up onto this shaded back wall. What I was seeing was no more mysterious than patterns in the water reflecting back up onto a shaded stone.

Tinkinswood chambered cairn, showing massive capstone (© John Higgs)

But what was striking was how similar these reflections were to textbook rock art. Ripples from insects or drips from the ceiling produced strong circular patterns. Eddies of water around rocks in the water produced the sort of swirls that no Celtic tattoo could be without. A gentle, consistent breeze produced a general shimmer of light that looked for all the world like a crosshatch pattern.

These ripples of light were very different to those you may find on the large, flat walls of an indoor swimming pool. The wind and the irregular surface of the rock produced very different imagery, tighter and more linked to the shape of the rock. It was a phenomenon that was very beautiful, to these eyes at least. I was reminded of a number of commentators who had highlighted the relationship between the shape of the rock and the lines of Neolithic art, a relationship which they explained away as evidence of the artist's genius. If you could somehow freeze the moment in time, immobilizing the luminous images as they played across the solid rock, then you would have produced a perfect example of abstract Neolithic rock art.

Thoughts Lost in Time

The strange patterns smashed into solid stone are, for me, physical remains from the time when our ancestors made the mental shift from animal to human consciousness. The circles, swirls and repeated patterns that make up the majority of these images are utterly incomprehensible to our modern sensibilities, yet we are constantly drawn to the idea that there must be an underlying sense to them; that they need to be solved. They fail to communicate with us like a bee performing a waggle dance in front of a philosopher, a form of visual expression so archaic and fundamental that, we like to think, we are just too advanced to comprehend. We recognize them as being the result of human endeavour, even though they are surely the least understood form of human expression.

Of course, rock art could simply be little more than good-old Neolithic mucking about, the product of people who had yet to invent straight lines or modern ways of wasting serious amounts of time. But this argument isn't completely convincing, and not just because of the amount of effort involved in carving a rock when the only tool you have is another rock. The language of rock art appears to be universal. The forms of pre-figurative art are found across the globe, executed with surprisingly similar imagery by very different people. There must be something else behind this, the argument goes, other than the whims of local culture.

There have been many theories have been put forward to attempt to explain how this could be. Over the years it has been argued that they are maps (of the moon, the heavens or the locality), representations of sound, early pictograms, or genealogical information. The current favourite explanation is that the symbols are *entoptic*, inner images experienced by the human nervous system in trance or other altered states.

This explanation arises from research into altered states of consciousness conducted in the early part of the twentieth century, in the days before that troublesome trickster Timothy Leary made such research highly disreputable. Early researchers studied the effects of mescaline, and went to great lengths to formally categorise the visual hallucinations experienced whilst under the influence of the drug. In particular, it appeared that the abstract visions at the onset of the trip – visions which would eventually gain complexity and discard their abstract nature for more representational imagery – could be classified into a number of distinct forms. These forms include spirals or tunnels, cross-hatch patterns and curved, parallel lines. It was eventually noticed that these categories matched to a remarkable degree the categories that researchers of abstract Neolithic rock art were using. A good overview of all this research is included in Paul Devereux's 1997 book *The Long Trip: A Prehistory of Psychedelia* (a book which has very helpfully been republished recently by Daily Grail Publishing).

Rock art swirls at entrance Newgrange (credit: Nomadtales)

The 'entoptic' argument for rock art, then, goes like this: Abstract rock art is a representation of visions that a prehistoric shaman figure experienced at the onset of a trance state. This trance state may have been triggered by drugs or other means, such as chanting, flickering lights, mental illness, extreme physical fatigue, or a combination of such causes. The shaman's trip was an integral part of the local culture, to the extent that the community extended the effort to build stone chambers to aid the shaman (and in Tinkinswood's case, coerced some local trolls into lifting up the damn capstone.) The carving of entoptic imagery in the cairn, therefore, is either to celebrate the shaman's inner journey or aid him in leaving these more earthly realms.

It is a fascinating and exotic argument, but after my experience at Tinkinswood I can't help but wonder if there is a simpler, more mundane explanation.

Could the reflections of light bouncing off water be the reason for the universality of the images in rock art? The phenomenon of light bouncing off water is identical, of course, in cultures across the globe. Could those ungraspable dances of light have been quickly sketched on to the solid rock with chalk, and then hammered into existence? Did our ancestors attempt to cling on to these fleeting immaterial images by trapping them in the most solid material they had? It struck me that, if this was the case, then it was a very human thing to do.

More importantly, does the study of this idea – which I fancy should be called archaeoaquatisthetics – shed any light on our history and mental evolution? I sat back on the damp grass and watched the light-show for a while, and I came to the conclusion that it just might.

Reflecting on Ancient Reflections

The obvious problem with the theory was that the images were constantly shifting and flowing. There seemed to be no reason why any one moment should be selected over all the others to be immortalised. The problem was the wind, blustering in through the gaps into every part of the chamber. It was clear that our ancestors would have understood the role of the wind in producing the images, because when the breeze picked up you simultaneously felt it on your skin, heard it and saw it's affect on both the water and on the reflected images. Drafts were a constant fact of life back then, unavoidable in wattle and daub or wooden buildings. The problem in this instance was that one side of the Tinkinswood chamber is ruined and now missing. The hole that let in the light also let in the wind.

I wondered if it would be possible to avoid the wind whilst simultaneously letting in the light. It seemed to me that this would be quite a feat of engineering. The water would have to be surrounded by a solid, draft-proof chamber, and the light would have to enter down a long, straight passage. It struck me immediately that this was exactly the design of most of the chambered cairns in north-west Europe. There is a central chamber, built from rocks and covered over with earth, making it wonderfully draft-proof. Then there is an entrance passage, usually fairly long, which is typically orientated to let in beams of sunlight at dawn or dusk on significant days of the year, such as equinoxes and solstices. I thought back to the chambered cairns I had visited in Ireland. The carvings were typically focused on the backstone facing this entrance, exactly what you would expect if the light that entered was bouncing off water.

Was there any evidence, though, that these buildings were designed to have water inside? They are typically on high ground, to give a clear view of the horizon, so they would not habitually be flooded. However, there is a famous 'cauldron' stone in the chamber at Knowth. This rounded stone does appear to be a shallow basin for holding liquid, and it has been argued that hot stones were dropped into the water in these stone cauldrons to produce a 'sweat lodge' effect. The cauldron appears to be integral to the purpose of the cairn because the building was built around it. It is still within the chamber because it is not physically possible for thieves or archaeologists to get it out.

I also thought back to Cairn T at Loughcrew, where there are low flat stones at each side of the central chamber, like tiny walls, which have never really been explained. It might require a little clay to ensure that they are totally waterproof, but these small 'walls' could hold water in the central chamber, while people remained dry in the side chambers around it. And there is the strange 'skylight' above the entrance at Newgrange, from which light would advance down the sloping passage even if it had been blocked off and flooded. These thoughts are all highly speculative, of course, but I was delighted to stumble upon this 19th Century carving of Cairn L at Loughcrew, reproduced on the following page from Paul Devereux's book *The Long Trip*:

19th century engraving of rock-art carvings inside Cairn L, Loughcrew Island (credit: Paul Devereux, The Long Trip)

This engraving shows a low shallow stone dish placed under the carvings at the rear of the cairn. When the engraving was made, it was not known that light enters the chamber (in Cairn L's case, on or around the festivals of Imbolc and Samhain). With this knowledge, however, it is easy to see how light would have bounced off liquid in that low dish and produced an effect exactly like the carvings shown.

It seems clear that a study of the positions of the rock carvings inside such monuments, by someone more scholarly and respectable than myself, would go a long way to confirming or dismissing this theory. If we know where the carvings are and we know how the light enters the chamber, then we could check to see if the addition of a reflecting surface would connect the two. It wouldn't be an exact science, of course. There are examples of cairns being built using previously carved stones, possibly from an earlier monument. But in general, archaeoaquatisthetics has a great advantage over other theories in that a methodical survey would either strengthen the hypothesis, or allow us to dismiss it outright.

Of course, if we have light entering a draft-proof chamber and possibly reflecting off water, we hit our next problem. If the water was still, what would disturb it to produce the light pattern? And more importantly, why bother in the first place? Here we enter a wildly speculative world. We know that the cultures that built these monuments perceived the elements of rock and water differently than we do, dragging very specific rocks from South Wales to build Stonehenge, or casting high-status items into sacred lakes. It seems probable that they perceived in them some form of living or magical quality that most modern people do not.

Is it possible that they attempted to 'interpret' these immaterial patterns flashing across solid rock at a significant time of the year, in much the same way that some modern people attempt to tell the future by reading tea leaves? It could be that a shaman figure cast something in the water, or banged a rock or the ground at the climax of a ritual, in order to generate the light pattern and interpret the response from the immaterial world. I am also reminded of Paul Devereux's study of how a high number of these chambers resonate at a particular frequency, between 110 and 112hz, which is in the low male baritone. What would be the effect on still water, I wonder, of hitting this resonating frequency by chanting in such a chamber?

Such thoughts are wildly speculative, of course, but there was a lot to be said for entertaining them whilst sitting in the Welsh landscape in the autumn sunshine. If the rock art and chambered cairns of north-west Europe were shown to be designed to capture a message from the immaterial world, then we would be looking at a very significant moment in history. This would be the moment when humans stopped being simply aware of the larger world beyond them, and set about capturing it to use it for their own purposes. And if that was the case, it seems to me, it would be hard not to look at Neolithic rock art and see the point were our species proved that they had evolved into something that was undeniably human.

John Higgs is a BAFTA-nominated writer and producer from Brighton, England. His book *I Have America Surrounded* chronicles Timothy Leary's life of "flat-out epic grandeur." More information about the book can be found at www.ihaveamericasurrounded.com.

妖怪

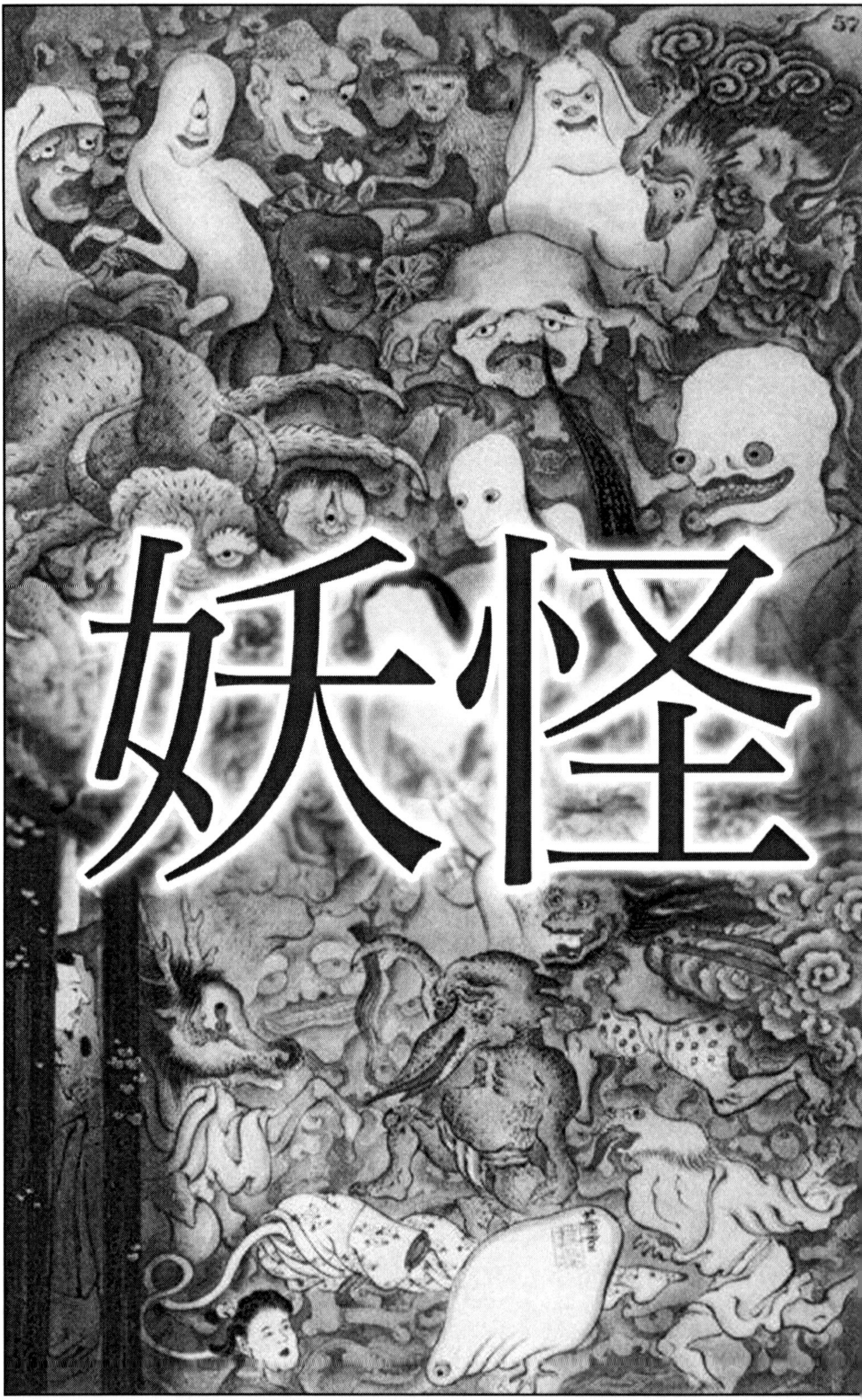

In Search of...

YOKAI!

Monster sightings in the Land of the Rising Sun

by *Richard Freeman*

Japan is a culture awash with monsters. Ask the man in the street to name ten Japanese things and the odds are that Godzilla (or Gojira to give him his Japanese name) will be amongst them. For many people their first exposure to Japan is through the wildly entertaining genre of giant monster movies, in which antediluvian or extraterrestrial beasts smash through Tokyo. Godzilla, Rodan, Gamara and their colleagues even have a collective name in Japan. Known as Kaiju, they have become an institution.

Yet Japan's monster fixation goes back much further than film. Japan has a folklore tradition unrivalled in richness and strangeness anywhere else in the world. Collectively the monsters and ghosts of

Japan are known as Yokai, and constitute a veritable supernatural menagerie. With a handful of exceptions these amazing creatures and characters are almost unknown in the west.

Origins of the Yokai

Yokai is really a catch-all term for any odd, un-natural, ghostly, or monstrous being. They can fall into a number of categories. Henge are shape-shifters. Unlike the western lycanthropes and other were-beasts, the Japanese Henge are usually animals that take on human form rather than vice-versa (such inversions of western conventions are not uncommon in eastern lore). Henge can include foxes (Kitsune), raccoon dogs (Tanuki) and cats (Bake-neko), animals that most of us would consider harmless. In Japanese legend all of these creatures can take on human form to spread chaos and misery. Ironically the wolf (Okami), so vilified in the west, was thought of as a force of good in old Japan.

Another class of Yokai are Tsukumogami, inanimate objects that can take on a life of their own. Household objects such as old sandals (Bakezouri), sake jars (Kameosa) and even umbrellas (Karakasa) can become Tsukumogami. When an object reaches one hundred-years-old it becomes sentient. Its behaviour then depends on how well the object was treated in the past century.

Obakemono or Bakemono means 'changed thing' and can include the previous two categories, but also includes changed humans. Many Yokai are people twisted beyond recognition, or having some feature extenuated to a grotesque degree. Examples include the snake-necked Rokuro-kubi and the doubled-mouthed Futakuchi-onna.

Finally there are a mixed bag of monsters who have always been monster, as opposed to changed humans, animals, or objects. These include the daemonic Oni, the Tengu bird-men, the turtle-like Kappa and Tatsu, the Japanese dragon.

The question arises: why is Japan's folklore so rich and so weird? The answer may come from Japan's unique history. Before the modern Japanese arrived the Ainu people had migrated into the Japanese islands from mainland Asia (probably Kamchatka in Siberia), possibly as much as 10,000 years ago in the Jamon Period (14000–300 BC). The Ainu, now mainly confined to Hokkaidō, once inhabited the whole of Japan and had a distinct folklore featuring many strange creatures. The Ainu religion is animist and believes that everything has a spirit, or Kamuy. They venerated spirits of earth, mountain, fire, and sea. There was no organized priesthood, with tribal chiefs preforming religious rituals including libations and prayers. The Ainu believed in the immortality of the spirit and in an afterlife.

The modern Japanese arrived some 2300 years ago in a second wave of migration during the Yayoi period (400 BC–250 AD). Their ancestors seem to have come from Korea. It is during this period that rice cultivation began. They brought with them their folklore and the beginnings of the Shinto religion, an animist religion with no central spirit or object of worship. It concentrates on getting along in this world, rather than preparing for the next. It has no defined prayers, but instead consists of rituals to mediate between humans and spirits, who in Shinto inhabit the same world as we do.

Chinese emissaries wrote reports on Japan in the mid-third century. They speak of thirty separate kingdoms each with it's own ruler. All of these rulers recognized a supreme power, a Yayoi queen called Pimiko (an archaic version of the word *bimiko*, meaning princess). She was unmarried and lived in a heavily-guarded palace. She served deities who in return gave her powers to foresee the future and bewitch people. A male associate acted as an intermediately between her and the people. Upon her death she was buried under a great mound and 100 attendants followed her to the grave.

Later writers speak of an Empress called Jingo who spoke with the gods and issued advice, including at one time recommending an invasion of Korea.

Could these early accounts be recordings of an early matriarchal society that flourished before the Japanese began to write their own records? Fifth century tumuli have yielded clay figurines of women in strange flat head-dresses. It is possible that some vestige of these old beliefs lingered into later times and manifested as Amaterasu, the sun goddess and principle deity of Shinto.

Buddhism first arrived in Japan in the Asuka period (538–710 AD) and was radically different from the previous religions. Indeed, Buddhism is more of a philosophy than a religion, with its ideas of self-improvement and negation of desire to thwart mortal suffering and re-incarnation. Spreading out across Asia from India it must have gathered up much folklore on its way, like a spiritual snowball. Buddha taught that nothing in this world is stable; no form of existence is anything more than flux. Ego and self are imaginary constructs and hence transformation is the truest form of being. Yokai are all about transformation.

Taoism had its roots in ancient Chinese religions of the 4th and 3rd century BC, but didn't reach Japan until the 7th century. It emphasizes the 'three jewels of Tao': compassion, moderation and humility. Tao itself is the force behind the natural order or the flow of the universe. A central concept in Taoism is *wu wei* (without action), with a goal of alignment with the Tao via the revealing of the soft invisible power in all things. There are several branches of Taoism including a philosophical one, an elite religious one, and a shamanistic one that is perhaps closest to its original conception.

Shugendo is a religion peculiar to Japan. It arose from the veneration of sacred mountains that were the dwelling place of *kami* (spirits). This became overlaid with symbolism and beliefs from both Taoism and Buddhism. The priests of Shugendo were known as *yamabushi,* meaning 'to lie down in the mountains'. They climbed to the peaks to perform special ceremonies said to endow them with magical powers.

In any country where there have been several dominant religions, cultural cross-pollination has occurred. Today many Japanese combine Buddhist, Taoist and Shinto beliefs. So we can see how the scene is set for a massively rich folkloric landscape.

This could be a clue to the weird nature of the Yokai. When one people conquer or assimilate another, the culture of the former is rarely destroyed totally. The gods and deities of the older culture may still be secretly worshiped in pockets here and there; and, alternatively, demonized by the newer religions. Christianity did this by changing the Greek gods Pan and Dionysus into Satan – many Biblical daemons were former gods, the Phoenician Moloch being a good example.

Buddhism is known to have done much the same thing. In his 1935 book *Men and Gods in Mongolia,* Henning Haslund writes of how the former animist gods of the Gobi-dwelling Mongols were transformed into daemons by Buddhism, becoming wild spirits of the desert that Buddha quelled. Still ferocious, they were now defenders of the Buddhist faith. In a festival Haslund witnessed in the remote Gobi he saw men dressed as outlandish daemons, the old lost gods of the Mongols now assimilated by Buddhism.

The same could be said for England. The great folklorist Reverend Sabine Bearing-Gould, writing in the *Transactions of the Devonshire Folklore Society*, says that in 1875 a farmer he knew had been suffering illness among his cattle. He sacrificed a sheep to the pixies, the little people infamous in the legends of the South West of England. Afterwards his livestock recovered. The farmer did not think his actions in the least odd. Black Annis of Leicestershire, Ginny Green Teeth the water hag of Cheshire and Shropshire, and Peg Prowler of the River Tees are all snaggle-toothed hags. They seem to be diminished and distorted versions of the 'hag', the winter aspect of the old British mother goddess. In her crone form she is known as the Morrigan or the Cailleach.

Similarly, in The Gambia and surrounding countries there is a widespread belief in a giant serpent that bears a crest on its head, known as Ninki-Nanka. It is thought that the creature is so lethal that it can strike a man dead just by looking at him. Gambia is a Muslim country, but prior to this its folkloric beliefs were animist. Python worship cults flourished in West Africa, and it seems that the Ninki-Nanka legend may have grown out of a demonization of the old serpent deity.

Could the same be true of some Yokai? The answer is almost certainly yes. The bizarre habits and appearances of some Yokai may have made sense in their original form if they were indeed some kind of god or divine being. With the religions and beliefs attached to them forgotten, and only the outlandish behaviour or appearance remaining, a monster is born.

Another factor in the richness of Japan's monstrous menagerie is the fact that when the public interest in the supernatural peaked in the Edo Period (1603–1868 AD), there was a very high level of public literacy. The printing press was in wide use at this time as well; additionally, it was a time when people could still recall the ancient stories of times past. Add to this the isolation that Japan had experienced during the Tokugawa Shogunate (which had banned foreigners, and travel abroad) and you have a potent mix for a well-preserved folklore. Such a combination did not occur in Europe or anywhere else in the world.

We must also take into account the physical nature of the Japanese islands. Dissected by huge mountain ranges, only 16% of the land is available for cultivation, and three tectonic plates meet beneath it causing regular earthquakes (around 1000 perceptible tremors wrack the country each year). Seismic activity also occasionally creates tsunami, and typhoons occur in late summer and autumn along the cost of Honshu. It is small wonder that such a country produces a rich folklore of strange beasts and spirits.

Many Japanese monsters are distorted humans with a certain feature such as the neck, face, limbs and tongue exaggerated. These could be based on medical conditions or physical deformities that were not understood at the time. Imagine, if you will some poor soul in a rural village afflicted by something like Proteus Syndrome, or hypertrichosis. These would surely become Yokai in the eyes of their contemporaries. Mental illness too may have given rise to ideas of possession by fox spirits or other malevolent entities. The concept of foxes, raccoon dogs, otters, cats and other creatures being evil spirits may have had its genesis in diseases such as rabies (which may also be behind the vampire myths of Europe).

The idea of the stranger as monster is also an interesting one. The foreigner or outsider bringing different ideas or concepts into an area might be perceived as threatening to an insular community. On a larger scale foreign appearances and ways may have seemed so alien as to render them sub-human. Indeed the tribesmen in the Japanese Alps were referred to as 'Earth Spiders' (Tsuchigumo) due to their squat hairy appearance. Battles with them entered into history, and the hairy little men became giant spiders.

Fossil bones of dinosaurs and other large prehistoric animals have long been associated with legendary beasts. Dragons in China were supposed to shed and re-grow their bones with their skin; fossil bones were collected and used, in ground form, as medicine. Dinosaur bones are not as common in Japan as they are in China, but in one area near the town of Mifune, Kumamoto Prefecture, many fossil bones have been unearthed – including the skull of a hadrosaur and a large theropod resembling *Tyrannosaurus rex* (possibly *Tarbosaurus bataar*).

In my capacity as a cryptozoologist I have investigated mysterious creatures in many places around the world. Certain kinds of monster turn up in almost every culture on Earth no matter how widely separated by time and distance those cultures are. Creatures that occur time and again are dragons and other monster reptiles, little people, hairy giants, monstrous birds, and giant or supernatural dogs and cats. I call this 'The Global Monster Template'. Japan is no exception, and in the coming pages you will find examples of some of them.

The monsters bear an uncanny resemblance to the creatures that would have co-existed with, or menaced, our australopithecine ancestors on the planes of East Africa over 3 million years ago. Moving onto the grasslands from the forest to exploit new food sources such as carrion brought them into conflict with other hominids and primates, including massive baboons. Crocodiles, pythons, large eagles, hunting dogs and big cats would all have preyed upon our ancestors. It can be no coincidence that they all fit quite nicely into the Global Monster Template.

Perhaps many of the world's monsters are a massive, collective, subconscious, thought form. The thought form, or tulpa, is said to be a three-dimensional, semi-solid image created by the power of the mind; Buddhist lamas in Tibet are said to be able to summon up tulpas during intense meditation. Western explorer Dame Alexandra David Kneel was said to have created a tulpa of a monk whilst studying in Tibet. Polish medium Franek Klusk was said to have summoned up huge cats, birds, and even ape-men during séances. Perhaps, considering the types of beast he called up, he was creating tulpas.

If individuals can create tulpas, imagine what the collective, gestalt mind of humanity as a species could do. Perhaps monsters are a giant worldwide thought form emanating from our innermost fears, summoning the prehistoric terrors of our past.

Finally, and in my opinion most interestingly, some Yokai may be based on garbled reports of real animals, both known and unknown. The Bkau – the weird, trunked Yokai said to devour dreams – may have been based on the tapir of mainland Asia. The red-haired, sake-swilling Yokai known as Shojo may have had its ancestry in the orang-utan. The noble Kirin, a kind of Japanese unicorn, may have been based on descriptions of a giraffe brought to China from Africa, and some of the Japanese dragons or Tatsu may have been inspired by encounters with the huge and dangerous Indo-Pacific crocodile that occasionally strays into the waters around Japan's southern-most islands. Alternatively, some Yokai may have been based on unknown species, some now extinct or very rare. Others may still be awaiting discovery. From time to time people report encounters with elongate reptiles in the world's oceans and seas. It is more than likely that the sea harbours some large undiscovered animals. Some of them bear a striking resemblance to Asian dragons.

Not satisfied with being relegated to the realms of myth and history, there are a number of Yokai that have been reported in the 'age of reason'. It is to them that we now turn our attention.

Kappa: The Water Goblin Pervert

One of the most famous of all Yokai – along with the Tatsu (Japanese dragon), Tengu (the bird men) and the Oni (Japanese daemon) – is the Kappa. Kappa has the shell of a turtle and frog's arms and legs. It has a human-like face but with a beak instead of a mouth. It has fringe hair, known as *oKappa-atama*, like that of a western monk about its head. The top of a Kappa's skull is concave and holds a magic liquid that gives the water goblin its phenomenal strength. Despite being only the size of a small child, a Kappa is strong enough to overpower a horse or cow.

Kappas are said to often challenge an unsuspecting human to a sumo match and easily overpower them with their magical brawn. The defeated victim would have his bowels devoured after they were ripped from his anus. Animals would be killed by Kappas in this way as well. Kappa was particularly fond of the *shirikodama*, a fabled ball said to be found near the anus. A Kappa victim will usually have a distended anus and is known as a Gappadoko. Some victims, oddly, seemed to be smiling after their fatal, anal violation!

Kappa would often lurk in toilets and fondle women's thighs and buttocks. Indeed Kappa were said to rape women if they got a chance. In Matsuzaki village, Iwate Prefecture, women allegedly bore hybrid children from Kappas for two generations. The creatures were so grotesque that they were hacked to pieces upon birth and buried in wine casks.

The easiest way to defeat a Kappa is to make it spill the liquid from its concave skull. Despite their predatory nature Kappas were surprisingly polite. If an intended victim bowed to a Kappa the water goblin would be obliged to bow in return thus spilling its power-giving liquid. In such a weakened state a Kappa could hardly move. If it is at the mercy of a human a Kappa will often make a promise or impart wisdom in return for its life. A Kappa is a most trustworthy Yokai, and any promise it makes will always be honored.

Another way of foiling a Kappa attack is to exploit its love of cucumbers – Kappas love to eat cucumbers even more than intestines. By carving the names and ages of your family members into cucumbers, and tossing them into a Kappa-haunted body of water, you can guarantee that they will be safe from the monsters depredations. Kappa's strange love of cucumbers may stem from the tradition of floating the first

of the year's cucumber and egg plant (which Kappas also like) onto rivers to appease river gods or hungry ghosts. It was said to be unwise to swim at this time or to swim after eating cucumber, lest the scent attract a hungry Kappa.

There are over 80 different regional names for Kappas in Japan. These include Kogo, Kawaso dangame, and Eneko. The Kappa legend may have its origins in the floating of stillborn fetuses down river – a badly deformed fetus might give rise to the idea of a water Yokai or even Kappa-human hybrid. Some also say that Kappa may be descended from a character in the famous Chinese story *Hsi-Yu Chi* ('Journey to the West'). It was written as a book by Wu Cheng'en in the 16th century, although the legend existed long before. It is based on a real person named Xuan Zang (602–664 AD), a Buddhist monk who journeyed to India in search of Buddhist sutras. Protecting him on his journey are three companions the Monkey, the Pig, and a water demon called Sandy (Sagojou in Japanese). Sandy is depicted with a shaven head and a necklace made from the skulls of his victims.

Alternatively Kappa may be based on garbled reports of some kind of strange turtle. The big-headed turtle (*Platysternon megacephalum*) of mainland Asia has a vaguely Kappa-ish look about it. Or perhaps the Kappa is based on a species unknown to science.

There are rare accounts of Kappa sightings today. In the late 1950s Japanese-American folklorist Hiroko Ikeda was touring rural areas of Japan. A number of families proudly showed agreements written with Kappas. In these contracts the Kappa swore to leave the families alone and in some cases even to protect them.

At around 11pm on August 1, 1984, in the town of Tsushima in Nagasaki prefecture, squid fisherman Ryu Shirozaki was walking home from the local pier after work. As he passed near the Kuta River, he came upon a small group of children playing at the water's edge. While it was not entirely uncommon to encounter people fishing in the river at night, it was rather surprising to see youngsters there.

As Shirozaki approached the children, he was struck by how bizarre they appeared in the moonlight. He could make out swarthy faces, unusually spindly arms and legs, and glistening skin. Suspicious, Shirozaki called out to them as he neared, but they seemed startled and quickly disappeared into the water.

The next morning when he returned to the same spot, Shirozaki discovered a set of moist, teardrop-shaped footprints on the nearby pavement. The prints, which appeared to consist of a slimy substance that had begun to coagulate under the hot morning sun, stretched for about 20 meters. Each footprint measured 22 centimeters (about 10 inches) long and 12 centimeters (5 inches) wide, and they were spaced about 50 to 60 centimetres (about 2 ft) apart.

Shirozaki and a few curious onlookers immediately suspected the footprints belonged to a Kappa. People began to gather around as the news spread quickly through town, and all agreed the prints belonged to a Kappa. In the minds of many residents, the footprints confirmed the existence of the river imps they knew through local legends.

When police forensic investigators arrived on the scene, they determined that the slimy footprints consisted of an unknown secretion. They took a sample to the lab for analysis, but the results unfortunately turned out to be inconclusive because the sample was too small. The police eventually dropped their investigation, and the mystery was never solved.

Another modern-day Kappa encounter occurred on June 30, 1991 in the town of Saito in Miyazaki prefecture, when an office worker named Mitsugu Matsumoto and his wife Junko returned home for the evening. Upon opening the front door, the Matsumotos were confronted with a strange smell inside their home. Inside, they found dozens of small, wet footprints around the front door and in the hallway, bathroom, and two *tatami* rooms (traditional Japanese mats consisting of a straw core, a cover of softer reed or rush and a cloth edging). At first they suspected a burglar, but they soon realized nothing had been stolen.

The police briefly surveyed the house, but found nothing except a floor soiled by thirty footprints, each measuring about 7 centimeters long and 6 centimeters wide, and having 4 or 5 toes. To Matsumoto, the footprints did not look human, nor did they appear to belong to any animal he could imagine.

Later that night, as Mrs. Matsumoto was putting laundry away, she discovered an unusual orange stain on some clothing. The next morning, as Matsumoto inspected the house more closely, he discovered a deposit of orange liquid on the portable stereo in the *tatami* room. He took a sample to the local public health center for analysis, and the results indicated the liquid had an extremely high iron content and chemical composition resembling spring water.

Troubled by the incident, Matsumoto decided to visit a shaman. After listening to Matsumoto's story, the shaman encouraged him not to worry, explaining that the Kappa indigenous to the nearby swamp enjoyed playing the occasional prank on local residents. The Kappa were harmless, the shaman told him.

Matsumoto tried using detergent, paint thinner and gasoline to remove the footprints and orange stains, but nothing seemed to work.

The Devilfish of the Ainu

In the legends of the Ainu people, the original inhabitants of Japan, Akkorokamui was a monster resembling a giant octopus or fish. It lurked in Funka Bay and adjacent waters off southwestern Hokkaido. The beast was supposed to be 110 meters long!

The Akkorokamui was said to attack boats, similar to the Scandinavian Kraken. Ainu fishermen carried sickles on their boats to protect themselves from it (though how sickles could protect you from a 110 meter monster escapes me!).

John Batchelor was an English missionary who lived among the Ainu in the 19th century. In his book *The Ainu and their Folklore,* published in 1901, he recounts an attack by the Akkorokamui on some fishermen:

> In the morning, we found the whole village under a cloud. Three men, it was said, were out trying to catch swordfish, when all at once a great sea monster, with large staring eyes, appeared in front of them and proceeded to attack the boat. A desperate fight ensued. The monster was round in shape, and emitted a dark fluid and noxious odor. The three men fled in dismay, not so much indeed for fear, they say, but on account of the dreadful smell. However that may have been, they were so scared that the next morning all three refused to get up and eat; they were lying in their beds pale and trembling.

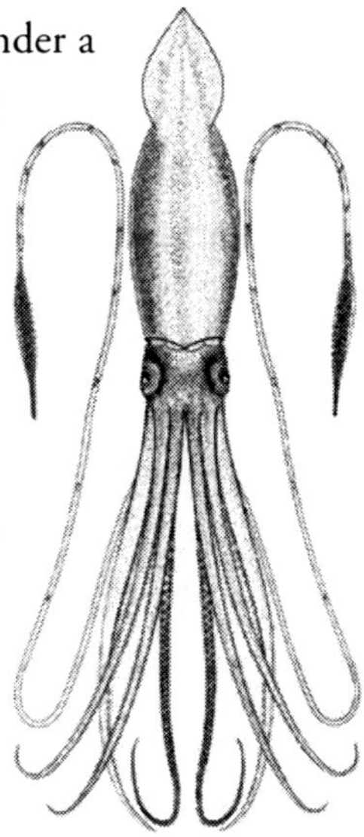

Brent Swancer, an American cryptozoologist living in Japan, has translated another 19th century account from the original Japanese. Once again the witness is a fisherman:

> And I saw ahead something huge and red undulating under the waves. I at first thought my eyes deceived me and that I was merely seeing the reflection of sun upon the water, but as I approached, I could see that in fact it was an enormous monster, 80 meters in length at least, with large, thick tentacles as big around as a man's torso. The thing fixed me with a huge, staring eye before sinking out of sight into the depths.

The Akkorokamui sounds very much as if it may be based upon reports of some vast, unknown species of octopus.

Tsuchinoko, the Flat Snake

Tsuchinoko, the 'flat snake', is a Yokai that may have its roots in reality. Tsuchinoko is reported to be one to three feet long with a dorsoventrally compressed body. It has horn-like ridges above the eyes and dorsal pits. The head is triangular and the neck well defined. It is thought to be venomous. It is described as being black or rust-colored, and is supposed to have an odor like chestnut tree flowers! In legend it has a liking for alcohol, can speak, and can hold its tail in its mouth and roll along like a hoop (such stories are common in western snake legends as well). It is also said to progress in a series of hopping motions.

The creature is known as Bachi hebi in Northeastern Japan and is also said to live in Korea. This Yokai has a particularly long history: drawings resembling Tsuchinoko on stoneware dating back to the ancient Jōmon Period (14,000–300 BC) have been discovered in Gifu and Nagano. Accounts of the Tsuchinoko can also be found in the Kojiki, Japan's oldest surviving book from 680 AD. An encyclopedia from the Edo Period contains a description of the Tsuchinoko under the name Yatsui hebi.

But Tsuchinoko is still reported in modern times. In June 1994, 73-year-old Kazuaki Noda was cutting grass with his wife when they came across a huge snake with a thick body like a beer bottle, and a head described as being like that of a tortoise. On May 8, 2000, 90-year-old farmer Sugie Tanaka was out looking for bamboo shoots in Mikata, Hyogo prefecture, when she happened across two metallic coloured snakes with what she described as "tails like rats." Two weeks later, on May 21 in Yoshi, Okayama prefecture, a farmer cutting grass saw one of these weird serpents slithering across his field. He said its face reminded him of the popular Japanese cartoon cat Doraemon. He slashed at it with his weed whipper, but it escaped into a stream. He said he had heard of the creatures before, and thought they made a kind of chirping sound.

Four days later 72-year-old Hideko Takashima found the creature's body lying beside a stream. Government officials collected the body and sent it to Kawasaki University of Medical Welfare to be examined. Professor Kuuniyasu Saton examined and said that the creature may indeed have been the beast referred to as Tsuchinoko in ancient legends but "scientifically speaking, it was a kind of snake." If the professor ever established the what type of snake it was, or if it was indeed a new species, is unknown.

A live Tsuchinoko was reportedly captured in Mikata on June 6, 2000. It was supposedly put on display in a glass box in the Mikata visitor center. It may well have been a hoax to drum up publicity for the Tsuchinoko hunts held each year in the area.

Also in June, 2000, 82-year-old Mitsuko Arima saw a Tsuchinoko swimming along a river. She described its eyes as being the most striking feature, saying "I can still see the eyes now. They were big and round and it looked like they were floating on the water." She added "I've lived for over 80 years but I've never seen anything like that in my life."

On August 30, 2000, the *Mainich Daily News* reported that a bounty had been put on Tsuchinoko's head. People throughout Kansai and from as far away as Kanto thronged to the town in central Okayama Prefecture, in order to try and catch a Tsuchinoko and claim the reward of twenty million yen from the Yoshi Municipal Government. Though the scaly little Yokai remained elusive, local sales of Tsuchinoko wine and Tsuchinoko rice cake sky rocketed…

Other supposed bodies of this animal have turned up. In Mikata, (the area said to have the highest concentration of sightings in Japan) a corpse was found by four loggers in the Spring of 2001. The body was actually turned over to the Japan Snake Center in Gunma prefecture, where an analysis was done on it that confirmed it as a common grass snake. Another body was found by a villager near Mikata around the same time in May that year, and it too was turned in to the same center for examination. It was determined to be a rat snake.

Back in 1969 a live Tsuchinoko was reportedly captured by an M. Tokutake in Mikata. He supposedly captured it with a forked stick and kept it for a couple of days before deciding to eat it.

According to Naoki Yamaguchi, who has interviewed over 200 eyewitnesses, and is author of the book *Catching the Illusory Tsuchinoko*, the specially organized mass searches are of little use. The searchers do not go far enough into the wilderness – most sightings of Tsuchinoko are by hikers, fishermen and loggers.

If Tsuchinoko is a real creature then it seems probable to me that it is an aberrant species of pit viper (*Crotalinae*). The flattening of the body could enable the snake to hide in rock crevices; a reptilian precedent is the chuckwala (*Sauromalus*), a genus comprised of five species of Iguanid lizards of the arid areas of the southern USA. They are dorsoventrally flattened and once in a crevice inflate their bodies to make extraction by a predator near impossible. The Pancake tortoise (*Malacochersus tornieri*) of eastern Africa has a flattened shell so it can slide into crevices. It is not impossible that Japan, a country with a surprising number of snake species, plays host to an undiscovered pit viper of unique form. One of the most ancient Yokai may in fact be very real!

Dragons: the Rain Gods of Japan

The dragon is the most ancient and widespread of all monster archetypes. Before daemons, giants, vampires or werewolves, dragons haunted the dreams of mankind. A cave painting in southern France, 25,000-years-old, depicts a fanged serpentine dragon dwarfing mammoths. Ten thousand years ago a dragon image was carved on cliffs in Shanxi province, China. Dragons were known in Mesopotamia and Babylon. Britain alone has around one hundred dragon legends. They slither and crawl through all known cultures, and Japan is no exception.

The Japanese dragon known as the Tatsu or Ryū looks very like its Chinese counterparts. It has a head with piercing eyes and jaws furnished with formidable teeth. It has branching antlers on its head and barbles like those of a catfish on the snout. Its vast body is elongate, scaled and serpentine. Japanese dragons usually lack the massive bat like wings of their western relations but some sport small fin-like wings (or wing-like fins) just behind the front legs. Some individual dragons such as Mazuchi, the water-father and O-Gon-Cho had bat wings akin to western dragons. The dragon's four legs are small in comparison to its immensely long body. Unlike the Chinese dragon that has four (or five if it is the Imperial Dragon) claws on each foot, the Japanese dragon has only three.

Japanese dragons are less aerial than other Asian dragons but like those on mainland Asia they are intimately associated with water and the sea in particular. Most Japanese dragons are benevolent towards mankind, but if treated with disrespect they can wield god-like power. An angry dragon could cause earthquakes, tsunami, typhoons, floods or droughts. The length of the largest dragons are measured in miles. Asian dragons rarely breathe fire but their breath condenses and forms rain.

Japanese dragons hatch from eggs that resemble gems. They take 3000 years to hatch. Unlike the Chinese dragon with its long, staged development in several forms, Japanese dragons generally grew to a great size almost as soon as they hatched. In some stories snakes grow into dragons.

Black dragons guarded the north, red ones the south, white the west and blue the east. The yellow dragon ruled the center. Four great dragon kings governed various aspects of the world. They were the Celestial Dragon, the Hidden Treasure Dragon, the Earth Dragon and the Spiritual Dragon. Other renowned dragon kings include…

- Sui Riu is a rain-dragon, which when in pain causes red rain, coloured by its blood.

- Han Riu is striped with nine different colours and is forty feet long. This dragon can never reach heaven.
- Ka Riu is a small dragon; only seven feet long. It's said that Ka-Riu is scarlet, a fiery red. Some sources even say that its body is all flame.
- Ri Riu has wonderful sight and can see more than 100 miles.

In ancient Japan dragons were also thought to cause tsunami and waterspouts, also known as *tatsumaki* ('dragon's roll'), and caused by dragons ascending to heaven. A tatsumaki arose in 1733 in the vicinity of the Detached Palace in Shiba district, in the Yedo bay, and destroyed the roofs of many houses in Kyobashi and Nihonbashi districts; at the same time a heavy rain came down and it became pitch-dark.

In 1744 a tsunami which destroyed a little Shinto shrine near Yedo bay, as well as several houses and trees in Yedo, killing a large number of people, was ascribed to a dragon. Another tatsumaki happened in the Temmei era (1781—1788), when a dragon was said to ascend from the famous Shiuobazu pond in Ueno (Yedo). A black cloud arose from the pond and destroyed the houses in the vicinity. In 1790 four fisher boats sank and the crews all perished when pursuing a whale in the sea near Kashima no ura in Hitachi province. They were caught by a 'dragon's roll'.

In 1690 German explorer Englebert Kaemfer was shown a dragon that was worshipped in a Japanese temple. He describes it thus…

> A huge four-footed snake, scaly all over the body like a crocodile with sharp prickles along the back; the head beyond the rest monstrous and terrible.

Was Kaemfer describing a crocodile? Crocodiles are not native to Japan but the Indo-Pacific crocodile (*Crocodylus porosus*) may occasionally stray outside of its northern range into the waters around some of Japan's most southerly islands. The Indo-Pacific crocodile is at home in both salt and fresh water. It ranges from northern Australia up through New Guinea, Indonesia, Malaysia, Indo-China and India. Its northernmost outpost is southern China. Known for spending weeks at sea these huge animals sometimes stray as far a field as New Zealand, where they may have generated the legend of the Maori dragon or Kihawahine.

Crocodylus porosus is the largest known reptile in the world reaching thirty feet long and having a bite pressure three times as powerful as that of a great white shark. It has been know to devour water buffalo, leopards, tigers, sharks and men. In China the Indo-Pacific crocodile was sometimes called the 'flood dragon', perhaps because floods sometimes washed specimens into human habitations. The people may have even thought that the crocodiles were to blame for the floods.

We know the Japanese traveled in China. The *Kinmou Zui*, Japan's first illustrated encyclopedia was published by Nakamura Tekisai in 1666 and contains pictures of many animals unknown in Japan but found on mainland Asia including elephants, pythons, and tigers. There is also a picture of a crocodile. However the book lists dragons separately from the crocodile, which has its own Japanese name: Wani. So it may be that crocodiles were responsible for some Asian dragon legends, but they cannot account for all of them. But the strong link with water is worth noting.

The dragon is not content to merely coil through ancient legend. Creatures resembling dragons have been reported in modern times. On August 18, 1901, First Officer F. Wolfe, in charge of the Chinese customs launch Lung-tsing, was off Tai Yue Shan Island, Hong Kong. He spotted a dragon-like animal coiled on the sea's surface. It held its head around three feet out of the water; it bore a crest and had two fins high on the neck. Wolfe rather stupidly ordered Second Officer V. Kuster into a gig with a number of men and told them to attack the creature. The men attempted to attack the animal with a boat hook, an endeavor that strikes me as akin to attempting to knock over Nelson's

Column with a flywhisk. The monster reared fifteen feet out of the water, bit one of the oars in two, and then dived. The mariners were indeed lucky that it didn't turn on the gig. They estimated its length at fifty feet.

From July 1897 to 1904 marine creatures strongly resembling dragons were reported in Along Bay, Vietnam. The French gunboat Avalanche was the first to encounter them. A Lieutenant Lagresill described how he and his crew watched a pair of grey and black serpentine animals some sixty-five feet long. They sported saw-like crests running along the spine, and blew jets of vapor from their nostrils. This last detail recalls the rain-bringing breath of Asian dragons. Revolving guns were fired at them from a range of six hundred yards but seemingly had no effect on the animals whatsoever. The Avalanche gave chase but was outpaced by the creature.

Lieutenant Lagresill was laughed at by many of his fellow officers when he recounted his story a week later at a reception for the Governor General of Indo-China. He invited the naysayers to return to Along Bay with him. Lagresill was vindicated when the animals returned in front of a collection of officers who watched them for thirty five minutes from the deck of the Avalanche. In his own words...

> Undoubtedly these animals, known and feared by the Annamites, must have provided the idea of the Dragon, which modified and amplified by legend, has been, if I may so term it heraldized into their national emblem.

Admiral de la Bedolliere of the French navy wanted to try and capture a specimen but a diplomatic crisis in China saw to it that his plan was never carried out. Another one of these beasts was seen again from the Vauban the following year. Jean Baptiste, a marine guard, noted scaly skin and a snake-like head. The Charles-Hardouin was on passage from Nantes to Hong Kong when in December 1903 it ran into a latter day sea dragon. The helmsman wrote...

> I think that the Taiwan embroidered the beast on Imperial and Annamite is just a stylized version of this animal.

Later the same year a number of passengers on board the Gueydon observed the dragon. On February 14, 1904, Lieutenant Peron saw the serpent of Along Bay from the steam launch Chateau-Renault. He observed the sixty-foot serpentine creature shoot jets of vapor from its nostrils. A fortnight after Peron's sighting another gunboat, the La Decidee, met with a monster that Lieutenant L'Eost and his crew estimated to be one hundred feet in length. Finally in May of 1904 the Gueydon mat again with the dragon off Along Bay. On this occasion over one hundred people saw the creature.

The reports from this period were remarkably consistent. An animal sixty to one hundred feet in length, scaled, serpentine, moving in vertical undulations, having a saw-like crest along the back, grayish black in colour and snorting vapor from the nostrils. All in all one could hardly ask for a better description of an Asian dragon.

Similar beasts have been reported from Japan's coast. In 1879 the steam ship Kiushiu-maru – one of a fleet belonging to the Mitsubishi Company – observed a serpentine monster attacking a whale in the Sea of Japan. Captain Davidson stated that he saw a whale leaping from the water with the monster biting into its belly. He observed the whale disappear beneath the surface as its assailant reared up thirty feet before plunging down after it. He said the creature was as thick as a junk's mast.

Japan's lakes are also haunted by elongate monsters that recall ancient dragons. The most famous of these is Lake Ikeda, created from a collapsed, extinct volcano near the city of Kagoshuma on the Island of Kyushu. It formed only twenty thousand years ago and is, by geological standards, a young lake. The modern media has dubbed the strange creature of Lake Ikeda 'Issie', after Nessie, the more familiar beast alleged to inhabit Loch Ness, Scotland. Issie is one of the few Yokai reported in the modern age, and may well have a basis in fact.

In 1961, a large-scale search was conducted for a US military jet believed to have crashed in the lake. Sonar equipment used in the search reportedly revealed a large object moving through the water below, and records indicate that divers on the lake floor were nearly attacked by a large, unidentified creature.

On December 16, 1978, folklorist Toksiaki Matsuhara was visiting the lake to study its legends. He saw a whirlpool form in the middle of the lake and watched it through a telescope. He saw two hump backed creatures close together near Metow-Iwa ('married couple') Rocks. He took photographs that appear to show two animals together, their humps creating waves. Mr Matsuhara was the individual who christened the creature(s) Issie.

Many respectable people have seen something weird in Lake Ikeda. Yutaka Kawaji, the president of a construction firm, and twenty members of his family observed a black-skinned animal showing twenty to thirty feet of its body at the surface. The children of the family alerted their elders to a pair of humps protruding two feet above the water. Mr Kawaji pursued the beast in a motorboat and saw it dive several times.

Iamu Horiouchi says he saw a row of humps sixty five feet long in the lake in October 1978; he took eight photos but none turned out clearly. A mere four hours later Hiromi Nakahuma watched for nearly four minutes as two massive humps rose and fell in the water. In 1991 an alleged video tape of Issie was shown on the Nippon TV special *World's Mysterious Phenomena*. The author has not seen the film but apparently it is lacking in detail.

Lake Kussharo-ka on Hokkaido is the biggest crater lake in Japan, covering 80 square kilometers. It is said to be the home of a monster akin to Issie, named 'Kussie', and local people have formed a protection society on its behalf. The beast first raised its head in 1973 when 40 schoolchildren saw it and drew pictures afterwards. A team of biologists from Hokkaido University saw it in the same year. In 1974 alone there were 15 sightings.

Kusshe is said to be 10 to 20 meters (30 to 60 ft) long and has humps on its back, a long neck and a pair of horns on its head. It can swim as fast as a motorboat. In 1988, eight men in a boat saw a black and white long necked creature in the lake; in 1990 some odd wave formations were filmed on the lake but the footage was inconclusive. Locals say the creature preys on deer, and Ainu legends state that a giant snake is supposed to dwell in the lake.

Aquatic, serpentine creatures are still reported today and are referred to as 'dragons', but what kind of animal could they be? Witnesses' testimony points to some kind of huge marine reptile. Most known reptiles flex in the horizontal plane but the sea dragon flexes in the vertical plane. Some species of marine reptile from the fossil record are thought to have been able to do this. Thalattosuchians were a group of marine crocodiles that flourished during the Mesozoic era 180 million to 65 million years ago. Unlike many other marine reptiles of the period such as plesiosaurs and icthyosaurs, the crocodilians survived the mass extinction at the end of the Mesozoic. It is not impossible that one of the thalattosuchian group was amongst their number.

'Mossie' is the monster supposed to inhabit five volcanic lakes at the foot of Mt Fuji, Lake Kawaguchi, Lake Motosu, Lake Saiko, Lake Shoji and Lake Yamanaka. Lake Motosu is connected to Lake Saiko and Lake Shoji by a system of underground waterways. The five lakes are relatively recent, having been formed by lava flows in the 9th and 10th centuries. They are also landlocked with no rivers running to or from them. Whatever is in the lakes got there via the land or was placed there by man.

The dragon-like beast is supposed to look like a crocodile, and be up to 30 meters (100 feet) long. Some say it also sports a shark-like fin. Mossie first drew attention to itself in the 1970s when odd wakes and surges were reported, as well as dark shapes in the water. A group of fishermen erected a series of nets in the hope of catching the creature (or creatures). The nets were torn to shreds by something large and powerful. Boats equipped with sonar also picked up strange readings.

In October 1987 the beast was supposedly caught on film. A Mr. Yoneyama and three friends were out taking pictures of the lake when they saw a large surge form on the still waters. At its center they could discern 4-5 meters of the back of some large animal. They described it as resembling a crocodile. They managed to take some film but it was not good enough to make any conclusions from.

Another candidate is a surviving member of the Mosasaurs, a group of giant sea-going lizards also from the Mesozoic. They were closely related to the modern Varanids, or monitor lizards, that include the infamous Komodo dragon (*Varanus komodoensis*). With 65 million years of evolution to play with, either of these animals could have radically changed in form between then and now.

Hibagon, the Japanese Yeti

Hibagon is a modern day Yokai, and is described as an upright walking ape-like beast. It has been reported from the forests around Mount Hiba in Hiroshima prefecture. The first known sighting occurred on July 20, 1970, in the area around Mt. Hiba near the border with Tottori prefecture. Three days after the initial sighting, the ape-like creature was seen again walking through a rice paddy in the nearby rural town of Saijo. A total of 12 sightings were reported that year, and mysterious footprints were found in the snow that December.

In the Autumn of 1972 Reiko Harada and her son encountered a Hibagon whilst walking home near Hiwa. It stood at the roadside and raised its hands as if signalling her to stop. Both mother and son ran home terrified. A search later revealed crushed shrubs and a stench like that of a rotting cadaver.

月耕隨筆
龍昇天
月耕

Yokio Sazawa was digging wild sweet potatoes in the foot hills of Mount Hiba when he encountered the beast:

> All of a sudden, this thing stood before me. It was about five feet tall with a face like an inverted triangle, covered with bristles. Having a snub nose, and large, deep, glaring eyes.

Mr Sazawa was certain that what he had seen was not a monkey.

Albert Kubo was spreading fertilizer on his rice fields when he saw a figure standing on a path. It seemed to be holding a paper bag. Not knowing who it was Mr Kubo approached it.

> He seemed to be lost in thought or puzzled...I was just about to say something when I realized it was the Hibagon. I was petrified, but the stench was what really got to me. He must have bathed in a septic tank and dried off with cow dung. I nearly passed out. Luckily enough, though, I managed to turn and run before it realized I was there. I ran five miles straight home without ever looking back over my shoulder."

Numerous Hibagon sightings were reported in areas surrounding Mt. Hiba in the summers between 1971 and 1973, possibly due to the hunting season forcing the creature down from the mountain. On July 15, 1974, a woman saw one near her house and described it as very ape-like, like a gorilla walking around on two legs, and about 1.6 meters tall. There was even film footage taken of one walking along a remote mountain road, however the footage is blurry and of poor quality. On August 15, 1974, the Hibagon was photographed as it hid behind a persimmon tree. The photo only shows a dark shape obscured by bushes – it might even be a tree trunk. Unusual footprints measuring 20 centimeters (9 in) long were found nearby.

After the photo was taken, the creature was only to be seen three more times. In 1980 one was seen fleeing across a river with a bounding gait near the town of Yamano, and another sighting was made in 1981 in the same area. This time it was standing by a road near a health center. Finally in 1982 in Mitsugi, the Hibagon was described as being somewhat larger at 2m tall. Could people have seen a male and female or an adult and young? In this final account it was said to be holding what looked like some sort of stone tool like an axe. A nervous populace began to attribute livestock and even human disappearances to the creature, even though it never behaved in an aggressive manner.

What was Hibagon? The Japanese macaque (*Macaca fuscata*), or snow monkey is found throughout the wilder, mountainous areas of Japan. But the macaque is a quadruped, and reaches a size less than half that of Hibagon.

Another idea is that Hibagon was an escaped pet chimpanzee (*Pan troglodytes*). Exotic pets are popular in Japan and strange as it may seem a number of these savage and dangerous apes are kept. Chimps can walk on their hind legs for a while but they are knuckle walkers by nature. This clashes with the description of Hibagon as a bipedal creature. It is likely that an escaped chimp would have also attacked humans.

Hibagon is more like other short, upright hominids or pongids reported elsewhere in the world. On mainland Asia there are supposedly three types of Yeti: the giant Dzu-Teh, possibly a surviving form of the giant Pleistocene ape *Gigantopithecus blacki*; the man-sized Mi-Teh, perhaps a mainland species of orang-utan; and the smaller Teh-lma. This last kind is four to five feet tall. In Malaya the Batutut is also a small upright walking primate. It is said to be fond of stealing shiny objects from human camps. On the island of Sumatra the orang-pendek or 'short man' is well known. It is a five foot tall muscular bipedal ape of great strength. It has black or honey-coloured hair and a long mane that hangs down from its head. The author has twice taken expeditions into the deep jungle in search of orang-pendek, and even followed its tracks. I have spoken to many witnesses including Debbie Martyr, head of the Indonesian tiger conservation group, who has seen orang-pendek no less than four times. I have no doubt it exists. My colleague Adam Davis brought back hair from Kerinchi National Park in Sumatra that was examined by Professor Hans Brunner, the world's leading expert on animal hair. He announced that it was from a new species of ape related to the orang-utan.

Could Hibagon be related to one of these creatures? Japan is certainly not tropical like Malaya or Sumatra, but the Teh-lma inhabits cooler mountain climates. There have, as far as I know, been no recent sightings of Hibagon. The animal might have died out, or it just might still be awaiting discovery in Japan's trackless mountain forests.

Hibagon may be one and the same as several other ape-like Yokai described from times past, such as the Hi-Hi. This Yokai was covered in long silver hair that could turn back the blows of a sword. Those who drank its blood were said to be able to see daemons usually invisible to the human eye. It may be the same species as Hibagon, but with mystic attributes grafted onto it. Some say the Hi-Hi was a monkey that rolled in turpentine to make its pelt bullet proof. Just how turpentine can turn back musket shots is unclear!

A soldier named Daijirō was fleeing from Sendai, capital city of Miyagi Prefecture, with his family. His brother and his family were following behind Daijirō when a Hi-Hi killed his brother's daughter. Daijirō and his brother killed the beast. The monster, and the weapons used to kill it, were supposedly buried in the grounds of a primary school. Another Hi-Hi was said to have been killed in Sannai Village, Hiraka District, Akita Prefecture. Strangely enough, this beast was also alleged to have been buried in land where a modern primary school now stands. As far as I am aware no excavations have been undertaken. Perhaps the remains of some kind of unknown primate lie there to this day.

Modern-Day Monsters

You might think that Yokai are restricted to the more remote parts of Japan, but it seems that new breeds of urban monster are developing in the neon-lit folklore of the cities. A fine example is Kuchisake-onna, the slit-mouthed woman. Legend has it that centuries ago, during the Heian Period (794-1185), there was a beautiful woman who was the wife or concubine of a samurai. But the woman cheated on her lover, and the enraged samurai slit open the sides of her mouth leaving her with a gaping maw, telling her that "no-one will find you beautiful now".

She was supposed to have become a Yokai and the story goes that she still wanders around on foggy night till this day. Kuchisake-onna is said to cover her mouth with a surgical mask. She approaches victims (usually children) and asks "Do you think I am beautiful?" If they answer yes then she removes her mask and reveals the jagged tear that extends her lips all the way into her cheeks. She again asks "Do you think I am beautiful?" If the victim answers either yes or no the Kuchisake-onna will attack them and slash open their mouths with a knife or scalpel so that the resulting wound resembles the mouth of the Kuchisake-onna. Reputedly there are two ways of stopping her attacking. One is to answer her question by saying "you look normal to me" or by offering her a piece of candy.

The Kuchisake-onna has become one of the most well-known urban legends in modern Japan. She seems to have stepped out of mythology and into the modern era in the 1970s, with new stories of her origins emerging to fit in with the times. For example, in the modern version her disfigured face is sometimes caused by botched plastic surgery, other times by environmental pollution, which also gave her seven toes on each foot. In 1979 rumors abounded in Japan that the slit-mouthed woman was hunting down children. The scare stories spread via playground lore and within one year had covered most of urban Japan. She has even traveled abroad – in 2004 a similar scare occurred in South Korea.

This modern-day Yokai has differing attributes in the various parts of Japan. In Gifu she lives in a hut near the water supply near the city limits. The Kuchisake-onna of Kitaku (a district of Tokyo) has a red sports car, can run 72km per hour, and can be foiled by offering her rock candy. Meanwhile, to thwart her advances in Kanagawa, you face her, chant "garlic" three times, write the Chinese character for 'dog' on your palm, show said palm to her and shout "HAAAAAAAAAAAAAA!" In Hokkaido she is 170cm (5' 7") tall, slender, and beautiful, wears a raincoat, and can run 100km per hour.

Kuchisake-onna even became the subject of a record. "Catch Kuchisake-onna" was recorded by Pomâdo & Kometiô on King Records in August 1979, and featured a trio of girl singers wearing surgical masks. The single was not released however, due to the fact that the advertising director of King Records had received a phone call from a woman claiming to be the Kuchisake-onna herself, accusing the company of trying to profit from her "distinct physical characteristics"! In 2005 the single was released as part of a CD from Teichiku Entertainment.

Shigeru Mizuki, the creator of the popular Yokai-related Manga series *GeGeGe no Kitaro*, mused over the disappearance of Yokai from the modern world in an interview with Tomoko Otake in *The Japan Times* on February 6, 2005:

> They say Yokai disappeared as electric lights came in. Monsters prospered in the pre-electricity days, when people used andon (a standing lantern with a wooden frame and paper shade) and oil lamps. Electricity was too bright for Yokai to survive. The darkness, with a touch of light like that of paper lanterns and oil lamps, was great for Yokai, and it inspired people to imagine Yokai.
>
> In New Guinea, old people believed Yokai were really alive because there was no electricity. In fact, when I was there I asked the people

> to let me see "the head Yokai," who supposedly lived in the river. They were dead serious as they woke me up in the middle of the night and took me there, pointing to a certain location, shouting, "there it is!" I couldn't see anything. Electricity is dangerous. Not many people say this, but it's absolutely the electricity that made Yokai vanish.

I must respectfully disagree with the grand old man of Japanese goblins. I think Yokai are alive and well in the 21st century. Far from being relegated to the distant past they are still manifesting and evolving in the modern age.

Richard Freeman is the zoological director of the Centre for Fortean Zoology in Devon, England. He is one of the few full time cryptozoologists in the world. He has hunted the orang-pendek in Sumatra, the naga (a giant crested serpent) in Indo-China, the Mongolian Deathworm in the Gobi, the dragon-like ninki-nanka of West Africa, giant anacondas in Guyana and the relic hominid called the almasty Russia He attributes his facination with monsters to a boyhood (and manhood) love of *Doctor Who*.

the WATSEKA WONDER

The strange case of Mary Lurancy Vennum

by *Michael E. Tymn*

Put Watseka, Illinois (USA) into a search engine and you'll find that it is a small town of about 5400 people located some 90 miles south of Chicago near the Indiana border. "There isn't much excitement happening in Watseka at any given time, but the town is still a beautiful one," a real estate web site states, adding that it is rich in history – though telling nothing of that history.

Perhaps it is necessary to go back more than 130 years, to 1877, to find some "excitement" in the town. Watseka was then a farming community and train 'whistle stop' of about 1500 people, but a curious event was to bring it to national prominence: "Watseka, Illinois has been swept by a tidal wave of excitement, on account of the presumed insanity of one Lurancy Vennum, a young girl belonging to an unpretentious family in the suburbs of the city," began an article appearing in the September 1879 issue of the *Religio-Philosophical Journal.* It was written by Dr. E. Winchester Stevens and titled "The Case of Lurancy Vennum." The case would later be referred to as "The Watseka Wonder."

On July 11, 1877, 13-year-old Mary Lurancy Vennum, who went by "Rancy," was sewing a carpet when her mother told her to begin preparing supper. "Ma, I feel bad; I feel so queer," Rancy replied, holding her left breast. According to the story later related to Dr. Stevens, Rancy then went into "what seemed like a fit, falling heavily on the floor, lying apparently dead, every muscle becoming suddenly rigid. There she lay for five hours." After retuning to consciousness, she told her family that she felt "strange and queer," but she rested comfortably that night.

"The next day the rigid state returned, and passing beyond the rigidity, her mind took cognizance of two states of being at the same time," Stevens further recorded what was told to him by Rancy's parents. "Lying as if dead, she spoke freely, telling the family what persons and spirits she could see, describing them and calling some of them by name. Among those mentioned were her (deceased) sister and brother, for she exclaimed, 'Oh, mother! Can't you see little Laura and Bertie? They are so beautiful!' Bertie died when Lurancy was but three years old."

Over the next two months, Rancy had a number of similar trances, describing heaven and the "angels." However, sometime in September she appeared to return to her normal self. Then, on November 27, she began experiencing severe stomach pains five or six times a day, and on December 11, she entered a trance state and again began seeing "angels." These trances continued over the next seven weeks and Rancy would often appear to be in a state of ecstasy, claiming that she was in heaven. Two physicians and the family's Methodist minister concluded that she was insane and recommended an asylum.

Upon hearing of the situation at the Vennum home, Asa Roff, a lawyer and one of the town's founders, called upon Rancy's parents and persuaded them to let Dr. Stevens of Janesville, Wisconsin, some 200 miles northwest of Watseka, examine the girl before having her committed to an asylum. Although Roff and his wife had only casually met the Vennums, who lived on the other side of town, they were very sympathetic to the Vennum's situation as they had experienced a similar ordeal with their daughter, Mary, a dozen years earlier.

Mary Roff had died in 1865 at age 18. Rancy was just a year old at the time. Mary began suffering from "fits" at an early age and would often become violent. Her physicians diagnosed it as "catalepsy." According to reports gathered by Stevens, she would become "a raving maniac of the most violent kind" and later would enter a clairvoyant state in which she had no normal sense of sight, feeling, or sound and seemed not to recognize anyone, including her family members. She could see as if blindfolded and could even read a book without the cover being open.

Asa and Ana Roff were forced to put Mary in a sanatorium for a time, something which they regretted after they were converted to Spiritualism and came to believe that there were spiritual forces at work in Mary's case. It was due to the mistakes he felt he had made with his daughter, who died during one of her fits, that Asa Roff was prompted to call upon the Vennums and suggest that Dr. Stevens, a Spiritualist as well as a physician, examine their daughter.

Beginning in 1848 with the so-called "Rochester knockings," Spiritualism had spread throughout the United States and Europe. It started with strange communicating raps and taps, sometimes very loud knocks, purportedly coming from the dead (so many raps, taps or knocks for each letter of the alphabet, or the human sitters would recite the alphabet and would get a rap, tap, or knock at the desired letter). It was communicated that Benjamin Franklin, the American statesman and inventor, and Emanuel Swedenborg, the Swedish scientist and mystic, worked together on the "other side" to invent this method of communication. Apparently, efforts were made by the spirits to communicate for several years before two young girls, Margaret and Kate Fox, who lived with their parents in Hydesville, a suburb of Rochester, figured out that they could communicate with the "raps" by asking for so many raps for a "yes" and so many for a "no." When their parents and neighbors were called in, the alphabet system was employed for more detailed communication. During the 1850s, faster and more sophisticated methods of communication with the spirit world were established to replace this slower and more cumbersome method.

Spiritualists came to understand that low-level or "earthbound" spirits (not necessarily evil spirits) were more adept at communicating than more advanced or higher spirits and that the advanced spirits had to employ lower-level spirits to relay their messages. This was due to the vibratory aspect of the spirit world. That is, the lower-level spirits were closer in vibration to human vibration than the higher spirits.

It was also very easy, Spiritualists determined, for "earthbound" spirits to communicate without any guidance or direction from higher spirits. It soon became clear to the investigators that many human mental disorders were a result of spirit possession – depraved earthbound spirits would attach themselves to the aura or energy field of the human and thereby influence his or her actions. In most cases, the "possession" was limited to influences, but occasionally the spirit entity would completely take over someone's body. "It is an incontestable fact that there are among them bad, crafty, and profoundly hypocritical spirits, and against these we must be on guard," said French researcher Allan Kardec, "but because we meet in the world with bad men, is it a reason for withdrawing ourselves from society? God has given us reason and judgment to appreciate spirits as well as men."

Spiritualism became popular at a time when the 'Age of Reason', and then Darwinism, had both significantly undermined belief in God and an afterlife, especially among the educated. It helped many restore their faith in the supernatural, but, seeing some of it in conflict with Scripture and as a threat to their authority, orthodox Christianity vehemently resisted it. Citing Old Testament passages warning against "talking with the dead," Christian leaders condemned Spiritualism, referring to it as "demonic." However, there were a number of open-minded people, like Stevens, who believed that some good could come of it and that one had to "test the spirits whether they are of God" and "discern" the messages, as advised by the New Testament.

J. C. Bundy, the publisher of the Religio-Philosophical Journal referred to Stevens as "a man of pure life and great benevolence. His honesty, candor, modesty, and deeply religious nature combined to make him one of the noblest of men. His wonderful cures and good deeds have embalmed his memory in thousands of hearts."

Mary and 'Mary'

Accompanied by Asa Roff, Dr. Stevens visited the Vennum family on January 31, 1878. "The girl sat near the stove, in a common chair, her elbow on her knees, her hands under her chin, feet curled up on the chair, eyes staring, looking every bit like an 'old hag'," Stevens observed and reported. "She called her father "Old Black Dick" and her mother "Old Granny." When Stevens asked her name, she replied somewhat antagonistically that it was Katrina Hogan, giving her age as 63 and saying she was from Germany. After carrying on a conversation with Stevens, she suddenly changed personalities and claimed to be a man named Willie Canning. 'Willie' then started asking Stevens who he was, what his beliefs were, whether he went to church, liked to smoke, liked to drink, and other odd questions. After about an hour and a half, Rancy fell on the floor and went into a trance. She then began answering Stevens' questions "with rationality and understanding." She apologized for having such evil conditions about her and said she knew the evil spirits calling themselves Katrina and Willie.

Stevens suggested that she look around her for a higher, purer, more intelligent, and more rational spirit to control her. "Then, on being advised, she looked about and inquired of those she saw, and described, and named, to find someone who would prevent the cruel and insane ones from returning to annoy her and the family," Stevens continued the story.

Rancy said there were a great many spirits there willing to come, but that one "angel" who stepped forward gave her name as Mary Roff. "Mr. Roff, being present, said, 'That is my daughter; Mary Roff is my girl. Why she has been in heaven 12 years'," Stevens noted. "Lurancy, after due deliberation and counsel with spirits, said that Mary would take the place of the former wild and unreasonable influence."

Mary Lurancy Vennum Binning and daughter

After apparently discussing the matter with some spirits, Rancy announced that she was going to let Mary Roff take over her body for a period of time. A more mild, docile, polite, and timid voice then began speaking through Rancy's vocal cords. She knew none of the Vennum family and asked Asa Roff to take her home. Asa explained to the girl that she was at home and must remain there. The following day, 'Mary' continued to plead with the Vennums that she be allowed to return to her home.

Upon hearing of the situation, Mary Roff's older sister, Minerva Alter, paid a visit to the Vennum home with Ana Roff. "There comes my ma and sister Nervie!" "Mary" exclaimed, using her pet name for Minerva, a name not heard by anyone since Mary had died. After that reunion, Rancy, as Mary Roff, became even more homesick and begged to "go home." Reluctantly, the Vennums consented. According to Dr. Stevens:

> On the 11th day of February 1878, they (the Vennums) sent the girl to Mr. Roff's, where she met her 'pa and ma' and each member of the family, with the most gratifying expressions of love and affection, by words and embraces. On being asked how long she would stay, she said, "The angels will let me stay until some time in May," and she made it her home there until May 21, three months and ten days, a happy and contented daughter and sister in a borrowed body.

When Mary had died, the Roffs lived in another home not far from the one they now occupied. As the Vennums accompanied their daughter to the Roff's house, they passed by the Roff's old house. Rancy insisted that the old house was her home and had to be persuaded to continue on to the Roff's current home.

During the first month in the Roff home, 'Mary' refused to eat, explaining to her 'parents' that her nourishment was coming from heaven and it was necessary for her to refrain from food until the body was ready. Gradually, she came to eat with the family.

While at the Roff's house, Rancy – as 'Mary' – recognized old neighbors and friends. When Mrs. Parker and her daughter-in-law, Nellie, came calling, Rancy greeted them as "Auntie Parker" and "Nellie." Rancy asked Auntie Parker if she remembered when she (Mary Roff) and Nervie used to come to her house and sing, something which both Mrs. Parker and Nervie both clearly remembered. When another neighbor visited, Rancy called her Mrs. Lord, even though Mary Lord, a widow when Mary Roff knew her, had remarried and had become Mrs. Wagoner.

As a test one day in March, Asa Roff asked his wife to retrieve a velvet hat which their daughter wore before her death. It was placed on the table while 'Mary' was outside. When Rancy entered the house, she said, "Oh, there is the headdress I wore when my hair was short." On another occasion, Asa Roff asked "Mary" if she remembered their trip to Texas in 1857. "Yes, Pa," she replied, "and I remember crossing

Red River and of seeing a great many Indians, and I remember Mrs. Reeder's girls, who were in our company."

Lawyer that he was, Asa Roff tested "Mary" in other ways and became satisfied that his deceased daughter was indeed occupying the body of Rancy Vennum. On February 19, he wrote to Dr. Stevens, who had returned to his home:

> ...she recognizes everybody and everything that she knew when in her body twelve or more years ago. She knows nobody nor anything whatever that is known by Lurancy...she has been nothing but Mary since she has been here, and knows nothing but what Mary knew. She has entered the trance once every other day for some days. She is perfectly happy.

In another letter to Dr. Stevens, Asa Roff wrote that while Rancy was in trance one day, the voice of someone who claimed to have lived and died in Tennessee spoke through Rancy and told him that Mary would retain control of Lurancy's body until it was restored to good health.

On May 7, 'Mary' called her mother (Ana) to a private room and told her that Lurancy Vennum was coming back. A change of personality then took place and the girl asked Ana where she was, began crying, and said she wanted to go home. However, after about five minutes, Mary returned to Rancy's body. On May 21, Asa Roff recorded in a letter to Dr. Stevens:

> Mary is to leave the body of Rancy today, about 11 o'clock, so she says. She is bidding neighbors and friends good-by... She tells me to write to Dr. Stevens as follows: "Tell him I am going to heaven and Rancy is coming home well." She says she will see your dear children in spirit life... She talked most lovingly about the separation to take place, and most beautiful was her talk about heaven and her home.

At 11 o'clock, Rancy 'returned' and, speaking to Asa Roff as if a stranger, asked where she was and then asked to be taken to her home, where she recognized all members of her own family.

Rancy continued to live with her parents until her marriage to George Binning on January 1, 1882. She and her husband then moved west in 1884. It was reported that Mary would occasionally take control of Rancy's body in subsequent years, but apparently the possession was brief and caused no problems.

On April 12, 1890, Dr. Richard Hodgson of the American branch of the Society for Psychical Research visited Watseka and interviewed various people familiar with the story. "I have no doubt that the incidents occurred substantially as described in the narrative by Dr. Stevens," Hodgson reported, adding that the only explanation other than the spiritistic one was that Lurancy had a "secondary personality" with supernormal powers, a theory which seemed more fantastic than the spiritistic hypothesis. "My personal opinion," Hodgson concluded, "is that the 'Watseka Wonder' case belongs in the main manifestations to the spiritistic category."

Michael E. Tymn graduated from San Jose State College in 1958 with a degree in journalism. He has been a freelance writer since his college days, having contributed more than 1,400 articles to some 35 publications over the past 50 years. His primary interest now is in the metaphysical arena – he is the editor of *The Searchlight*, a quarterly magazine published by the Academy of Spirituality and Paranormal Studies, Inc.

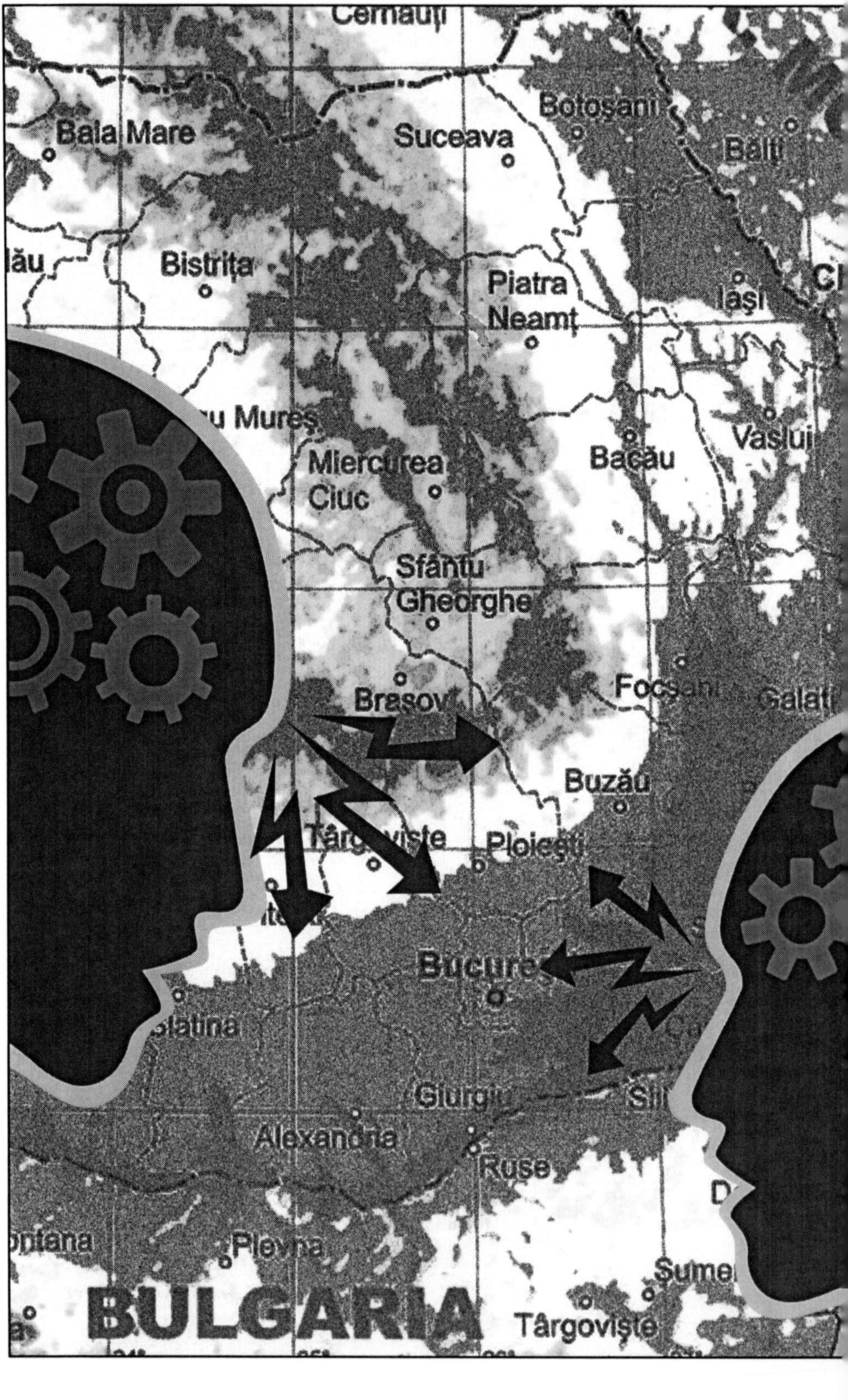

Baia Mare
Suceava
Botoșani
Bălți
Bistrița
Piatra Neamț
Iași
Vaslui
Bacău
Miercurea Ciuc
Sfântu Gheorghe
Brașov
Focșani
Galați
Buzău
Târgoviște
Ploiești
Giurgiu
Alexandria
Ruse
Plevna
BULGARIA
Târgoviște

INSTIGATING CHAOS IN ROMANIA

Was Psychotronic Warfare used during the December 1989 Revolution?

by *Robert M. Schoch and Oana R. Ghiocel*

Romania, 16 through 22 December 1989: the government of Nicolae Ceauşescu, the iron-fisted communist president, collapses. Opposition to the regime had been growing over the years, but when protests over the government's attempts to evict a dissident priest break out in Timişoara (a major city in the west of Romania) on 16 December, the anticommunist sentiments quickly grow, with crowds gathering, protests spreading, and riots ensuing. The army is sent in, but fails to establish order and active fighting escalates.

On the evening of 20 December, Ceauşescu delivers a televised address condemning the protests and violence in Timişoara, and blames the unrest on foreign influences. The next morning he speaks to a mass rally (roughly 100,000 people in attendance) from the balcony of a government building in downtown Bucharest, attempting to reinforce his speech of the night before. Far from garnering support for his fragile regime, the Bucharest rally has the opposite effect. Sounds interpreted as bombs or gunfire are heard, chaos breaks out, and voices blare from bullhorns announcing that the Revolution is underway. The rally turns into a massive protest.

Bucharest is in turmoil, while Ceauşescu and his personal contingent escape into the building and try to hide. To make matters worse for Ceauşescu, the dramatic rally and the ensuing chaos are captured live on national television (the censors could not cut the video feed in time). Ceauşescu tries to calm down the masses of confused people. The crowds disobey and Ceauşescu becomes angry and distraught. Those watching the events look on in disbelief.

Confusion and anxiety grow to the highest levels, with screaming hysterical masses trying to escape the scene – many injuries occur as people overrun one another trying to flee the now violent scene. Nobody knows what is happening. Ceauşescu continues to try to calm down the masses, but he is pulled from the balcony by security. The live broadcast continues to show masses of people fleeing the scene in horror. Eventually, the camera broadcasting the event pulls up from the crowds to the sky, in an effort to censor what is happening. An estimated three quarters of the Romanian population are watching...

Ceauşescu and the Christmas Celebration

On the morning of 22 December 1989, Ceauşescu and his wife Elena (who was also Deputy Prime Minister of Romania), along with a few high ranking members of his regime, made their exit from Bucharest by helicopter. Their dramatic escape, broadcast live on television, was followed by the announcement that he was now on the Romanian most wanted list.

With the apparent duplicity of Ceauşescu's newly appointed Minister of Defense, Victor Stănculescu (his predecessor died under suspicious circumstances earlier the same morning), as well as that of the helicopter pilot and others who were ostensibly helping them to flee, the Ceauşescu contingent was captured later in the day by the opposition. Ceauşescu and his wife were tried and summarily executed by an army firing squad on Christmas Day – the most important Romanian celebration. The brief trial and photos were broadcast on national television many times in the days to follow, right into the New Year. These are certainly the most celebrated holidays in Romania, apart from Easter. Coincidence? Was the execution part of the celebration? The execution presented a gruesome scene – photographs circulated of Ceauşescu and his wife in a pool of blood, with eyes frozen wide-open.

Can any situation be more dramatic than this? The finality of Ceauşescu's life was so extraordinary that it created shock and disbelief for days following the execution. This was an end that the Romanian people had desired for years, but could never imagine would happen so suddenly, and so perfectly. It was such a great story (with suspense, dramatic crescendos, and a climactic end) that it seemed too extraordinary to have happened by circumstance. To some observers, it all seemed staged.

The National Salvation Front (*Frontul Salvării Naționale*) established a new interim government. In the final days of the Romanian Revolution, sides in the fighting were not always clear as various factions vied for power. Orders were ambivalent, contradictory, and convoluted as chains of command broke down and loyalties shifted. Military contingents at times ended up fighting one another somewhat indiscriminately. The violence and chaos in Bucharest and elsewhere in Romania did not finally end until around 27 December.

During the ensuing chaos and violence, the National Library, where so many of the politically and historically important documents had been kept, was completely destroyed. By the end of the Revolution approximately 1100 people had died, and thousands were injured. Terrorists were blamed for these acts. A number of so-called authorities appeared on television urging the general population to stay calm and remain in their homes because terrorists had arrived in Bucharest to protect Ceauşescu. Nobody knew of course where the terrorists had come from – only that they were present in high numbers. Troops once loyal to the Ceauşescu regime were branded as terrorists. In the aftermath of the chaos, no genuine terrorists were ever identified, alive or dead. How is this possible? Were the reports pure fabrications?

During that frightful week confusion and panic reigned; fiction and reality blurred into one. Was this all a supreme example of media manipulation, or was it something even more insidious than that? Years after the revolution a number of top military officials broke their silence, and told of the manipulation of the masses via the application of psychological, radio-electronic, parapsychological, and psychotronic warfare techniques. Their version of events is shocking and controversial, presenting a totally new perspective on the Romanian Revolution.

Foreign Intervention and Non-conventional Weapons

The accounts given by these high-ranking military officers make the case that Romania was essentially a testing ground for unconventional, asymmetric warfare carried out using any techniques available, including blatant malefic psychic manipulation by domestic and foreign interests opposed to the Ceauşescu regime.

Teodor Filip was a key military commander during the Romanian Revolution, holding a number of important posts. He was Chief Commander of the USLA (*Unitatea Specială de Luptă Antiteroristă*

[Special Unit for Anti-Terrorist Protection]), he was in charge of security for President Ceauşescu, and he headed security operations at the Bucharest Otopeni International Airport (since renamed the Henri Coandă International Airport), the Parliament House, and other critical areas. In his book *Războiul Parapsihologic Împotriva României* [*The Parapsychological War Against Romania*] Filip writes...

> ...the moments of the beginning of the Romanian Revolution from December 1989, as well as the events that preceded it, raise many questions and doubts. Many of these events were marked by deeds that make one think of the premeditated action of a 'film director' from outside the masses of those revolting. Some elements make one realize that during the Romanian Revolution, against Romania took place a true parapsychological war, where all unconventional weapons of psychological, psihotronic [psychotronic], and psychic warfare were widely used.[1]

Other Romanian military and ex-military officers, as well as specialists in parapsychology, have supported Filip's assertions. Indeed, in present-day Romania books on the use of psychotronics (defined below) and related techniques during the Romanian Revolution have become a minor industry. But then Romania is the original source of the Dracula legends, and Filip, among others, suggests that the Romanian people have a predilection for paranormal phenomena.

In addition to Filip, other prominent Romanians speaking out about the military and terrorist applications of parapsychological and psychotronic techniques are:

• Emil Străinu, Romanian military scientist and Brigadier General who specializes in psychotronic spying, psychotronic warfare, and geophysical warfare.

• Florian Gârz, retired Colonel who had a long and distinguished military career from the late 1950s until June 1984, when he was accused of misconduct against the Ceauşescu regime and he resigned; after the Revolution, from 1991 to 1997, he served as adviser to the Department of Defense, National Security, and Public Order, and he was Head of the Secretariat of the Supreme Council of Defense of the Presidency of Romania.

• Dan Alexe, former Romanian police officer and ex-revolutionary; after the Revolution, he was in charge of security for the Romanian National Bank and State Treasury, 1991 to 1993; in 1993 he began a school for police officers; in 1994 he was chief commander in charge of guarding the Ammunition Factory Mija.

• Eugen Celan, a specialist in parapsychology, who served as President of the Romanian Association for Psihotronic [Psychotronic] Research after the 1989 Revolution.

Perhaps not coincidentally, the Romanian Revolution of December 1989 began in Timişoara, and it was in Timişoara a quarter century earlier that Professor Doctor Edouard Pamfil, Chief of the Psychiatric Department of the Timişoara Medical School, sponsored an unofficial, illegal, and politically dangerous study group that explored such topics as the influencing of public opinion through the media, methods of mass manipulation, and Soviet-style terror tactics to control the public. Topics discussed are likely to have also included parapsychological and psychotronic techniques. According to a United States Defense Intelligence Agency report – released under the Freedom of Information Act after being heavily redacted:

> Source stated that if these subjects were analyzed and/or publicized, they would reveal the full extent of the deception practiced by the East Bloc political leaders in their unscrupulous manipulation of the masses, and would thus endanger the Communist political system.[2]

Romania, with an independent nationalistic streak, was long a thorn in the side of the Soviets. By shrewd political and psychological manipulation, Romania avoided invasion by the Soviets, as Czechoslovakia was in 1968.[3] Teodor Filip contends that a number of countries (he names specifically the United States, England, "some European countries," Russia, Hungary, and Israel) were actively attempting to destabilize Romania, and by 1989 Romania was the only European country opposing Soviet Union President Mikhail Gorbachev's reforms. Furthermore these foreign powers were developing unconventional weapons and warfare techniques that needed to be tested under real wartime conditions in the field. Romania during December 1989 provided the perfect situation to secretly put them into operation.

Fake Fire

Although unconventional weapon use occurred before and throughout the December 1989 Revolution, such techniques escalated from 22 through 27 December, and then suddenly died down. Romanian military radar detected lines of enemy aircraft, and in some cases these could even be seen by naked eye from the ground, but when fired upon there were no aircraft present! Noises accompanied the faux aircraft, but not the proper sounds that should emanate from such aircraft. It became difficult or impossible to detect the difference between real and decoy or virtual targets.

As the events of the Romanian Revolution unfolded, an interesting phone conversation between two generals arguing about helicopters was aired on television.[4] One general asked his cohort if the helicopters flying across Romania, and picked up by radar, were his, but the other denied it. The two officers involved were General Ştefan Guşă, chief of the General Staff of the Romanian Armed Forces (1986-1989), and General Iulian Vlad, Minister of State, Secretary at the

Ministry of the Interior, and Head of the State Security Department. During the televised conversation, Vlad – when questioned about the helicopters – said to Guşă, "No they are not my helicopters. We do not have helicopters!" Guşă responded, "Well, if they are not yours, or mine, whose helicopters are they? Someone explain to me what is going on!" This conversation is very telling as it was between the top commanders of the very forces, the army and the state security forces, which were supposed to protect Ceauşescu.[5]

In the air, for pilots it was even worse. To give but one example, here is the testimony of Major Vasile Marcău, a helicopter pilot, as quoted by Filip:

> Starting with the night of 22 December we started chasing a non-existent enemy which was also attacking us. I was the first to take off at 10 p.m. On the coordinates indicated by the radio there were enemy targets present with light systems and other similarities to helicopters. I got close to the first enemy target that appeared to be a helicopter. I gave report of the position and prepared to fire. I opened fire. The enemy target vanished. After two seconds, the 'adversary' re-emerged and fired at me. I thought he will destroy my helicopter, but he did not. Around me, other luminous 'adversaries' appeared as if they wanted to capture me by surrounding my helicopter. I executed a few maneuvers at low altitude, and shocked that nobody opens fired against me I fired again with missiles and machine gun. A few of the targets vanished, and then re-emerged again firing at me. At first the fact that I was not hit I attributed to luck, then realized something very strange was happening. I attacked again. I fired a single missile. The enemy responded by firing a single shot of the same caliber as mine. Oops! Something was not right here. I got closer to the enemy. I fired twice; the enemy fired twice. I could not see the actual enemy in the night, but it felt in motion. I fired once more. The enemy fired once too. And then I realized the truth; I was fighting with simulated virtual helicopters gifted with a system

> that was able to capture and recreate any noise. It was noise without response. These targets' bullets did not exist – an excellent method of creating panic. A real adversary would have known, judging by my maneuvering, actions, and ammunition, by now how to respond to me in order to eliminate me. Somewhere near my right, another target emerged."[6]

Something very strange was indeed going on here. Were electronic means being used to jam radar and give false signals? Were hallucinations being induced in pilots and ground personnel? Clearly the intention was to confuse, distract, and destabilize the Romanian military apparatus while cutting into their supplies of fuel and munitions (wasting them on chasing and shooting at non-existent targets). Such strange, non-existent, aerial targets may possibly have been a more sophisticated form of the 'foo fighters', glowing lights that darted around flying aircraft, which were commonly reported during World War II. Former U.S. Army Lt. Col. Thomas E. Bearden, writing a decade before the Romanian Revolution, explained such phenomena as tulpoidal (essentially thought-form) manifestations from the collective human unconsciousness, stating "A war is a typical example of a situation where the group consciousness of a country is under enormous pressure. In such a situation, the 'targeted' population is often exposed to tulpoidal manifestations from time to time."[7] Bearden implies that such tulpoidal forms arise spontaneously, but during the Romanian Revolution could enemy forces have purposely induced similar, indeed more sophisticated, phenomena? We believe this may have been the case.

Terms

Parapsychology is a term used among Western academics to refer to the study of anomalous mental phenomena which generally fall into two broad categories:

(a) Mind-to-mind communication and interactions without the use of the normal senses (such as sight, sound, or touch), and the gathering of information by psychic means, including potentially from the past and the future; these are commonly referred to as telepathy and clairvoyance, or more generally extrasensory perception (ESP).

(b) Mind-over-matter, or anomalous energetic processes, such as moving or affecting matter by mental concentration alone (commonly referred to as psychokinesis, PK, or telekinesis) and the materialization and dematerialization of matter or energy (tulpoidal manifestations, and certain types of ghosts or discarnate entities, may possibly fall into this category).

Somewhat synonymous with the concept of parapsychology in the West is the older concept of psychical research. Psi is a more recent term for ESP and PK. In Western academic circles the term paranormal is used as more or less an equivalent to the subject matter of parapsychology. In popular parlance, however, the concept of the paranormal (and parapsychology) is much broader, and often includes many unusual and unexplained phenomena, such as UFOs (alien visitors could quite conceivably be perfectly "normal" in the sense that their technology is based on the same physics as ours, or they might have "paranormal" attributes, such as communicating telepathically), Sasquatch and Yeti (the domain of cryptozoology, but not necessarily paranormal unless, as some suggest, they are perhaps manifestations of thought, such as the Tibetan concept of tulpas or tulpoidal forms,[8] or some other exotic phenomenon), or crop circles (if they are hoaxes, clearly they are not paranormal; if crop circles are manifestations of aliens or Earth Spirits, then who knows?). Bottom line, in a strict Western academic sense parapsychology is focused on unexplained mental phenomena. Thus, if something can be ultimately explained in terms of electromagnetic radiation, for instance, it might no longer be classified in the domain of parapsychology and the paranormal by most Western researchers.

In the former Soviet Union and the Eastern Bloc countries, the concepts and distinctions in the field differed. The emphasis was less on purely mental or psychic abilities, in many cases, but rather more on practical and applied approaches. Indeed, standard Marxist-Leninist doctrine stressed materialism and to even entertain the concept of mind, consciousness, or spirit apart from matter and energy could be dangerous under classic Communist regimes. Thus in the East such terms as psychoenergetics, biophysical fields, biocommunication, paraphysics, bioinformation, and bioenergetics have been applied to subjects that have various amounts of overlap with Western parapsychology in a strict sense. A particularly widespread term in the East is psychotronics (psihotronics), which is variously considered more or less synonymous with Western parapsychology,[9] but actually emphasizes "instrumentation aspects"[10] of paranormal mental functioning. To put it more simply, psychotronics in practice includes a mixture of strict parapsychological phenomena and any other methods or techniques, from radio-electronics, electromagnetics, and acoustic modulation to the purely psychological. If it works, use it! All is fair in love and war.

Real Fires: Military Applications of Psychotronics

There are a number of potential military applications of parapsychological and psychotronic techniques, many if not all of which were allegedly tested during the Romanian Revolution. Here there is only room to mention a few major categories with some examples.

1. The Use of Psychics by National and Military Leaders.

Filip, who was apparently in a position to know, contends that by the end of his regime Ceauşescu had surrounded himself with people having reputed paranormal abilities, including a Tibetan monk, people he believed could help him maintain good health and provide advice. Some psychics appear to have genuine precognitive ability, which of course can be extremely useful. Filip mentions the case of Florian Onitza who predicted in April 1989, in print, the death of Ceauşescu on 25 December 1989. However, the use of psychics can be a double-edged sword. According to Filip, such persons could convince Ceauşescu to take actions that he would not otherwise carry out. Rasputin and his relationship to the family of Czar Nicholas II immediately comes to mind.

Could Ceauşescu's dictatorial control, his "madness," and resulting downfall, have been induced or enhanced by parapsychological techniques? Could his delusions of grandeur have been the result of psychic spies or some other form of psychic manipulation, either from inside or outside forces? Ceauşescu was the supreme leader of Romania beginning in 1965, first as Secretary General of the Romanian Workers' Party (which became the Romanian Communist Party), and in 1974 he took the title of President of Romania. At first he was an extremely popular figure, but by 1989 he had become so hated that when he was executed the people danced for joy. Was his decline facilitated by the use of unconventional means? During the first half of his tenure as leader Ceauşescu was open toward Western Europe and the United States, but the latter portion of his regime was characterized by a strange personality cult. He seemed totally unaware that the Romanian people had come to hate him. He strongly believed the people were content and happy with their lives and his leadership. At his trial, Ceauşescu kept repeating that he was betrayed and that strong outside influences played a major role in the Revolution, clearly stating that the Revolution was a well thought out, premeditated plan – not a spontaneous happening.

2. Psychic Espionage (Remote Viewing).

The use of telepathy and clairvoyance (given the collective and apparently more respectable name of remote viewing, or RV) for espionage is, at least in the West, the classic military application of parapsychological techniques,[11] and such techniques are rightfully stressed in the Eastern European arena also. What better way to spy than to access the closed quarters and even minds of the enemy remotely? Străinu and other Romanian authors discuss such techniques at length, but it is unclear how widely or successfully psychic espionage was carried out during the Romanian Revolution.

3. Dowsing.

Classic dowsing, using a forked stick or any of a number of other paraphernalia, is an ancient technique that has been used successfully to find not only underground water deposits, but mineral and ore deposits, buried objects, and so forth. In a military context, it has reputedly been used to discover underground tunnels and mine fields (presumably the latter remotely). We cannot confirm that dowsing was actually used during the Romanian Revolution.

4. Communications.

Telepathy can potentially be used to send messages under adverse conditions or when conventional communications systems break down. Even if captured by the enemy and stripped of all equipment, properly trained personnel may be able to transmit a message telepathically. It is not clear that such uses of telepathy occurred during the Romanian Revolution.

5. Remote Influencing, the Manipulation of the Masses, and the Weakening of Enemy Personnel.

Telepathic espionage is only a step away from telepathic manipulation. Surveillance and influence blend together, as accessing another's mind leads to planting thoughts in that mind. All the Romanian authorities we have mentioned discuss the use of telepathy to send messages with the intention of exerting influence on military and political leaders so that they will make decisions and take courses of action against their own best interests (dubbed in some cases remote influencing, RI). Another aspect is the "telepathic" manipulation of masses of people and entire military units. In Romania and the Eastern countries this is often attempted (and apparently accomplished) using instrumentation such as electromagnetic or acoustical generators (thus to the Western academic purist such techniques may not be strictly telepathic). The idea in many cases is simply to disrupt human psychic equilibrium, destroy the human will, and put a populace in a hypnotic, catatonic, or fearful state.

There are persistent reports of the development of particular types of psychotronic devices, commonly referred to as Pavlita generators[12] after the Czechoslovakian engineer Robert Pavlita who invented them in modern times (or reinvented them, as arguably such devices may have been known in ancient times and among Medieval alchemists). Pavlita generators supposedly store or concentrate psi energy, bioenergy, or biophysical energy, much as a Leyden jar stores an electrostatic charge, and then release the psi energy again, performing or amplifying paranormal feats. A person or other biological entity may charge a Pavlita generator, though some of these devices are said to be possibly charged by the cosmos. Străinu and others insist that different types of Pavlita generators can perform different functions, such as serving to enhance the psychic powers of spies, induce psychic disruption or hallucinations among a target audience, or act as a direct weapon that may even have the potential to kill from a distance. Could psychic manipulation of physical objects (psychokinesis) be used in a military setting to cause damage to the enemy? For instance, a well-trained psychic might conceivably be able to remotely influence enemy computers or other electronic equipment at a micro-level, causing a destructive scrambling effect. Or could PK be applied to macroscopic objects? Such controlled and directed uses of PK are at this point speculative at best.

Teodor Filip cites engineer Gheorghe N. Popescu as a direct witness to the potential use of manipulative techniques during the Romanian Revolution. Popescu, who attended the Ceauşescu speech of 21 December 1989, believes that a coherent transmission of electromagnetic radiation at the correct frequency (probably in the ELF, extremely low frequency, range) was able to produce both psychic effects among the human crowd and also initiate localized fires. The source of the 'broadcast', which may have included emissions from a Pavlita generator as well as acoustic emissions, was possibly set up in the Continental Hotel in downtown Bucharest, located in proximity to Revolution Square. Members of the crowd experienced strange, unsettling, and inexplicable sensations including the feeling of being stabbed. At this time, fires ignited in the Central Library, the Art Museum, and Small Hall of the Palace almost simultaneously. Filip argues that these buildings were so completely and thoroughly destroyed by the fires that it is unlikely only conventional techniques of burning were used.

6. Virtual Attacks and Tulpoidal Manifestations.

We already discussed 'virtual' aircraft attacks during the Romanian Revolution. Străinu describes an example of similar phenomena, this time apparently an accidental release of such weaponry, in his book *Psychotronic Warfare.* Even though it allegedly took place in the United States, we believe it is so interesting that we find it worth including here.

> One of the strangest events with psychotronic undertones happened in the morning of 12 March 1984 when Thomasville and Tucks, Nebraska, were suddenly attacked by strange military troops. The National Guard, and later the Army, intervened, but to everyone's surprise the attackers were not affected by bullets. The eyewitnesses confessed that the attackers looked very strange -- they looked as if

> they had been dead for a long time. The biggest surprise was that during the night of the attack, the dead soldiers 'came alive' and started to attack again.
>
> The following day and night things happened the same way as before, and the two towns became literal battlefields. Under the command of a short Chinese man, the troops that had just arrived were able to defeat the enemy all of a sudden, a very surprising occurrence, and then disappeared into an unknown direction taking with them the remains of the attackers as well.
>
> Much later, in the American mass media there was a big scandal involving a top secret U.S. Army project initiated by a Chinese psychotronic savant, named Shi Chang, also called 'the father of horror' because he had created specialized 'Zombie' troops; a certain number of soldiers had escaped control in unclear circumstances and revolted – which caused the above-mentioned incident. The American authorities covered up the event and made the public believe that the destruction of the two towns was caused by a tornado. Then the American authorities presented a report to the mass media stating that the Chinese professor Shi Chang had died a year before, indicating even the burial place. But military specialists confirmed that the experiment was real and it was continuing."[13]

We have not been able to confirm this report, but if there is any element of truth to it, might the "zombie" troops have been some sort of psychotronically induced thought manifestations?

Did Ceauşescu Know the Truth?

Ironically perhaps, as his regime came crumbling down, Ceauşescu may have known what was going on. He may have understood that paranormal and psychotronic methods had been used against him. During his trial he asserted that the secret services of various Western countries were involved in the Revolution. He demanded that he be judged in front of the Romanian people, have a proper trial, and let the general public decide his fate. Of course, looking back, perhaps he knew too much. Perhaps Ceauşescu had to be eliminated quickly, because he was indeed very aware of what was going on. His captors asserted that he was delusional, but at his trial Ceauşescu seemed sharp, clear, focused, and very much aware of the whole plot. Arguably, he had a very realistic perspective of what was going on. So perhaps, toward the end of his regime, he had been manipulated into believing that the general public loved him; at his trial he appeared capable enough to comprehend true reality and realize what had happened.

Today, many Romanians view the hasty and merciless Christmas execution of Ceauşescu much differently than back in 1989. Many people now wonder if his statements regarding foreign manipulation and intervention may be true.

The Parapsychological War Continues

Filip concludes his book with comments on the state of post-revolution Romania. He is convinced that the parapsychological war against Romania continues to this day. Dark, occult, forces are attempting to subjugate and conquer the spirituality of the Romanian people, using any and all means at their disposal he says, through both religious cults and infiltration into established religious and sectarian institutions. Especially nefarious, according to Filip, is the use and subversion of techniques that seem benign or even healthy in order to subjugate the population. Examples include forms of meditation, yoga, and hypnosis. Filip writes:

> The main role in the parapsychological war of spiritual subjugation of the Romanian nation belongs to the persons with 'paranormal' abilities, the Illuminated, who, using oriental relaxation techniques, turn masses of people into subjugated people. A person that 'relaxes,' 'meditates,' is under 'hypnosis,' is a person who has the subconscious open.[14]

And, by Filip's way of thinking, a person with an open subconscious is easily influenced and subjugated. His advice? "To survive the parapsychological war one needs to have a strong personality and a great ethical code. The knowledge of human psychic abilities, of the methods of psychic terror, and intuition are methods of defending oneself."[15]

One can argue that Romania during December 1989 presented an extreme, perhaps even anomalous, situation that surely does not apply to most of modern society. Even if Filip is correct, and the parapsychological war against Romania continues, surely Romania is an isolated example. Surely such parapsychological and psychotronic techniques are not being applied against the populations of more enlightened, more sophisticated, countries? Denial, we would note, is often a powerful and irrational emotion. Another view, one that we find more compelling and coincident with the evidence, is that Romania represents but a microcosm of the world at large. Parapsychological and psychotronic means of manipulation and warfare are real, and utilized widely. Of course authorities that are actively engaged in the development and use of these weapons deny that such techniques are even feasible, but what else would you expect them to say? The goal is to control and manipulate, not to inform; it is better for the aggressors to keep such weapons secret.

A final word from Teodor Filip:

> Society will be destroyed by a series of parapsychologists and 'illuminated' people who will subjugate the human spirit through the practice and perpetuation of techniques that started around 5500 B.C. They have the objective of destroying humanity. This will happen if measures against these practices are not taken.[16]

Being aware and understanding the dangers and powers of parapsychological warfare is the first step in the process of change. Now, should we take action or continue denying a very plausible, even probable, reality?

You have been warned.

Robert Schoch received a Ph.D. in Geology and Geophysics from Yale University, and since 1984 has been a full-time faculty member at the College of General Studies of Boston University. His books include the trilogy with R. A. McNally: *Voices of the Rocks*, *Voyages of the Pyramid Builders*, and *Pyramid Quest.* His most recent book is *The Parapsychology Revolution: A Concise Anthology of Paranormal and Psychical Research* (Compilation and Commentary by Robert M. Schoch and Logan Yonavjak, Tarcher/Penguin, 2008). Dr. Schoch's personal website is located at: www.robertschoch.com.

Oana R. Ghiocel received an M.A. in Documentary and Audio Production from Emerson College and she holds previous degrees in screenwriting and filmmaking. She was born in Bucharest, Romania, and was a witness to the Romanian Revolution of 1989. She is an award-winning media producer, consultant, and screenwriter, and currently is the Vice-President of Hyperion Media Inc. She has appeared on television and has a strong interest in history, human evolution, and parapsychology.

THE NEWHALLVILLE TERROR

THE DAY SPRING-HEELED JACK ARRIVED IN AMERICA

by *Theo Paijmans*

In the fall of 1881 an inexplicable phantomlike creature haunted the streets of Newhallville, a neighborhood of the town of New Haven in the state of Connecticut. During those cold October and November months Newhallville was in the grip of something that the local newspaper baptised 'the Ghost', or more evocative 'Newhallville's Terror'. The thing that stalked Newhallville's streets late at night was described by horrified eyewitnesses as a very tall white ghost, but also as "a man at least six feet tall" wearing black clothes, with "a capelike garment of black, probably rubber" over his head and shoulders, and on his forehead and nose a "shining phosphorus, or some luminous material." A phantom taking "monstruous strides as he went." New research into these strange events through contemporary sources places the scare in a surprising context and terrible tradition. For with the scare that befell Newhallville, the infamous 'Spring-heeled Jack' had finally arrived in America.

A Most Hideous and Frightful Appearance

Spring-heeled Jack: a tall, thin demonic figure with supernatural agility, metal claws for hands, eyes like balls of fire, a cloak and tight fitting garment, a helmet and a shining lantern on its chest, belching blue flames from its mouth and able to jump to impossible heights. This is how the world has come to know one of the most horrifying creatures in the annals of the anomalous. One fateful day Spring-heeled Jack leaped out of the shadows of Victorian England, and he has never quite gone away. Worldwide sightings of similar entities are said to have continued well into the 21st century, and the scare that befell Newhallville in 1881 is among the long list of sightings.

London, late February 1838. It is around a quarter to nine in the evening when 18-year-old Jane Alsop hears someone ringing loudly at the gate in front of the house where she lives. On opening the gate, she sees a cloaked man standing there who identifies himself as a policeman and exclaims: "For God's sake, bring me a light for we have caught Spring-heeled Jack here in the lane." But then, as Alsop fetches a candle and hands it over to the man, things take a turn for the worse. As the story goes...

> ...he threw off his outer garment, and applying the lighted candle to his breast, presented a most hideous and frightful appearance, and vomited forth a quantity of blue and white flames from his mouth, and his eyes resembled red balls of fire. From the hasty glance which her fright enabled her to get of his person, she observed that he wore a large helmet, and his dress, which appeared to fit

> him very tight, seemed to her to resemble white oil skin…

The thing attacked Alsop and tore at her dress, neck and arms, shredding lumps of hair from her head with what she thought were "metallic claws." Her testimony was published in *The Times* of February 22, 1838, and in a number of American newspapers.[1] The same month Spring-heeled Jack also attacked 18-year-old Lucy Scales, again at an evening when she and her sister were returning home. Passing along Green Dragon Alley, they saw someone standing there who was "enveloped in a large cloak." Lucy, who was slightly ahead of her sister, was about to pass the cloaked figure when all of a sudden he spurted "a quantity of blue flame right in her face, which deprived her of her sight, and so alarmed her, that she instantly dropped to the ground, and was seized by violent fits, which continued for several hours."[2]

But more than anything, Alsop's graphic and detailed description was influential in how Spring-heeled Jack was seen in the next 150 years or so. Alsop's recollection was so formative, in fact, that the complex and uncertain origins of Spring-heeled Jack – which lie far beyond those events in the 1830s – were largely forgotten. We need to take these murky origins into consideration for a proper appraisal of the events at Newhallville, as they reveal certain similarities between the British monster, and the entity (or entities) responsible for the Newhallville Terror scare.

What was to become known as Spring-heeled Jack evolved out of a series of partially overlapping ghost scares with names such as The Hammersmith Ghost, The Hammersmith Monster and The Park Ghost, that infested London and its environs as early as 1803.[3] At the beginning of 1804, an English newspaper picked up on these unusual occurrences and published accounts of encounters with a ghostly apparition said to have "eyes…like a glow worm" and breathing "fire and smoke."[4] In 1825 the London suburb of Hammersmith was again plagued by this fire-belching spectre.

Spring-heeled Jack's progeny appeared in various shapes. They were seen around London as a harnassed phantom, as a black bear, as shrouded ghosts with fiery eyes with or without horns and occasionally belching flames. Towards the end of December 1837 something prowled the London environs which would be given the name 'Spring Jack' by a newspaper. It was said that the prowler resembled a man wearing a bearskin, as well as a pair of "spring shoes" – the earliest reference to Spring-heeled Jack's unique and highly characteristic jumping ability.[5] That same year a ghost which took the shape of a large, white bull with horns had attacked "several persons, particularly females" in the neighbourhood of Barnes, Surrey.[6] And at the beginning of 1838 a ghost in the shape of a white bear was said to stalk the outskirts of London.[7]

Spring-heeled Jack in America

From this brief outline it's clear that at this time a specific, definite image of Spring-heeled Jack still had to emerge from the many reports and descriptions of a broad variety, but also with some key elements already in place such as luminous eyes and the belching of flames. This would arrive in February 1838 with the often repeated account of Jane Alsop as published in *The Times*. The now-famous name 'Spring-heeled Jack' was published for the first time, together with Alsop's graphic description of her phantom attacker. Spring-heeled Jack finally had its unique appearance and iconic image, and in the following years and decades similar scares erupted in different places in England well into the 20th century. But also in America, where for instance in 1939 a similar agile phantom named 'The Black Flash' terrorized Provincetown in Massachusetts,[8] and in 1951 in

Baltimore where the 'Phantom of O'Donnell Heights' struck fear in the hearts of the inhabitants of that neighborhood.[9] However, sudden appearances of extremely agile creatures with the uncanny ability to make enormous leaps or jumps, and sometimes belching flames or fire from their mouths occurred in various parts in the United States long before the brief reigns of terror of Provincetown's Black Flash and the Phantom of O'Donnell Heights.

Although news of Spring-heeled Jack's exploits in his various guises was reported in the American press from 1804, the earliest suggestion that Spring-heeled Jack had crossed the Atlantic and had taken root in America was not published until 1961. The theory was presented in a speculative article on Spring-heeled Jack written by one J. Vyner. It was published in *Flying Saucer Review*, a specialised UFO magazine based in England,[10] and in *Fate Magazine*, a monthly magazine on various Fortean and supernatural phenomena published in America.[11] Lacking sources or references, it did offer a small collection of cases, out of which four concerned alleged Spring-heeled Jack sightings in America. The article became a highly influential source for subsequent authors on the topic of Spring-heeled Jack and his presence in America. Vyner's description and examples of the supposed presence of Spring-heeled Jack in America have been cited many times. Some have done so with measured degrees of caution, while others simply copied Vyner's data as fact.[12]

In truth though, Vyner's treatment of American 'Spring-heeled Jack' incidents proves to be a dead-end. The four examples Vyner listed as evidence of the presence of Spring-heeled Jack in the United States actually have nothing to do with the phenomenon. Vyner added the unrelated 'Mad Gasser of Mattoon' scare to the lore of Spring-heeled Jack, and the other three cases consist of an entirely different form of anomaly. They are not concerned with extremely agile, jumping and fire-belching creatures, but instead involve brief sightings of furtive flying humanoids, engaged in none of the activities that Spring-heeled Jack was famous for and which could be considered as his unique 'signature'. These cases are well-known Fortean events, involving the Chehalis flying man sighting (1948) and what was come to be known as the Houston Batman (1953). The third is the most puzzling, an incident that allegedly occurred in Louisville, Kentucky in 1880.

Though full of errors, Vyner's article was the single most influential article on Spring-heeled Jack in America, and it set the tone and general direction of future researchers and authors on Forteana and the paranormal. The unfortunate effect has been that we now often find references to flying humanoids and even the occasional 'mad gasser' intertwined with the Spring-heeled Jack phenomenon. The consequence is that the true history of Spring-heeled Jack in America has remained largely hidden from view.

Vyner situates the earliest appearance of Spring-heeled Jack in America in Louisville, Kentucky in 1880 and was the first to do so. The later treatment of the incident by author Jim Brandon is often copied on websites and in books on Forteana and the paranormal, but has all the hallmarks of a false assertion and in my opinion does not exist. Vyner devotes very few words to the event and does not offer a reference, merely stating that it was "Seen Louisville, Kentucky, July 28, 1880".[13] Vyner also offers no description of its appearance, nor any other details. Jim Brandon subsequently did in his *Weird America,* published in 1978, where Vyner's sparse entry is transformed into the sighting of a "tall and thin weirdo" who was

> ...agile as a monkey and with a long nose, pointed ears, and long fingers... He wore a sort of uniform, made of shiny fabric, and with a long cape and metallic helmet. On his chest under the cape was a large, bright light. His big thing seemed to be scaring people – particularly women – sometimes getting so familiar as to pull their clothing off. His favorite method of escape was by springing smoothly over high objects like haystacks or wagons, then vanishing on the other side.[14]

Brandon too, left this entry unreferenced. In extensive searches over prolonged periods of time, I have found no trace of an original source for these details, not in the *Louisville Courier-Journal* of 1880, not in any other Kentucky newspaper, nor for that matter in any American newspaper from that period available to me. Not only that, the researchers and writers that I contacted who listed the 1880 Louisville event in their writings had used either Vyner or Brandon as their source. In my own discussion of this case with Brandon he was unfortunately unable to locate his source in his files and could not remember where he had originally got the information from.[15] Analyzing and comparing Brandon's description with Alsop's account and the sparse data in Vyner's article, we find a mixture of separate and unrelated ingredients which in Brandon's entry conjured up a phantom that supposedly visited Louisville, but one that never existed; that Brandon's entry is composed of that part of Vyner's article where Vyner offers a description of Alsop's English Spring-heeled Jack, and not the American one that supposedly terrorized Louisville in 1880.

What was seen in Louisville on July 28, 1880, was – and this is in tune with Vyner's other two cases of flying humanoids – a flying man. On the evening of July 28, 1880, two perplexed Louisville residents C.A. Youngman and Ben Flexner were standing at a side window of Haddard's drug store in that city when they saw…

> …an object high up in the air apparently directly above the Ohio river bridge which they first thought was the wreck of a toy balloon. As it got nearer they observed that it had the appearance of a man surrounded by machinery, which he seemed to be working with his feet and hands. He worked his feet as though he was running a threadle, and his arms seemed to be swinging to and fro above

> his head, though the latter movement sometimes appeared to be executed with wings or fans... They could see the delicate outlines of machinery, but the object was too high up to make out its exact construction. At times it would seem to be descending, and then the man appeared to exert himself considerably, and ran the machine faster, when it would ascend again and assume a horizontal position. It did not travel as fast as a toy balloon, and its course seemed to be entirely under the control of the aeronaut. At first it was travelling in a southeastward direction, but when it reached a point just over the city, when it tucked to the southwest, in which direction it was going when it passed out of sight in the twilight of the evening...

This sighting was published a day later in the *Louisville Courier-Journal*.[16]

The Newhallville Terror

It would be a simplification to state that Spring-heeled Jack 'arrived' in America, if it implied the arrival of just one entity or phantom (or perhaps human agent). For there never was just one Spring-heeled Jack, rather a long tradition of various manifestations which can be grouped together through their uncanny similarities in appearance and action. The emergence of this Spring-heeled Jack phenomenon in America, though, was not in Louisville in 1880, but a year later in Newhallville. From then on we find a continuation of outbreaks throughout the years in various parts of the United States. In my paper on Provincetown's Black Flash (published in 2007 in *The Anomalist #13*) I assembled a preliminary list of thirteen cases where the Spring-heeled Jack phenomenon had manifested itself in America between 1885 and 1927.[17] For my larger study on Spring-heeled Jack in America (to be published in a collection of papers devoted exclusively to Spring-heeled Jack, entitled *Spring-heeled Jack: Sources and Interpretation*), I was able to expand the list of cases to more than thirty events up to 1975 – but which begin in 1881 with the Newhallville Terror.[18] It is there that the history of Spring-heeled Jack in America truly begins.

On October 26, 1881, the evening edition of the *New Haven Register*[19] commented in a lengthy article that for some time things had not been well in the neighborhood of Newhallville.

> An awful dread overshadows all that region of the town lying easterly of the Hamden line and known to people generally as Newhallville. A fear that could not have been engendered except in contemplation of the deep systems of the night side of nature, prevails in nearly all the families within a radius of several blocks contiguous to the corner of Shelton avenue and Division street, and the time has come when it is no longer judicious to refrain from a revelation of some of the principal facts. The women and children of that section of the town talk of nothing but the ghost, and as the stories of the sudden appearance, by night, of the spook, whenever women or children are out in the evening alone, are told and retold by the people with every variation of horror in the recital.

On the basis of a "careful investigation" of the matter, "throwing aside all that is improbable," the author of the article offered the following incidents which had sparked the "awful dread":

> Something like three weeks ago it was talked among the people of the neighborhood that it was unsafe to be outside of the house after dusk, as the ghost was likely to be met. If met, it was uncertain what dire transaction might take place, and young ladies began to refrain from evening walks, and finally from a ride into the city by the horse cars. Something happened last night which has added to the fearful excitement which prevails. Miss Jennie Burton, a handsome, sprightly young lady, with bright, black eyes, residing

> in the Comstock house, on Dixwell avenue, had been into New Haven during the evening. She returned by a late car. After getting off the car, Jennie and her friend proceeded homeward by Division street. After going about half a block, the two girls were stricken with fright by meeting the ghost face to face. Jennie fainted and was taken on board an up-bound car by persons near who had been alarmed by the excitement, and was carried to the house of Mrs. Milander, where it was feared for a time she would die. Dr. Lines attended the case. A call was made at the Comstock house this morning. The young girl was in better condition and described the apparition as being that of a white man wrapped in a yellowish white covering which might, if of material substance, have been a dirty table cloth. The figure was entirely enwrapped in this ghostly garment and held up its hands and moved its fingers in a weird manner, like clawing the air. The inside of the hands shone with mephitic light and there was a gleam of phosophoric radiance on the face. The moment the girls shrieked the ghost disappeared, and an immediate hunt that was instituted availed nothing to discover a trace of him.
>
> Last night Mrs. Charles S. Meeker, of 240 Division street, was walking in company with her friend, Mrs. H.W. Hindsley, of Hazel street, on Dixwell avenue between Ivy and Brewster streets. Mrs. Meeker says: "When we saw him or it, the ghost walked toward us about twenty yards and stopped. He was all covered up in a dirty, white sheet or cloth of some kind, and appeared to be partly leaning against the fence. Mrs. Hindsley was scared before I was.

These incidents were just the latest in a string of sightings in the area. Locals were moved enough to put together a group of nearly twenty-five men to patrol the woods and fields of "the ghost-visited district," but no sign "of the unwelcome prowler from the under-world" was found. We can be certain though that they meant business:

> Night after night, parties of a dozen, more or less, have hunted the thoroughfares, visiting the sheds and vacant buildings and peering between every fence rail and tree. Some of the committee have had the happiness of seeing the ghost, as they believe, in the distance, but never near enough for a pistol shot to take effect. Many of the young men of Newhallville go out of nights armed, fully prepared to shoot the ghost on sight and it will be a dead ghost, if the expression may be allowed, should one of these young men get a good range of its outline with a revolver.

For all the ghostly elements to the story though, there was no doubting that many locals felt the "author of the mischief" was probably still residing on this plane of existence. Rumors abounded as to the identity of the culprit. The newspaper reported, for example, that one explanation for the "terror" centered on a man who had previously lived in Newhallville, but had been "treated with some injustice" and gone away:

> Time elapsed, and brooding over the wrongs which had been done him he had returned and went prowling about and frightening women and children in revenge for what he had endured. A milkman going his rounds before the break of day, has seen the ghost and reported the circumstance to some of his customers, which has served to strengthen the fears which exist. A woman, living on Shelton avenue describes the ghost as being a black man. This does not agree with the description furnished by other intelligent ghost seers.

Nevertheless, one of the primary elements that ties the Newhallville reports to the Spring-heeled Jack mythos is his speed and agility. One lady "favored with a sight of this mysterious being" reported that "he lightly vaults into the air in acceleration of his speed, and that he has – must have – some kind of springs on his shoes to enable him to mount upward and scale over fences whenever his ghostship chooses to disappear." And despite numerous sightings and pursuits (at least six in one night on one occasion), nobody could lay a hand on the attacker: "He eludes the swiftest on foot, and those who know all the unevenness of the ground and are familiar with every hole or stone or stump, cannot move fast enough to catch the mighty disturber of the public peace. So far, beyond frightening people, no harm has been done."

One peculiarity of the "ghost" was, that when seen by women it would be dressed in white, and when afterward seen by men, it would be "clothed from head to foot in entirely black raiment, like a pall."

Phosphoric Radiance

In the coming days and weeks, more sightings of the ghost were reported. Beginning of November, it was seen thrice on Howard avenue, and a theory was current that "the ghost is that of a colored woman murdered about twenty-five years ago."[20] A man chased the ghost one November night, "I gave chase and in the flight it dropped a sheet... I am under the impression he is a large coloured man over six feet high... he formerly lived in Allingtown and takes a pleasure in frightening women and children. He is fleet of foot and hard to catch. He is said to be the quickest runner in the state..."[21]

Notwithstanding, the ghost kept manifesting itself. "Women and children continue to suffer from fright, on account of the appearance of the Newhallville ghost in different parts of the city. The figure is white and disappears when a man is in company with the woman."[22] Embedded in the confusion of sightings, hearsay, stories and possible explanations, we find a number of very curious encounters:

> There is current in York street and vicinity a story that a man having a business occupation on that street during the day has

> had an experience with the ghost… The other night…while he was out alone with a stout club the ghost rose. The man boldly engaged him, planting as he believed a telling blow. The ghost "lit out" with his fist, or something hard – perhaps an electric club – and the ghost killer was dazed…
>
> A young gentleman who lives in the north eastern part of the city, thinks he saw the ghost an evening or two ago about ten minutes before six o'clock. He was going up Whitney avenue thinking of anything but seeing an apparition, when upon reaching the gateway leading into the Footehouse, at the corner of Humphrey street, he was startled by an animated figure against one of the posts. It was that of a man at least six feet tall, who with his hands back of him against the post, straightened himself up to his full length. Over his head and shoulders was a capelike garment of black, probably rubber. His clothes were black and in no way noticeable. On his forehead and nose was shining phosphorus, or some luminous material. Owing to the darkness the man could not tell whether the man was white or colored. Neither party said anything and the man in black soon turned and went off in a bee line beneath the trees, taking monstruous strides as he went. This description of the ghost does not correspond with those given by most of those who have seen it, or think they have.

The description "given by most", as the article earlier explained, was that of "a colored person, dressed over all other clothing, in a white sheet."[23]

Dwight S. Tyrell had a Saturday night encounter with the ghost, during which it seized him by the arm. He retaliated, striking his attacker with his cane, "but the blows resounded on wood or sheet iron, and it is believed that some defensive armor was concealed under its clothing." Once again we find recurring elements: "Phosphoric radiance shone from the face and hands of the ghost, and immediately after the encounter this mysterious being sprang into the air and disappeared over a high board fence."[24]

To add to the confusion, the ghost was seen the night of November 21 by two policemen in different locations. Officer Pickering sighted the ghost on Ashmun street, "nor far from Grove street cemetery." Pickering pursued the ghost, but try as he might, he "could not get nearer than within about thirty feet of the frightful being. Its head and the upper part of his person were enveloped in a white wrapping of some kind – perhaps a shroud." The officer kept the ghost in view and continued the pursuit until the figure, "which appeared to float airily over the ground, gently lifted itself upward and disappeared over some neighboring buildings." A little after midnight that same night, Officer Bergin saw the ghost in Fair Haven:

> [H]e was met full in the face, and very unexpectedly, by the ghost, who raised both hands, the palms turned outwards in a threatening manner, the face and the hands of the ghost gleaming with phosphoric light, and in a horrid voice he or it said: "B-b b-b-boo-oo oo," and before the officer could catch him, the ghost had vanished into the circumambient darkness.[25]

It Wore a Cloud of Mist or Smoke

The endings of ghostly flaps and phantom scares are always unclear; the newspapers are usually marked by a sudden stop in the reporting of incidents. After the end of November, I did not find any other accounts on the Newhallvile ghost. I was able to reconstruct an indication of the length of the scare by way of a retrospective on the mysterious affair that was published half a century later in the *New Haven Register*:

> ...how many there are living today who remember the Newhallville Ghost scare of about 52 years ago? The newspapers were filled with accounts of this hopping, jumping, galloping, drifting apparition that performed almost nightly in the Newhallville or Southern section of Hamden for several weeks, frightening women, children and even men into hysterics, sometimes causing them to flop down in a dead faint right in the street. Self-appointed posses roamed the section night after night, their members armed with revolvers, rifles, shotguns, clubs and pitchforks in a vain endeavor to round up the Ghost, but without success. Those who claimed to have seen the ghastly night roamer, fixed its height at from 8 to 12 feet. On one thing all of these agreed; the wraith was invariably arrayed in white. Some said the unearthly visitant was clothed in a robe, while others insisted that it wore a cloud of mist or smoke. Another matter on which those who made its closest acquaintance agreed, was that the apparition made no bones whatever in leaping over fences as gracefully and easily as a running deer, no matter how high the fence might be.

Its writer, William H. Avis, recalled the scare well, as he had experienced the events himself: "The writer remembers the Ghost scare quite as vividly as if the demonstration were taking place right at the present time. While I never got a glimpse of the visitant, yet with many others armed to the teeth, I tried to assist in rounding the invader up, but without success. In fact, the Ghost was never rounded up, and the mystery was never solved..."[26]

The Newhallville Terror was not to be entirely forgotten. In 1988 another retrospective was published in the *New Haven Register* by

Connecticut folklorist Neil Hogan,[27] using the 1930s article and the first account on the Newhallville Terror published on October 26, 1881. Hogan's retrospective in turn was to become the source for a brief appearance of the Newhallville Terror in the 1996 book *Passing Strange: True Tales of New England Hauntings and Horrors,* by Vermont author Joseph Citro.[28]

Precisely how many strange creatures stalked the streets of the neighborhood of Newhallville will perhaps forever be a mystery. The various descriptions suggest that at least more than one person or entity was at work. Since the reporting on the Newhallville Terror in the *New Haven Register* stopped as suddenly as it had began, we have no way of knowing how or why the scare came to an end, nor do we have details of its aftermath. How many more sightings were made, and what other stories about the phenomenon circulated?

But from the various descriptions it is clear that something (or some things) very strange stalked the streets of Newhallville that fall of 1881. Whether a hoax, scare or truly anomalous phenomenon – and all of these possible explanations were offered in the pages of the *New Haven Register* in the 1880s – is impossible to fathom. But it is not the most important aspect, as the larger history of Spring-heeled Jack is riddled with these same problems of assessment and identification. What matters more is that we find the same crucial elements in the Newhallville Terror as we do in the various unique aspects of the original and early Spring-heeled Jack scare. Both have mentions in their descriptions of invulnerability, of phosphorescent faces, "phosphoric radiance," of smoke and luminous eyes, and in both cases capes or cloaks are mentioned. But most especially, how the Newhallville Terror was to be remembered half a century later, as a creature adorned with an uncanny agility "leaping over fences as gracefully and easily as a running deer, no matter how high the fence might be" – not to mention its preference for a certain type of victim: mostly young women. We will probably never know the true nature of the scare that befell Newhallville, as the events have since long faded from history. But with this strange moment in New Haven's history, Spring-heeled Jack had entered America.

Theo Paijmans has authored two books, a history of the UFO phenomenon published in 1996, and *Free Energy Pioneer: John Worrell Keely*. Published in 1998 it has been reprinted and saw a translated version published in Japan in 2000. His articles and papers have appeared in various publications including *All Hallows, Strange Attractor, The Anomalist, Gazette Fortéenne, The Centre for Fortean Zoology Yearbook 2009* and *Fortean Times*, where he is a regular columnist. His papers on the History of Spring-heeled Jack in America and Spring-heeled Jack in New Zealand were published in an academic collection under the editorship of Mike Dash. Theo was invited to speak and participate in the panel discussion at the 2008 Fortean Times Unconvention, and has recently appeared as expert in a Discovery Channel documentary on the Vril Society (*Dark Fellowships: The Vril Society*), the subject of his book slated to appear at a later date.

THE SACRED LANDSCAPE OF RE

Are the Old Kingdom Pyramids Interconnected?

by *Robert G. Bauval*

In 1990, the aging French Egyptologist, George Goyon, – who had once been the private Egyptologist of King Farouk of Egypt and had studied the pyramids for many years – could not help asking the following question: "Did the Egyptians of the Pyramid Age have much more astronomical and geographical knowledge than hitherto assumed by us?"[1] After so many years of investigating the pyramids of Egypt, and having studied their astronomical qualities, then my answer is a resounding 'Yes'.

It all began for me back in 1983 when I was working in Saudi Arabia. Having made the observation that there was a correlation between the layout of the Giza pyramids and the stars in Orion's belt, I had written a short dissertation and mailed it to various eminent Egyptologists including Dr. I.E.S Edwards and Dr. T.G.H. James, both senior members of the British Museum. I presented to them for the first time the so-called Orion Correlation Theory (OCT) which argued that the placing of the Giza pyramids was based on a plan inspired by the pattern of Orion's belt. And although I then also strongly suspected that all other pyramids may have been also positioned relative to each other, based on religious ideologies derived from astronomical observations, I nonetheless refrained from discussing this at the time lest it would at this stage complicate the OCT.

Much later I would note that some prominent Egyptologists had also suspected a 'religious' rather than practical/engineering motive for the positioning of pyramids in the vast Memphite necropolis. Miroslav Verner, for example, was to point out that "limestone occurs almost everywhere in the area of the Memphite necropolis and the technical difficulties in obtaining it and transporting it to the building site did not vary substantially between the different places."[2] In other words, the apparent unruly scattering of the pyramids over a vast area running nearly 40 kilometres from Abu Ruwash to Dashur, was not due to the availability of quarries, as often suggested, but to some other motive which could only be 'religious'. Jaromir Malek seems to support this idea when he writes that:

> The idea that the distribution of the pyramids is governed by definable ideological (religious, astronomical, or similar) considerations is attractive. After all, if there were such reasons for the design of the pyramid and for the relationship of monuments at one site, why should we shut our eyes to the possibility that similar thinking was behind the apparently almost perverse scatter of the pyramids over the Memphite area? The argument that the Egyptians would not have been able to achieve this had they set their mind to it cannot be seriously entertained.[3]

The same views were also cautiously expressed by Mark Lehner, today's perhaps foremost expert on the Egyptian pyramids. Lehner wrote that:

> ...some religious or cosmic impulse beyond the purely practical may also have influenced the ancient surveyors.[4]

Lines of Sight

The first time that someone noted an interrelationship between the Giza pyramids and the Sun Temple of Re at Heliopolis was in 1752 when Hekakian Bey noted that the south-west and north-east diagonal of the Great Pyramid extended to the distant obelisk of Sesostris I at Heliopolis.[5] In the 1970s the French Egyptologist George Goyon also proposed another line of sight from the north-south axis of the Great Pyramid to the ancient town of Letopolis, 16 kilometers north of the Giza Plateau, where he believed that a sighting bollard or tower once stood to aid the ancient surveyors to maintaining a precise alignment towards due-north.[6] What made Goyon's hypothesis very convincing was that it was well-known

Line of sight from Abu Ghorab

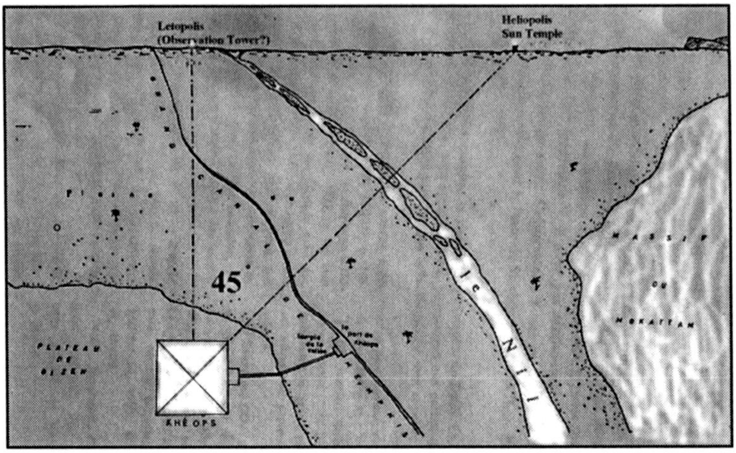

The Pythogorian triangle formed by Giza, Heliopolis and Letopolis

that from earliest times Letopolis had been the capital of the second Nome of Lower Egypt, and very much related to the sun-priests of Heliopolis and those of the Giza pyramids.[7] Goyon also pointed out that Letopolis was precisely due west of the sun-temple of Heliopolis, so that the three locations – the Giza Plateau, Letopolis and Heliopolis – form a huge and perfect Pythagorian triangle.

Nothing much was made out of these discoveries until the 1990s when the British Egyptologist David Jeffreys noted other lines of sight between the 5th dynasty sun-teemples of Abu Ghorab and the sun-temple of Heliopolis. Jeffreys cleverly noted that whereas one could have a clear and unobstructed line of sight towards Heliopolis from the Abu Ghorab sun-temples, this was not the case if one moved a little further south to the site of the 5th dynasty pyramids at Abusir. This was because the view from Abusir was obstructed by the Muqattam hills in the east.[8]

In Jeffreys own words:

> A re-examination of the location of Pyramids whose owners claim or display a special association with the solar cult betrays a cluster pattern for which a political and religious explanation suggests

> itself...The Giza pyramids could also be seen from Heliopolis... It is therefore appropriate to ask, in a landscape as prospect-dominated as the Nile Valley, which sites and monuments were mutually visible and whether their respective locations, horizons and vistas are owed to something more than mere coincidence.[9]

In 1997 Mark Lehner sensed yet another interrelationship between the 4th dynasty pyramid of Djedefre (a son of Khufu) at Abu Ruwash and the sun-temple of Heliopolis:

> ...the pyramid built by Djededfre, Khufu's son and successor, (is) 8 km (5 miles) to the north on a hillock overlooking the Giza plateau. By moving to this spot (Abu Roash), Djedefre's pyramid was *nearer* due west of Heliopolis, centre of the sun cult, than Giza. Perhaps he was motivated by religious reasons since Djedefre is the first pharaoh to take the title 'Son of Re'.[10]

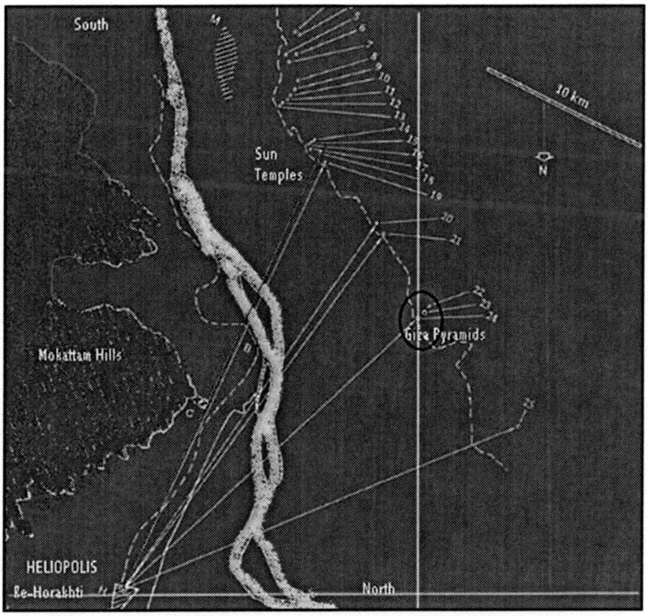

Line of sight from Abu Ghorab to Heliopolis

Measuring from various maps of the Memphite necropolis[11] and also from Google Earth satellite imagery, I determined that the sun-temple of Heliopolis was at 26.5° north of east from the pyramid of Djedefra. From my studies on the astronomy of the pyramid builders I was acutely aware that the angle 26.5° north of east had immense significance to the 4th dynasty pyramid builders. At the latitude of this region (30° N) 26.5° north of east marked the position of sunrise on the first day of the calendar year when the 'Birth of Re', the Sun God, was celebrated in the Old Kingdom. In c. 2500 BC, the epoch of the 4th dynasty pyramid builders, this event fell 4 days *after* the summer solstice, which also was the time of the heliacal rising of the 'birth star' Sirius, the marker of the religious New Year in ancient Egypt. This cosmic event also heralded the yearly flood of the Nile which, on average, came around the end of June.

Considering how crucially important this event was to the ancient Egyptians, and also how much focus was given to the first dawn rising of Sirius at this time of year – not only because it marked the start of the flood season but also because it symbolized the rebirth of Egypt and, by extension, the rebirth of the king –

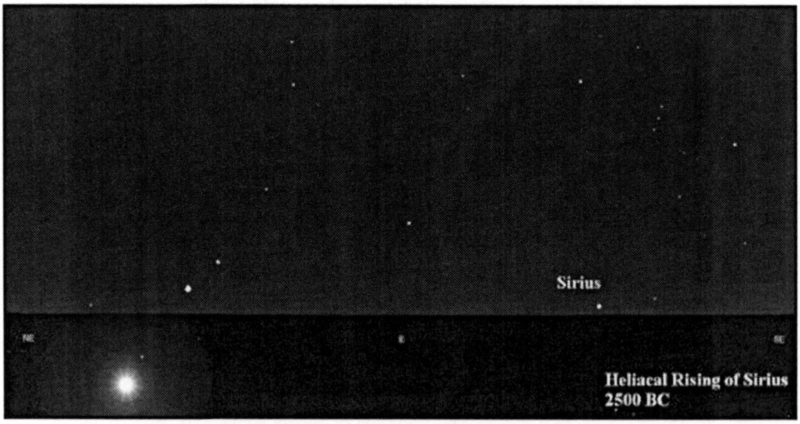

The sun about to rise at 26.5° north of east on the day of the heliacal rising of Sirius in c. 2500 BC

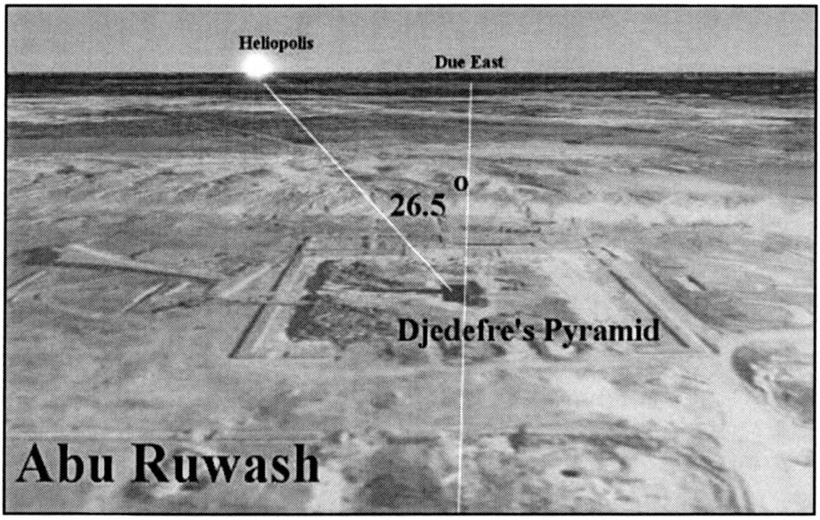

The line of sight from Djedefre's Pyramid to Heliopolis

then it must be taken as not being a coincidence that Djedefre's pyramid and the Great Sun Temple of Re at Heliopolis were interconnected by a line of sight that ran 26.5° north of east from the Djedefre complex.[12]

In the Spring of 2008, while investigating this matter further, I also noted that the there was another line of sight shooting from the Great Pyramid to the Abu Ruwash pyramid at 45° west of north. Considering also that Hekekian Bey (as mentioned earlier) had shown that there was also a line of sight shooting 45° north of east from the Great Pyramid to Heliopolis, as well as a due-north line of sight from the Great Pyramid to Letopolis and a further line of sight due-west from Heliopolis to Letopolis, then it would much appear that what is being discerned here is a deliberate topographical plan to interrelate the Great Pyramid, the Djedefre Pyramid and the Sun Temple at Heliopolis in some sort of sacred scheme surely associated with the rebirth rituals of the pyramid builders.

Temple of the Sun

The importance of the sacred city of Heliopolis in the Old Kingdom when the pyramids were built was immense. Heliopolis was the principal centre of initiation and teaching of the Old Kingdom sun-priests of the cult of Re, especially during the 4th Dynasty when the Pyramid Age was in full expansion. The 'solar' connotations of Heliopolis are well known: its main temple was dedicated to Re, the Sun-God and supreme deity of the pyramid builders. There was also another temple at Heliopolis, probably within the heart of the Re Temple, called in the Pyramid Texts the 'Mansion of the Bennu (Phoenix)', in which was kept a sacred conical stone called the *Benben* that symbolized the Primeval Mound of Creation upon which the sun first appeared. It is most likely that the pyramids of the Memphite necropolis, including those at Abu Ruwash and Giza, were the brainchild of the priests of Heliopolis.

We also know that the great sun temple of Re at Heliopolis was especially dedicated to Re-Horakhti, Re-Horus-of-the-Horizon, the

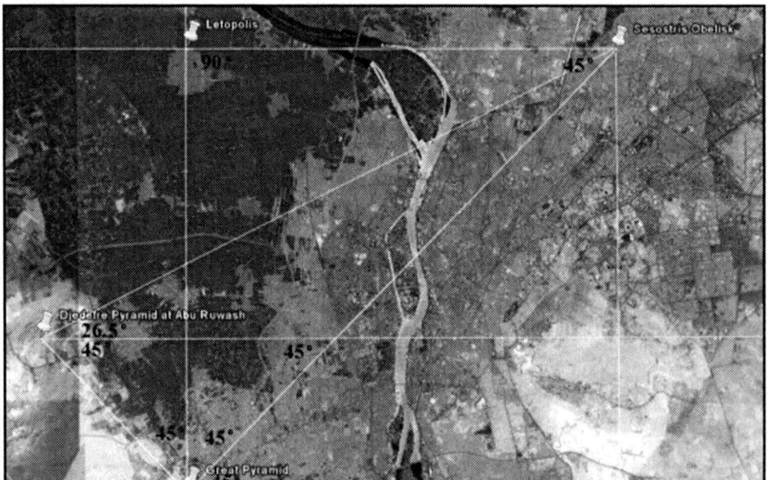

The lines of sight joining the Great Pyramid of Giza, to Heliopolis, to Letopolis and to the Djedefre Pyramid at Abu Ruwash

falcon-sun-god of the Old Kingdom. Heliopolis, in fact, was *the* 'City of Re-Horakhti'.[13] Indeed, the high priest of Heliopolis was known as the 'Chief Seer of Ra-Horakhti', and the *Benben* relic, according to Egyptologist Labib Habachi, was "sacred to Ra-Horakhti, the rising sun."[14] The term 'Horakhti' i.e. Horus-of-the-Horizon, is eponymous with the Great Sphinx of Giza which was, in the New Kingdom, called 'Horemkhet', i.e. Horus-in-the-Horizon, a very slight variation of Horus-of-the-Horizon. All Egyptologists agree that the Sphinx was a creation of the 4th dynasty, and that it was given the body of a lion and the head of a man deliberately made to gaze at the rising sun in the east horizon.[15] In the Pyramid Texts the dead king is said to join Horakhti in the eastern horizon at the moment of sunrise:

> The reed-floats of the sky are set in place for me that I may cross on them to Ra; the reed-floats are set in place for me that I may cross on them to Horakhti and to Ra. The Fields of Rushes are filled (with water) and I ferry across on the Winding Waterway… (Pyramid Texts 263)

> The Winding Waterway is flooded that I may be ferried over thereon to the horizon, to Horakhti…(Pyramid Texts 360)

> The king will be the companion of Horakhti and the king's hand will be held in the sky among the followers of Ra. The fields are content, the irrigation ditches are flooded for this king today… Raise yourself, O King, receive your waters… receive this pure water of yours which issues from Elephantine (the mythical source of the Nile)…O King, your cool water is the Great Flood which issues from you…(Pyramid Texts 865-6)

> The reed-floats of the sky are set in place for me that I may cross to the horizon, to Ra and to Horakhti. The nurse-canal is opened, the Winding Waterway is flooded, that I may be ferried over to

> the eastern side of the sky, to *the place where the gods were born…* (Pyramid Texts 351-3)

It was at Heliopolis that the calendar was invented, probably immediately prior to the Old Kingdom. A date favoured for the calendar's invention is 2780 BC when the summer solstice coincided with the heliacal rising of Sirius and also, as we have seen, the beginning of the Nile Flood. The summer solstice thus originally marked the New Year's Day, variously known as *I Akhet 1*, meaning 1st month, Season 0f Akhet (Flood), 1st Day. This day was also known as the 'Birth of Ra-Horakhti'.[16] In the epoch when the 4th Dynasty pyramids were built the sun transited in the constellation of Leo, the lion, during the time of the summer solstice. According to Egyptologist Richard Wilkinson…

> …an important mythological aspect of the solar god in the heavens is found in his identity as a cosmic lion…the stellar constellation now known as Leo was also recognized by the Egyptians as being in the form of a recumbent lion…(and that) the constellation was directly associated with the sun god…[17]

It can easily be shown that when the sunrise was positioned at 26.5° north of east (i.e. azimuth 62.5°) in the epoch 2500 BC – that is, when Djedefre built his pyramid on the high Abu Ruwash site – it was smack within the constellation of Leo, a fact that surely did not escape the attention of the sun-priests of Heliopolis and one, we presume, which was given much importance. And since the same 'Horakhti' applies to the Sphinx and was also the cult figure of the Sun Temple of Heliopolis (i.e. the Temple of Re-Horakhti), then it can be seen why both the Djedefre pyramid and the Great Pyramid of Giza were interconnected with Heliopolis by a sacred geometry based on the rising position of the sun when the latter was in Leo, at 26.5° north of east as viewed from Abu Ruwash.

Conclusion

It is very tempting, to say the least, to conclude that the vast region encompassing Abu Ruwash, Giza, Heliopolis and Letopolis – and perhaps even Abu Ghorab – was developed as a unified plan interrelated by lines of sight that locked the scheme into the time of the heliacal rising of Sirius which, in c. 2500 BC, marked the 'Birth of Re-Horakhti' and thus the moment of the supposed resurrection of the king in the eastern horizon at sunrise.

Robert Bauval has long been fascinated with the mysteries of Ancient Egypt and the pyramids. In 1994 he shot to public prominence with his book *The Orion Mystery*, in which he put forth his theory that the famous pyramids of the Giza Plateau near Cairo were laid out to mimic the three 'belt stars' of the constellation Orion. He has followed up with other books investigating the enigmas of Egypt, including *Secret Chamber* and *The Egypt Code*. His website can be found at http://www.robertbauval.co.uk.

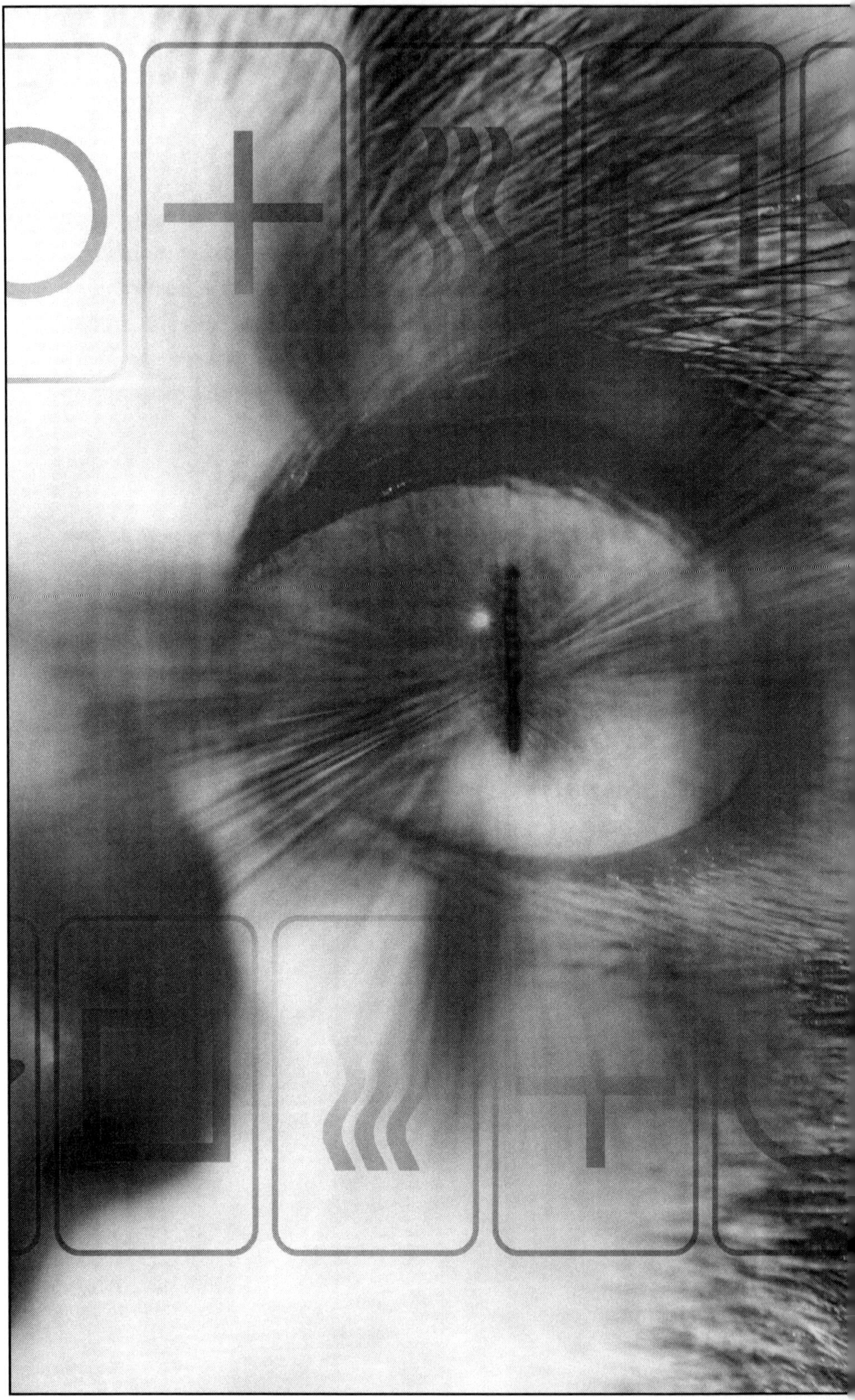

animal E.S.P.

Opening the government's files on the psychic powers of animals

by *Nick Redfern*

As the U.S. Freedom of Information Act has shown, over the years elements of the American military, defense community, and intelligence world have opened files on some distinctly unusual and eye-opening subjects, including UFOs, dowsing, spontaneous-human-combustion, crop circles, cattle mutilations, and much more. But, without doubt, one of the strangest areas of research that the world of officialdom has delved into is that pertaining to extrasensory perception (ESP) in animals. Does man's best friend possess extraordinary psychic powers? Do animals have souls? Is there life after death in the animal kingdom? Before you dismiss such questions out-of-hand, you may wish to acquaint yourselves with the following, startling data...

Tessie & Binnie: Canine Spies

Declassified United States Army files reveal that, in the early 1950s, Dr. Joseph Banks Rhine, Ph.D., of Duke University, North Carolina was secretly hired by the American military to determine if dogs, cats, and even pigeons, possessed extra-sensory perception, or ESP as it is more commonly known. The purpose of the *X-Files*-style research was to ascertain if, in the event that such out-of-this-world skills were confirmed, animals could be trained to use their psychic powers to locate landmines on battlefields. Notably, the final report submitted to the Army by Rhine in 1953 suggested that ESP was a reality, and that as a potential tool of warfare it should be seriously investigated further.

Rhine, regarded as the "Father of Modern Parapsychology," and the person single-handedly responsible for coining the term Extrasensory Perception, received his education at Ohio Northern University and the University of Chicago, and obtained his Master's Degree in 1923 and his Ph.D. in 1925, both in botany. But it was while at Duke University in the 1930s that Rhine's ESP research began in earnest. Using a pack of 25 cards – known as Zener cards, after their creator Karl Zener – that were comprised of images of circles, squares, crosses, stars, and wavy lines, Rhine's experiments would involve the selection of a 'sender', trained to concentrate on certain images, while a 'receiver' would attempt to use his or her mind to 'see' those same images. By assessing the statistical likelihood of simply guessing correctly or incorrectly, Rhine believed that he was able to determine which results were due to chance and which, if any, were possibly due to ESP 'talents' such as clairvoyance and telepathy.

By 1940, Rhine had undertaken thirty-three experiments and, astonishingly, almost a million trials – the results of which appeared in his book *Extra-Sensory Perception After Sixty Years.* And it was Rhine's ever-growing reputation as a major force in the field of

ESP that led the military to quietly approach him with a view to determining if psychic powers could be used as weapons of war.

Secretly contracted by the Engineering Research and Development Laboratories at the Army's Virginia-based Fort Belvoir facility, Rhine enthusiastically took up the challenge. According to Rhine, after an initial 3-month period of in-depth training with six German Shepherd dogs provided by the Army, "…tests were carried out on the beach of the Marshall Ranch on the coast of California in June 1952, using two dogs, Tessie and Binnie."

The files do not reflect precisely how the two dogs were trained to use ESP, or even how Rhine and his team concluded that they potentially possessed psychic powers; but they do tell an intriguing story. On repeated occasions, dummy mines were carefully buried beneath the sands, and Tessie and Binnie were brought in by their handler, as the experiment to locate the mines began.

The results, apparently, were remarkable, as Rhine elaborated: "The success was high enough that it was soon evident that the dogs were alerted to the mines before they set foot on the surface above them." The Army's secret documents add that: "The result of the first day's total of fourteen trials was eighty-six per cent successful."

Far more ambitious, classified experiments followed, with dummy mines carefully buried under the waters off the California coast. Again, the dogs performed well, and Rhine provided the military with a glowing conclusion: "There is at least no known way in which the dogs could have located the under-water mines except by extrasensory perception."

With respect to similar research undertaken with cats, Rhine explained, "Most of the things reported about dogs that suggested the possibility of ESP as a factor were also claimed for cats. Psychologically, the animals are close enough together to make a transfer of findings from one species to the other fairly likely."

Turning his attention to pigeons, Rhine advised his Army contacts that: "The mystery of pigeon-homing and the possibility that extrasensory perception enters into that performance led us to undertake the solution of the problem of how these pigeons find their way home. At the termination of the contract the problem had not been solved." Nevertheless, stressed Rhine, "researchers have ruled out all existing sensory hypotheses, thereby making extrasensory perception a more plausible interpretation than it has been hitherto." Rhine concluded with respect to his experimentation:

> ...this research has opened up possibilities of importance not only within but far beyond the scope of the projects specifically dealt with. The problems raised on this project involve basic research that may remain in the category of the inapplicable for many years.

"Measured against this," he was careful to note in his conclusion, "is the enormous value, not only to intelligence but to application in a wide range of military uses of extrasensory perception."

If the mysteries of the mind could be harnessed to find landmines, then what else were they capable of? This is a fair question and one that intrigued the military. But it must be asked: how reliable were the Rhine experiments? Is it not possible, for example, that the dogs were simply using their keen sense of smell, rather than utilising more exotic skills, to locate the mines?

Rhine did consider this possibility, and the experiments and conditions were modified to ensure that Tessie and Binnie were not exposed to "strong cross winds" that could allow the dogs to detect "chemical stimuli from the mines." Again, this appeared not to affect their successes – at least, not for a while.

Curiously, however, the positive results would lessen over time, or would prove to be erratic in nature, at least. Indeed, Rhine recognized this when he wrote to the Army: "...the thing that stands out is that the ability that is being measured is a very elusive and delicate one."

More controversially, there were some who were critical not just of the idea that ESP existed, but specifically of Rhine's work, too.

Duke University
SECURITY INFORMATION
THE PARAPSYCHOLOGY LABORATORY

July 10,1953

COLLEGE STATION
DURHAM, NORTH CAROLINA

Project 8-07-04-009
DA-44-009 eng. 1039

UNOFFICIAL COPY
FOR INFORMATION ONLY

ASTIA FILE COPY

THE COMMANDING OFFICER
Engineer Research & Development Laboratories
Fort Belvoir, Virginia

Attention: Mr. Leonard O.Goff
Mr.Wilbert W.Toole

Dear Sir:

This is the final report on the two branches of the experimental work carried out under the contract between your laboratory and Duke University, for which this Laboratory has assumed responsibility. Professor Markee will, in his report, sho now only his own branch of the experimental work but the financial report for all three of the subdivisions. The two subdivisions with which this report deals may be designated as the mine-locatio branch and the project concerning extrasensory perception in dogs.

I. Abstract

The research project was begun with the question posed as to whether dogs could, as claimed, locate buried land mines under conditions that gave no normal sensory cues. It was necessary to devise reliable scientific methods for determining whether or not this claim was justified. A method was designed which, with modifications in progress and in trial, proved satisfactory for the purpose. Experiments were carried out on dogs that had, in the meantime, been especially trained for the purpose and significant evidence was produced that trained dogs could detect Schu mines to a highly significant and reliable degree when these were buried under moderately moist beach sand to a depth of a few inches and all surface traces removed. The next step under the assignment was to find out whether or not this was a sensory mode of perception or, more specifically, a wholly sensory response. This requirement called for new methods and the tests were then carried out essentially as before but with the mines buried under sand which was under water and the water moving under the influence of cross winds.

One was Nobel-Laureate in chemistry, Irving Langmuir, who visited Rhine's laboratory at Duke University at the height of his research. Langmuir was dismayed to learn that Rhine was seemingly failing to take account of all of the data secured during the course of his ESP tests. For example, Langmuir was astonished to discover that "Rhine believed that persons who disliked him guessed wrong to spite him. Therefore, he felt it would be misleading to include their scores." Without doubt, such a scenario would hardly provide accurate results.

In addition, in the wake of the publication of Rhine's book *Extrasensory Perception After Sixty Years,* others – including London mathematician Samuel Soal – attempted to replicate Rhine's results. Most failed to do so, including Soal who toiled for 5 years without success. Soal would later reevaluate his data and assert that one subject in particular did seem to possess precognitive skills. Until 1978, that is, when – amid accusations and counter-claims – it was shown that Soal had distorted his data and it was rendered effectively useless.

Today, Rhine's work is championed by those who believe in ESP and derided by those who see inherent flaws in the man's work. As far as the U.S. Army is concerned, however, additional files show that it continued to quietly dig into the issue of ESP in animals for decades.

Defense Secrets of the Animal Kind

The Defense Intelligence Agency (DIA) was created in 1961 by United States Defense Secretary Robert McNamara, and brought together the military intelligence branches of the US Army, Navy and Air Force. Currently, the DIA satisfies the foreign intelligence and counter-intelligence requirements of the Secretary of Defense, the Joint Chiefs of Staff, various components of the Department of Defense and provides the military intelligence contribution to national intelligence. In other words, the DIA is a highly respected and vital component of the US Government and the Intelligence world.

An examination of files that the DIA has declassified under the terms of the Freedom of Information Act reveals that, in the Cold War environment of the 1970s, the Agency spent considerable time researching the existence (or otherwise) of extra-sensory perception and psychic phenomena. Not only that; the DIA was predominantly troubled by one particularly nightmarish and nagging scenario: that the Soviets would succeed in using ESP as a tool of espionage and that the secrets of the Pentagon, the CIA and just about everyone else would be blown wide open for Kremlin and KGB psychic-penetration.

Acting on this concern, the DIA (along with the CIA and the Army) began to seriously address the issue of whether or not the powers of the mind would one day prove superior to – or at the very least, the equal of – conventional tools of espionage and warfare. And it was as a result of its intensive study of Soviet research into psychic phenomena for espionage purposes that the DIA learned of some of the notable advances made by both Russian and Czechoslovakian scientists, whose attention was focused on the links between psychic phenomena and the animal kingdom.

In a September 1975 document, *Soviet and Czechoslovakian Parapsychology Research*, the DIA reveals its findings on animals and psychic phenomena in the former Soviet bloc countries. Interestingly, the Defense Intelligence Agency learned that Soviet research into the world of psychic powers in animals began decades previously, and focused on attempts to determine the validity of mind-to-mind contact between human beings and dogs. One section of the document is titled "Telepathy in Animals".

> Soviet research on telepathy in animals in the 1920s and 1930s was devoted largely to proving that telepathy between man and animals did indeed exist. A good example of the early Soviet approach was research conducted by V.I.M. Bekhterev of Leningrad University, in collaboration with a circus performer, V.L. Bekhterev reported that Durov's trained dogs successfully

> solved arithmetic problems and identified or retrieved objects solely on the basis of their trainer's mental suggestion. The results of these tests were controversial, since the dog's performances were good when Durov was present and supplied the "suggestions", but deteriorated markedly when he was absent and another individual attempted to mentally control them.

The DIA's observations that the results of the tests were largely dependent on whether or not a trained circus performer was present should not be ignored. If telepathy is a real phenomenon, as the DIA suspected it was, then it is entirely possible, of course, that Durov had indeed succeeded in generating a mind-to-mind link with his dogs. That the results should have deteriorated markedly when Durov was absent, however, is a matter that must leave this aspect of such research open to question.

The DIA continued:

> Bekhterev's original objective was to demonstrate that telepathy between man and animals was mediated by some form of electromagnetic radiation (EMR), but by 1937, he and other Soviet parapsychologists had concluded that no known form of EMR was the carrier of thought transmission. The EMR theory of information transfer is still unresolved by the Soviets, but is still the major basis underlying much of their research.

Three decades after Bekheterev's original research, the Soviets were still working hard to make advances in this intriguing area:

> In 1962 B.S. Kazhinskiy advanced the theory that animals are capable of visual and aural perception and reflex understanding of the behavior of other animals or humans. He postulated that this ability resulted from the capacity of one animal to detect (via its nervous system), analyze, and synthesize signal-stimuli

> given off by another animal. According to Kazhinskiy, the signals were transmitted in the form of a "bioradiational sight ray" and analyzed by the percipient animal as a result of its Pavlovian conditioning. The term "bioradiational rays" is still used by some Soviet and Czech parapsychologists to refer to focusing and concentration of biological energy by the brain and the optical neural channels.

If Kazhinskiv's research into visual and aural perception was, and still is, considered valid, then it offers the possibility that the entire animal kingdom of our planet may somehow have the ability to utilize highly-advanced mental tools that, largely, elude human beings. The 1975 DIA paper then turns its attention to then-contemporary research undertaken by the Soviets.

> Present day Soviet and Czech parapsychology research with animals is devoted almost exclusively to investigation of sources of biological energy involved in physiological processes, the interactions of such energy with external fields, and the effects of externally generated fields on animal physiology. Reference to telepathy in the sense of communications by transmission of total, conceptual, mental formulations is seldom made.

Believing that they were on the verge of a major breakthrough, the Soviets channeled much of their effort into a project that was being undertaken at a major Russian university.

> A significant advance toward identification of the EMR source of biological energy transfer was gained from recent research conducted at the University of Novosibirsk. Scientists there investigated the release of energy during cell division and during cellular damage and repair resulting from viral infection or toxic chemicals. In over 5000 experiments with cell cultures

> and animal organs it was shown that damaged cells radiated some form of energy and that the energy released was capable of causing damage in adjacent control preparations of organs or cells. Further investigation revealed that a uniform pattern, code, or rhythm of radiation was emitted by normal cells. This pattern was disturbed when cellular damage occurred, becoming quite irregular. It was also found that the patterns were transmitted from experimental to control preparations only when the cells or organs were cultured in quartz containers. Since quartz transmits ultraviolet (UV) radiation and standard laboratory glassware does not, the Soviets concluded that UV radiation mediated cellular information transfer. The researchers subsequently correlated given irregularities of emission with specific diseases and are now attempting to develop techniques for diagnosis and therapy by monitoring and altering cellular radiation codes.

The DIA also learned that two decades of research undertaken in Czechoslovakia had led to some startling results pertaining to 'energy transfer' between biological tissue samples.

> Czechoslovakian research on energy transfer between animal muscle preparations from animals to man, and from man to man, has also demonstrated EMR as the vehicle of biological energy transfer. In experiments conducted between 1948 and 1968 at the Okres Institute of Public Health, Kutna Hora, Czechoslovakia, Dr. Jiri Bradna demonstrated contactless transfer (myotransfer) of stimuli between frog neuromuscular preparations. Bradna placed identical preparations side by side; stimulation of one preparation with electric pulses at frequencies between 10 and 30 pulses per second caused contraction and a recorded electromyographic response in the other. In other experiments, stimulation of muscle preparations influenced the oscillations of a pendulum

> and increased the muscle tension of a human subject. Bradna obtained objective proof that energy in the very high frequency (VHF) range mediated the stimulus transmission. He also demonstrated that myotransfer could be blocked with ferrous metal filters and aluminum, could be deformed with magnets, ferrites and other conductors, could be reflected and transmitted over waveguides, and shielded with grids. Bradna concluded that primary perceptual and informational pathways between animals are based on metabolic processes at the macromolecular level and that the magnitude of energy transfer depends on muscular adenosine triphosphate (ATP) energy release.

Of particular interest to the DIA was the research of Dr. Bradna that had a bearing on human behaviour and on the potential for altering or influencing that behaviour.

> Bradna has reported successful application of myotransfer in physiotherapy. It has been found to be effective for both individuals and groups. In the latter case, the summation of stimuli has been shown to enhance the neuromuscular responses of individuals within the group. Bradna feels that such stimuli influence the herd of animals and may also be a factor in altering human behavior under conditions of isolation or overcrowding.

It is quite clear from examining the now-declassified files of the DIA that Soviet scientists postulated numerous theories to try to explain extra-sensory perception and psychic phenomena in animals. According to the DIA, a Doctor Y.A. Kholodov had:

> ...investigated the effects of a constant magnetic field (CMF) on rabbits. Whole-body exposures to fields between 30 and 2000 oersteds resulted in nonspecific exchanges in the electroencephalogram but no other directly measurable

> physiological responses. Kholodov showed that weak magnetic as well as other externally generated radiation fields have a direct effect on nerve tissue, and for this reason he feels that natural and artificial fields in man's environment may have an influence on health and behavior via the nervous system and the hypothalamus. Kholodov's research is representative of current Soviet efforts to explain paranormal phenomena on the basis of known physical and biological parameters.

Conversely, another Soviet scientist, A.S. Presman, felt that biological energy and information exchange between living organisms was the result of electromagnetic field (EMF) interactions between individuals or between the individual and the environment.

> Presman and other Soviet scientists have recorded EMFs from man, frogs, and insects of various species at ranges from several centimetres to several meters from the body surface. The frequencies of the EMFs were found to correspond to various biorhythms of organs, rhythms of movement and acoustic signals and bioelectric rhythms. Presman thinks that in groups of animals, electromagnetic oscillations are synchronized by frequency matching and that the cumulative intensity may grow in proportion to the square of the number of individuals. Such cumulative emission is also thought to be possible as the result of synchronization of the emissions of many cells in animals in a highly excited state. Presman, like Kholodov, feels that the effects of sub-threshold stimuli are mediated through the hypothalamic region of the midbrain. The hypothalamus regulates diverse physiological processes in the organism (pulse, bodytemperature, oxygen consumption, carbon dioxide liberation, urine volume, urine nitrogen concentration, etc.) and these are the functions most commonly disturbed by changes in EMFs.

Presman also speculated on the reason for the apparent widespread telepathic abilities in animals versus the lack of such abilities in human beings:

> Presman believes that electromagnetic signaling is universal between animals, but not between humans who may have lost the capability for such communication as a result of evolution and the development of verbal and artificial communication channels. He does not rule out the possibility that "spontaneous telepathy" may occasionally occur, but regards such occurrences as rare cases of atavism. Consequently, he regards man as the least suitable animal for studying electromagnetic communication.

The DIA also noted that, by 1975, Soviet research into ESP in animals had been modified and now encompassed a whole new range of disciplines and terminology.

> It is important that the increased degree of sophistication which has occurred in Soviet ESP or telepathy research since 1960 be understood. At present the terms "ESP" and "telepathy" are seldom used. It is possible that the newer terms "biocommunication" and "psychotronics" will vanish in the near future only to be replaced by conventional high-energy physics terminology, or term such as "interpersonal subconscious reactions" or "mention" forces. In any event, the classical ESP experiments with animals are no longer of interest in the USSR. The typical Vasilev experimentation from 1920 to 1955 has been replaced with sophisticated research protocols which study complex interactions between man, animals and plants.

The file also addresses an intriguing Soviet Naval experiment that occurred in the mid 1950s and that, at least fifteen years later, was still considered classified by Soviet authorities. Despite the secrecy surrounding the event, however, the DIA was able to glean enough data to suggest that Soviet scientists were involved in research to determine what happens at the moment of death, the nature of death, and the possibility of an after-life in animals.

> Dr. Pavel Naumov, conducted animal biocommunication studies between a submerged Soviet Navy submarine and a shore research station: these tests involved a mother rabbit and her newborn litter and occurred around 1956, three years prior to the USS Nautilus disclosure (Note from the author: this is a reference to an ESP study allegedly undertaken by the US Navy in 1960 that will be discussed in another chapter). According to Naumov, Soviet scientists placed the baby rabbits aboard the submarine. They kept the mother rabbit in a laboratory on shore where they implanted electrodes (EEG?) in her brain. When the submarine was submerged, assistants killed the rabbits one by one. At each precise moment of death, the mother rabbit's brain produced detectable and recordable reactions. As late as 1970 the precise protocol and results of this test described by Naumov were believed to be classified. Many can be found in Soviet literature with dogs, bears, birds, insects and fish in conjunction with basic psychotronic research. The Pavlov Institute in Moscow may have been involved in animal telepathy until 1970.

Did the Soviet Navy's experiments of 1956 stumble upon the secrets of life after death in the animal kingdom? That the mother rabbit's brain produced, detected, and recorded reactions at the precise moment that her offspring were killed is both eye-opening and not a little disturbing. One is also prompted to ask if the results of this experiment were indicative of evidence for the existence of some form of soul in the animal world? We know nothing more as the Soviets immediately and effectively classified their findings in this area – and the U.S. Government isn't saying anymore, either...

The Name's Kitty...Acoustic Kitty

For the strangest animal espionage of all, and one that sounds straight out of the realm of science-fiction, we have to turn our attention to the Central Intelligence Agency. In the 1960s, declassified memoranda from the CIA's Directorate of Science and Technology reveals that the Agency attempted to probe the darkest secrets of the Kremlin by turning cats into what could arguably be termed walking bugging machines. In one particular experiment conducted at the height of the Cold War, a cat – dubbed nothing less than Acoustic Kitty – was wired up for use as a biological eavesdropping machine. CIA scientists, the files make clear, were hoping that the animal – which was surgically altered to accommodate transmitting and control devices – would be able to listen to secret conversations from particular locations such as park benches and dustbins. According to Victor Marchetti, a former CIA officer:

> They slit the cat open, put batteries in him, wired him up. The tail was used as an antenna. They made a monstrosity. They tested him and tested him. They found he would walk off the job when he got hungry, so they put another wire in to override that.

Not only that, but the operation was financially a disaster too, costing the American taxpayer more than ten million dollars. Then the real disaster occurred, says Marchetti. "They took it out to a park and put him out of the van, and a taxi comes and runs him over. There they were, sitting in the van with all those dials, and the cat was dead."

So much for the past; but: what of the present era? Responding to my inquiries, the U.S. Army declined to comment on allegations that similar research to the Rhine experiments continues to this day. "It wouldn't be prudent in today's climate to discuss matters like this," was their tight-lipped statement.

Perhaps Joseph Banks Rhine – and Tessie and Binnie, of course – will one day be vindicated, after all.

Nick Redfern is the author of many books on unexplained phenomena, including *A Covert Agenda, Body Snatchers in the Desert, On the Trail of the Saucer Spies*, and *Memoirs of a Monster Hunter*. His latest book is titled *There's Something in the Woods*. More information about Nick and his research can be found at his website, www.nickredfern.com, and at his blog, www.ufomystic.com.

The Mole of Edge Hill

The Underground Empire of Joseph Williamson

by ***John Reppion***

Mr. Charles R. Hand wrote the following words in 1926, which he read to his fellow members of the Historical Society of Lancashire and Cheshire. The essay was entitled "Joseph Williamson – The King of Edge Hill":

> I speak of Williamson's works from an intimate acquaintance with them during my early days. As a lad I, with a number of companions, made them the object of an almost regular Saturday afternoon expedition. Tied together, in single file, and carrying as many lighted candles as we could get, [...] we traversed these strange and wonderful passages, literally in 'fear and trembling,'

> afraid yet fascinated by the eeriness of it all, dreading we knew not what, yet going on.[1]

The name of Williamson – sometimes known as the Mole of Edge Hill, occasionally the King – is inextricably linked with the history of Liverpool and yet most people seem to know little about the man and his works. There was a time not so long ago that my own knowledge on the subject stretched no further than the fact that there were some tunnels somewhere in Liverpool and that there was a pub on Wavertree Road called The Mole of Edge Hill. Williamson's story is a fascinating one, and in a very literal sense the city of Liverpool is built upon his life's work.

Joseph Williamson was born in Warrington on the 10th of March 1769. Little is known of his home life there but it is said that at the age of eleven he was sent to the then thriving city of Liverpool to seek his fortune.[2,3] Williamson found employment at a tobacco and snuff factory on Parr street owned by the Tate family. Joseph was a hard worker with a head for business and, working his way up through the company, he gained the respect of his employers. So much so that in 1802 he married Elizabeth Tate, the sister of the

firm's owner.[4] The following year ownership of the factory passed to Williamson. Some say that he bought the business with money that he had accumulated through other ventures whilst others claim that he inherited the firm.[5,6] Soon after, Williamson purchased land and began to build houses on Mason Street in the Edge Hill district of Liverpool. Because these houses backed onto an almost sheer drop, Williamson had huge arches constructed behind each to provide his tenants with room enough for rear gardens.[7] Joseph's own abode was number 14 Mason Street, and it was beneath his home that the first of his tunnels began.[8]

Williamson, it seems, enjoyed spending time underground; it is said that his cellar served as his sitting room and his bedroom was described as a "cave".[9] The tunnel beneath his residence was eventually to provide direct routes for Williamson to his local church and his favourite pub, amongst other choice locations. Soon, Joseph set men to work digging and constructing tunnels beneath the arches at the rear of his other Mason Street properties. It is completely unknown how and why Williamson developed his subterranean fascination and for what exact purpose these excavations where intended, but their construction was to obsess him for the rest of his life. Eventually, a great network of single, double and even triple layered tunnels filled with complex archways and mysterious dead ends was to riddle the ground beneath central Liverpool. Williamson even went so far as to have two full sized houses –complete with sandstone spiral staircases – carved out of the solid rock. These dwellings now lie tragically neglected and inaccessible, deep beneath the foundations of a modern tower block. Unreachable as the subterranean houses may be, their location is at least recorded – unlike much of Williamson's work which remains largely uncharted.

In 1818 Joseph Williamson retired and sold his business, devoting all of his time and effort to the construction of his labyrinth.[10] It was a time of great poverty and mass unemployment, many men having recently returned home from the Napoleonic War to find their old jobs gone. It is estimated that Williamson employed over half the able bodied labouring population of Edge Hill, providing work and training for men who would otherwise have been living in abject poverty.[11] Indeed, it is now generally accepted that philanthropy was the motivation for the construction of the tunnels; old Joseph giving something back to the community and to the working class from which he came. Work on the tunnels did not cease until 1840 when Joseph Williamson died at the age of seventy-one.[12] The maze's entrances were sealed soon after.

The mythology surrounding Williamson's abandoned tunnels grew exponentially and in 1906 – a mere sixty six years after Joseph's death – local newspaper *The Liverpool Porcupine* reported that "some three hundred years ago a rich nobleman spent a fortune in making the excavations, but with what object in view we are unable to learn!"[13] Rumor spread that the catacombs were haunted or that huge populations of spiders and rats, made monstrous by their perpetual interbreeding, now resided within them. Hand himself wrote of such superstitions in his paper: "It is often said that in these workings are countless accumulations of spider's hammocks and armies of rats, but I have not seen either the one or the other".[14] Such beliefs have survived well into modern times with an eyewitness to an explosion in Edge Hill in 1941 apparently claiming to have seen "thousands of rats flee[ing] from there [sic] underground sojourn in fright".[15]

Although not teeming with grotesque vermin the tunnels did fill up with something unpleasant: rubbish. After their closure, many people living near the excavations began treating them as (seemingly) bottomless pits for dumping their refuse into. Hand's own expedition of 1926 was halted when he and his party came across tunnels entirely blocked with the accumulated waste of hundreds of homes and businesses.[16] This method of disposing of unwanted materials eventually reached its logical conclusion and scores of passages became completely packed with debris. For many, it must have seemed that the tunnels had finally outlived any purpose they may have had.

Underground History

Williamson's story could easily have been lost in the mists of antiquity; dismissed as a mere urban legend or simply forgotten had it not been for a small group of dedicated individuals. In September 1995, Mr. David Head and Mr. Steven Moran set up a small stall outside the old Lord Mayor's stable yard on Smithdown Lane. The yard had been opened to the public for the National Civic Trust Heritage weekend, being the site of two of the main tunnel entrances. Mr. Head and Mr. Moran, both keen historians, took the opportunity to make visitors aware of the fact that the site was set to be demolished in the near future to make way for student housing. All visitors who expressed an interest in saving the location were invited to a meeting at Liverpool's Central Library. From that initial gathering the basis of the Friends of Williamson's Tunnels organization was formed with the intention of acting as a pressure group campaigning to prevent any developments that would jeopardise the tunnels.[17] Today the stable yard is owned by the Joseph Williamson Society (a separate organisation to the FOWT) and is the site of the Heritage Centre: a small area of tunnels now cleared and opened to the public, complete with its own bar situated within one of Williamson's famed triple tunnels. The FOWT's own visitor site is located in the heart of the Williamson Student Village in Paddington, just around the corner from Mason Street.

Both organizations are campaigning to raise awareness of the works of Joseph Williamson and are working hard on opening up more and more of his tunnels to the public. As Williamson left no map of his structures, each time a new stretch of tunnel is cleared of its ancient rubbish – itself now a precious source of historical data – fresh discoveries are made. The tunnels are seen as something of a problem by Liverpool City council however. Whilst cooperative in many ways, the council are arguably somewhat guilty of downplaying their significance and size. Presumably this has something to do with the fact that it would be rather awkward to go ahead and build new housing estates and the like if people realised that large amounts of historically significant architecture would be lost in the process. Regrettably, many of Williamson's excavations have already been lost in precisely this manner. The remains some of the original Mason Street houses have recently been demolished and plans are afoot to develop the land immediately adjacent to the Smithdown Lane visitors centre into apartments.[18]

Digging for Answers

What of Williamson's motives then? Are we now any closer to understanding the reasoning behind Joseph's magnificent project? As mentioned earlier, philanthropy is the most commonly believed explanation but there is another: Sanctuary.

The 1800s were a time of great change; a new era of history in which science and industry altered people's perceptions of the world hugely. Liverpool was a thriving port and people of all nationalities and religions met and mixed each day on its cobbled streets. Amid all this modern multiculturalism and mechanisation new religious sects began to surface, many of which foretold the coming of the Apocalypse. It is believed by some that Joseph and his wife Elizabeth were members of such a cult and that the tunnels were in fact built to shelter the faithful when the time of Armageddon came.[19] It has even been alleged that the Williamsons had plans to rebuild the city after the catastrophe (whatever form that might have taken) using the very money and work force Joseph had spent much of his lifetime acquiring. Looking at the complex gothic architecture of the surviving tunnels, it is not at all difficult to think of the structures as holding religious significance; indeed, many of them remain positively cathedral like. Joseph was known to be extremely secretive about the tunnels; not only did he keep no maps but he is also said to have never allowed any but a select few to wander freely through the catacombs, which are notoriously riddled with hidden and secret passageways. Were the tunnels then built not only as shelters but also as mazes to baffle and ensnare any uninvited guests prior to or during the time of judgement? Comparisons to the pyramids of the pharaohs are, perhaps, not without foundation.

Though his tunnels may have more than a whiff of the tomb about them, Williamson was not interred within his life's work; he was buried in the Tate family vault at Saint Thomas's Church alongside his wife in 1840. Having fallen into disuse, the church was demolished in 1911. Headstones and monuments were removed and the land was eventually sold off for development. Even so, there were those who dared to dream that the Tate's crypt had somehow been left undisturbed. On Sunday the 23rd of August 2005 FOWT were excavating a disused car park near Canning Place, soon to become part of the new Liverpool One Paradise Street Development. Believing that the parking place stood upon the once hallowed ground of Saint Thomas's, the volunteers had until five o'clock that afternoon to unearth some evidence of Williamson's final resting place; construction work was scheduled to begin on the site the following morning. It was a little after lunch time when a 7 foot by 3 foot [2.13 metre by 0.91 metre] slab bearing the name of Tate was unearthed by one of the on-site archaeologists. The find was greeted with cheers from the assembled volunteers, representing as it did an end to ten year's worth of searching with barely four hours to spare. Once fully uncovered the grave stone could be clearly read, The Mole's modest epitaph at its bottom: "Also the remains of Joseph Williamson of Edge Hill who died 1st May 1840 aged 71 years". With its location properly noted and recorded, the slab was re-buried before the afternoon's deadline.

Newspapers at the time reported that Grosvenor, the company responsible for the Paradise Project, had agreed to preserve the grave site and pledged to turn it into a green space dedicated to Williamson.[20,21] Four years on and the memorial has yet to become a reality but, with work on the Liverpool One development now drawing to a close, FOWT remain hopeful. Members recently met with representatives of Grosvenor and the company currently working on plans for the space. Their proposed design incorporates a green space on two levels surrounded by low hedges, to be christened the Williamson Memorial Garden. Williamson's grave itself will not be uncovered, its exact location remaining unmarked, while a plaque placed in the garden will give information about the man and his work.[22] Perhaps it is only fitting that The Mole of Edge Hill should remain in death where he walked in life – just beneath the feet of the citizens of Liverpool.

John Reppion is a freelance writer with an interest in all things Fortean, folkloric and esoteric. In the past he has written for the likes of *Fortean Times, Strange Attractor Journal, Paranormal Magazine* and *The End is Nigh* on subjects as diverse as medieval revenants, exogenesis and Spring-heeled Jack. His book *800 Years of Haunted Liverpool* was published in 2008 by The History Press and covers much of the uncanny history and folklore of his native city. More information can be found online at www.MooreReppion.com

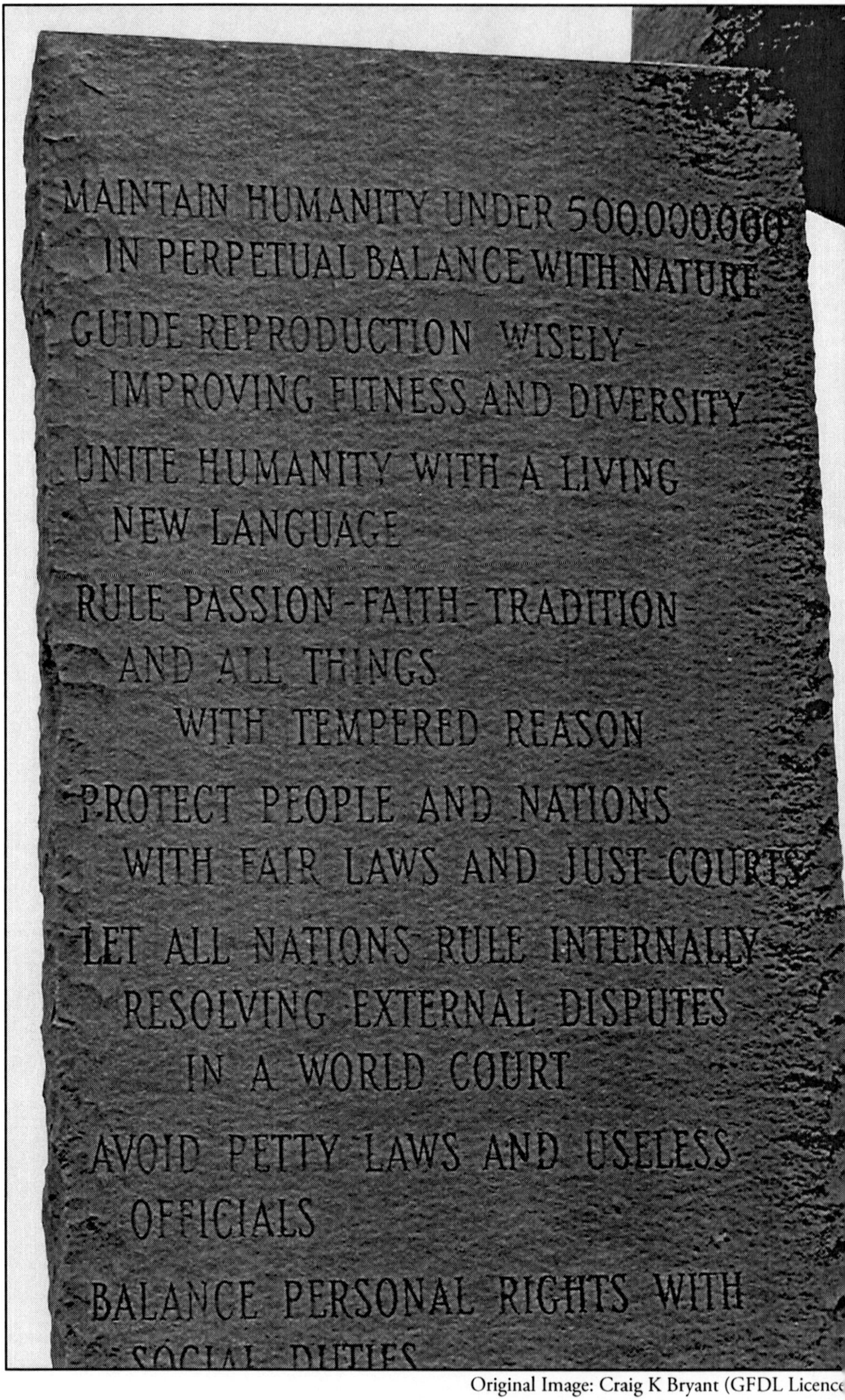

Original Image: Craig K Bryant (GFDL Licence

BEYOND THE APOCALYPSE

MYTHS AND LEGENDS CONCERNING THE GEORGIA GUIDESTONES

by *Greg Taylor*

Silently surveying the rural lands surrounding them, the giant stones impose themselves upon the grassy landscape. Raised by human hands, but dwarfing any man, they are neatly aligned to various celestial phenomena, such as the rising and setting of the Sun at the Solstices and the hitching post of the heavens, the North Star Polaris. Their designers are unknown; they remain a mystery to us – but the Stones give voice to their inner thoughts. Some see in their construction a guiding wisdom for humanity, whilst others feel threatened by the overt pagan overtones and, paradoxically, stark scientific simplicity, of the megaliths and their message.

Far from being the work of an ancient people though, this monument was raised just three decades ago by a group of stonemasons – in the literal sense of the word – from the South of the United States of America. Unlike that other famous megalithic site, Stonehenge, we know exactly how the stones were quarried, how they were finished, and then assembled into one interlocking marvel. And yet, the Georgia Guidestones remain a modern mystery.

Their story begins with the arrival of a neatly-dressed gray-haired gentleman at Elberton Granite Finishing Company on a Friday afternoon in June, 1979. He introduced himself as one 'R.C. Christian', acting on behalf of "a small group of loyal Americans who believe in God", and who wanted to "leave a message for future generations."[1]

Joe Fendley, president of the Georgian stone-working company, listened to the man outline the specifications of the monument that he and his small group were seeking. Christian explained that they had chosen Elberton due to its stocks of hard-wearing granite – a key element of the design was that the monument should be able to withstand both the slow erosion of time as well as possible catastrophic events. The monument was to serve as a compass, calendar, and clock, with celestial alignments which would encode the passing of time itself. And it would be engraved with a set of '10 commandments', written multiple times in eight of the world's major languages.[2]

Given the dimensions of the desired construction, Fendley made some notes, consulted his calculator, and offered a rough – and sizeable – quote to Mr Christian for the price of construction. The figure didn't seem to bother the enigmatic man though. He simply asked Fendley for assistance in locating a nearby bank through which to deliver the funding:

> Some 30-minutes or so after leaving Fendley's office, Christian appeared at the office of Granite City Bank president Wyatt C. Martin. After introducing himself to Mr Martin in the same

> manner in which he did to Fendley, he repealed his mission and desires to have a monument erected.
>
> Christian told Martin that he represented a group of individuals who had planned this project for more than 20 years, and that each one of the group was a loyal American who believed in God and country.
>
> He said the group of sponsors wished to remain anonymous and went on to say that his real name was not Robert C. Christian as he had introduced himself, but this was simply a name chosen because of his Christian faith.[3]

This explanation sounds a little suspicious – the name, and the philosophy of the group, suggest the name is more likely inspired by the famous Rosicrucians – the Brotherhood of the Rosy Cross. But more on that soon. For now, it's worth pointing out that Mr. Christian's explanation for the need for secrecy was that the group did not want to distract people from the monument or its meaning. More precisely…

> The message, to be inscribed on the stones, is to all mankind and is non-sectarian, nor nationalistic, nor in any sense political. The stones must speak for themselves to all who take note and should appeal to believers and non-believers , wherever. and at all times.[4]

Again, it seems a little odd that a man who introduces himself as being a 'loyal American', who "believed in God and country", should then say it is necessary that the monument be non-sectarian and not nationalistic. Perhaps though this presentation as being a loyal, Christian American was meant more to assuage any fears or hesitancy on the part of his new collaborators. He was looking to raise an odd monument – replete with strange 'commandments' on how future generations should maintain their society, and with references to that "dirty little Atheist", Thomas Paine – in the 'Deep South', after all.

Wyatt Martin wasn't born yesterday though, and informed Mr. Christian that "a pseudo-name and a promise of money for a project of this magnitude just was not enough." The mysterious man was thus forced to swear the banker to secrecy, before providing his real name and enough information for the project to progress financially. Martin remains the only man alive – outside of the secret group – who knows the true identity of 'Robert C. Christian'.

Christian returned several days later with a wooden model of the intended structure, and a message from the group:

> Stonehenge and other vestiges of human thought arouse our curiosity but carry no message for our guidance. To convey our ideas across time to other human beings we want to erect a monument. A cluster of graven stones...which will silently display our ideas when we have gone. We hope they will merit increasing acceptance and that through their silent persistence they will hasten in a small degree the coming Age of Reason.[5]

On this visit Christian also raised the matter of where the monument would be located. He said that Georgia had been chosen not just for its granite supplies, but also on account of its mild climate (to insure the permanence of the stoneworking), and distance from major tourist centers. With Wyatt Martin's assistance, he located a five-acre plot of land some eight miles north of Elberton, on the farm of Mildred and Wayne Mullenix. Standing atop an unwooded ridge in the middle of cow pastures, the site is the highest point in Elbert County and offers excellent visibility in all directions. With its prominent location, the monument itself can be seen from several miles away. In a happy coincidence (or was it?), the site is also less than 10 miles from Ah-Yeh-Li A-Lo-Hee, the Cherokee "Center of the World".

Money for the project arrived from different banks across the country, as did all future correspondence from Christian. According to Wyatt Martin, this was yet another measure to protect R.C. Christian's real identity, "because he wanted to make sure it couldn't be traced... He made it clear that he was very serious about secrecy."[6]

After nine months of intense work on the part of Elberton Granite and Finishing, the Georgia Guidestones were unveiled to a crowd of 400 people on March 22, 1980. The main structure of this impressive site is composed of four massive granite monoliths, each weighing around 20 tons, and a 9-ton central pillar, all of which support the square 11-ton 'capstone'. The completed monument stands some 19 feet (just under 6 meters) high. Perhaps taking a lesson from the discovery of the Rosetta Stone (an inscription in multiple languages which facilitated the decoding of the Ancient Egyptian hieroglyphs), the four Pyramid-Blue granite side-slabs are etched with 4000 individual characters, which present the 'guide'

The standing megaliths of the Georgia Guidestones

in eight different languages. The central support pillar features a 'mail-slot' through which observers can see the alignments to the rising sun on the equinoxes and solstices, while another angled hole drilled right through this center stone allows a person on the southern side of the monument to look through and see the North Star, Polaris, which sits almost directly at the North celestial pole. Meanwhile, a 7/8 inch hole in the capstone allows the light from the Sun to pinpoint the day of the year at noon of every day on the central column. The four side-slabs are oriented to the limits of the migration of the moon during the course of the year.

The eight languages which present the guide to future humanity are English, Chinese, Russian, Spanish, Swahili, Hindi, Hebrew, and Arabic. The ten instructions etched into the stones are:

- Maintain humanity under 500,000,000 in perpetual balance with nature;
- Guide reproduction wisely, improving fitness and diversity;
- Unite humanity with a living new language;
- Rule passion, faith, tradition, and all things with tempered reason;
- Protect people and nations with fair laws and just courts;
- Let all nations rule internally, resolving external disputes in a world court;
- Avoid petty laws and useless officials;
- Balance personal rights with social duties;
- Prize truth, beauty, love...seeking harmony with the infinite;
- Be not a cancer on earth – leave room for nature – leave room for nature.

In addition, the capstone has the words "Let These Be Guidestones to an Age of Reason" inscribed upon it in four ancient scripts: Egyptian hieroglyphs, Babylonian cuneiform, Classical Greek, and Sanskrit.

A Work of Satan

But with mystery and secrecy comes fear. Not all in the local area were happy with the project, perhaps confirming why R.C. Christian was so quick to announce his patriotic and religious nature. Local Christians in particular feared that the newly-constructed megaliths would become a 'sacred site' to heathens and occultists:

> The first rumor began among members of the Elberton Granite Association, jealous of the attention being showered on one of their own: Fendley was behind the whole thing, they said, aided by his friend Martin, the banker. The gossip became so poisonous that the two men agreed to take a lie detector test at the Elberton Civic Center. The scandal withered when The Elberton Star reported that they had both passed convincingly, but the publicity brought a new wave of complaints. As word of what was being inscribed spread, Martin recalls, even people he considered friends asked him why he was doing the devil's work. A local minister, James Travenstead, predicted that "occult groups" would flock to the Guidestones, warning that "someday a sacrifice will take place here."[7]

Some pounced on the date of the unveiling – March 22 – as confirmation that the Guidestones were the work of the devil. Christian pundits were quick to associate the date with various ancient pagan rites, as well as those of Wicca – seemingly oblivious that the date marks the Spring Equinox, one of the key alignments of the monument, and the original reason why these rites occur on that date.

But if the seemingly pagan nature of the monument was a concern, the instructions themselves induced near panic in various segments of the local, and national, community. Those who see conspiracy everywhere jumped on the first instruction, which suggests maintaining the world population at 500 million. As one hysterical author wrote, "To bring the population to this level means that nine tenths of the earth's population must die!"[8] Or in the words of another Christian writer, "that kind of sounds like the mass extermination of the earth's population during the time of tribulation."[9]

More recently activism against the Georgia Guidestones has become more fervent, with critics banding together to call for their destruction. A 2009 feature on the monument in *Wired Magazine* pointed out…

> …Among them is an activist named Mark Dice, author of a book called *The Resistance Manifesto*. In 2005, Dice (who was using a pseudonym of his own—"John Conner"—appropriated from the Terminator franchise's main character) began to demand that the Guidestones be "smashed into a million pieces." He claims that the monument has "a deep Satanic origin," a stance that has earned him plenty of coverage, both in print and on the Web. According to Dice, Christian was a high-ranking member of "a Luciferian secret society" at the forefront of the New World Order. "The elite are planning to develop successful life-extension technology in the next few decades that will nearly stop the aging process," Dice says, "and they fear that with the current population of Earth so high, the masses will be using resources that the elite want for themselves. The Guidestones are the New World Order's Ten Commandments. They're also a way for the elite to get a laugh at the expense of the uninformed masses, as their agenda stands as clear as day and the zombies don't even notice it."[10]

In the past year vandals have spray-painted messages across the inscriptions, and splashed the slabs with polyurethane, which makes cleaning the graffiti a difficult proposition. Messages on Internet forums suggest a petition to have them destroyed, and even debate whether it would be illegal to take it upon themselves to do the

Vandalism on the Georgia Guidestones

destroying.[11] Like Dice, they see the Guidestones as the calling card of the Illuminati, the New World Order, and/or various other groups intent on controlling the world's population. Though why some shadowy group intent on killing off 90% of the world's population would announce their plans on a monument in rural Georgia is beyond me…

The R.C. Brothers

At least the conspiracy theorists might have one thing right. The messages from R.C. Christian and his secret group certainly evoke the philosophy behind a number of secret societies of the 17th and 18th centuries, including the earliest incarnations of Freemasonry and the Illuminati. Arising out of the 'Rosicrucian' tradition, these secret societies had at their heart an embracing of the use of reason to guide humanity forward, with an ultimate goal of a 'brotherhood of man', a Pan-Sophist Utopia in which people around the world united in a peaceful quest for knowledge.

The public announcement of this goal came in the Rosicrucian manifestos, which circulated in the early 17th century and inspired many leading thinkers to join this 'quest'. Francis Bacon's *New Atlantis* followed in 1627, with its tale of a group known as 'Salomon's House', an order of priest-scientists who pursued research into all the arts and sciences in order to benefit humanity.[12] With officials wearing turbans decorated with "a red cross on the top", it is easy to see Bacon's affiliation – no matter whether official or self-announced. In the words of the great Renaissance scholar, Dame Frances Yates:

> The religion of New Atlantis has much in common with that of the Rosicrucian manifestos. It is intensely Christian in spirit, though not doctrinal, interpreting the Christian spirit in terms of practical benevolence, like the R.C. Brothers... The inhabitants of New Atlantis would appear to have achieved the great instauration of learning and have therefore returned to the state of Adam in Paradise before the Fall – the objective of advancement both for Bacon and for the authors of the Rosicrucian manifestos.[13]

Given the secrecy of R.C. Christian and his group, and the fear and loathing it has engendered in certain quarters, it is perhaps worth noting that Yates points out the effect of the 'invisibility' of the Brothers in Bacon's Rosicrucian parable. "[T]he travellers wonder whether they are not in the presence of divine powers and beings, whether the invisibility of the Brothers (whom we now know to have been R.C. Brothers) may not have in it something supernatural," says Yates. "[T]he New Atlantis is poised on a knife edge, depending for its favourable reception by the reader on whether that reader accepts the scientific influences in it as 'almost magical', or as diabolically inspired."[14]

Following this Rosy thread, we next spy the beginnings of the 'Invisible College', later to become that great bastion of scientific thinking and rationalism, the Royal Society. The Scottish chemist Robert Boyle mentions this group in a letter dated February 1647, describing its members as "men of so capacious and searching spirits... [who] endeavour to put narrow-mindedness out of countenance, by the practice of so extensive a charity that it reaches unto everything called man, and nothing less than an universal good-will can content it... [taking] the whole body of mankind to their care." Later members of the Invisible College/Royal Society would include some of the greatest scientific minds of the last four centuries. Esoteric scholar Manly P. Hall claims that the Rosicrucian tradition was simply the latest incarnation of a movement that was over three millennia old. "For more than three thousand years," announces Hall, "secret societies have labored to create the background of knowledge necessary to the establishment of an enlightened democracy among the nations of the world." Hall says the global, collective name of these secret societies is "The Order of the Quest".

In any case, when Freemasonry emerged into the public consciousness in the 18th century, bringing with it a large dose of the Rosicrucian ethos, we finally see the full flowering (pardon the pun) of the seeds planted by the Rosicrucian manifestos. Numerous founders of the United States of America would be initiated into Freemasonry, including Benjamin Franklin, George Washington and Paul Revere. Others, if not actually Masons, were certainly aligned in their thinking, such as Thomas Jefferson and Thomas Paine. And with Paine we come full circle, remembering that the message of the Georgia Guidestones is to lead future humanity toward a 'New Age of Reason'.

A Record in Stone

It is in the myths of the Freemasons that we find a curious ancient echo of the Georgia Guidestones. Or perhaps, more correctly, the blueprint – for in some of the Masonic legends we find the construction of stone monuments in order to transmit knowledge to a post-apocalyptic world. For example, in one tale the Biblical prophet Enoch is moved to create a lasting monument, inscribed with hieroglyphs, to ensure that certain secret knowledge is not lost:

> The degeneracy of mankind became so great , and their perversions of pure antediluvian Masonry so grievous, that, according to our traditions, Enoch feared the genuine secrets would be lost, and swallowed up in the predicted Deluge. To prevent which he hid the Grand Secret, engraven on a white oriental porphyry stone, in the bowels of the Earth; and being apprehensive that the morality and science which had been embodied in Freemasonry with such care would be absorbed in the general destruction; to preserve the principles of the science, he built two pillars near the spot where they were concealed, with an inscription in hieroglyphs, importing that near it was a precious treasure which had been dedicated to God.[15]

Arturo de Hoyos, Grand Archivist for the Scottish Rite Southern Jurisdiction, suggests another possible source for the myths of the Royal Arch degree:

> The writings of Flavius Josephus may also have contributed to the Masonic tradition. In his Antiquities of the Jews (Book I, Chap. II, vs. 3), he mentions that Seth, the son of Adam "made two pillars; the one of brick, the other of stone: they inscribed their discoveries on them both, that in case the pillar of brick should be destroyed by the flood, the pillar of stone might remain, and exhibit those discoveries to mankind; and also to inform them that there was another pillar of brick erected by them."[16]

Graham Hancock discusses Josephus' recounting of this myth in his seminal book *Fingerprints of the Gods,* adding details which further correspond with the Georgia Guidestones. Given the plethora of astronomical alignments incorporated into the Guidestones, it's worth noting that these antediluvian people were said by Josephus to be "the inventors of that particular sort of wisdom which is concerned with the heavenly bodies, and their order."[17] Hancock goes on to point out that similar myths of knowledge transmission through world-ending events can be found around the world. In the Indian Puranas, the fish god Vishnu warns his human protégé shortly before the Great Flood that "he should conceal the Sacred Scriptures in a safe place" to protect it from the impending disaster. In Mesopotamia's version of the Deluge, the god Ea tells Utnapishtim "to take the beginning, the middle and the end of whatever was consigned to writing and then bury it in the City of the Sun at Sippara," in order that the survivors of the Great Flood could return and search for the writings.

Perhaps most notable is the account of Oxford astronomer John Greaves, who collected local Egyptian myths when visiting the land of the pyramids in the 17th century. According to some local traditions, the three Giza pyramids were said to have been constructed by an antediluvian king, who dreamt that "the whole earth was turned over, with the inhabitants lying upon their faces and the stars falling down and striking one another with a terrible noise":

> And he awakened with great feare, and assembled the chief priests of all the provinces of Egypt...He related the whole matter to them and they took the altitude of the stars, and made their prognostication, and they foretold of a deluge. The king said, will it come to our country? They answered yes, and will destroy it. And there remained a certain number of years to come, and he commanded in the mean space to build the Pyramids...And he engraved in those Pyramids all things that were told by wise men, as also all profound sciences – the science of Astrology, and of Arithmeticke, and of Geometry, and of Physicke. All this may be interpreted by him that knows their characters and language.[18]

While investigation of the Giza pyramids has turned up very little 'engraving' – in fact, engraving of any sort is conspicuous by its absence on these imposing structures – certain knowledge is certainly 'encoded' and ready to be interpreted. The main passage descending into the Great Pyramid on its northern face is aimed directly into the firmament at the 'imperishable' polar stars, just as the Georgia Guidestones are now locked onto Polaris through the hole in its central pillar. And, through design or coincidence, the monument also encodes the values of *pi* and *phi*, in the slope of the pyramids sides and the dimensions of the 'King's Chamber' respectively. Certainly, we can at least give Greaves the 'astrology' and 'geometry' parts of his statement.

Maintain Humanity...

These myths about the purpose of stone monuments show that, far from being a New World Order directive to kill off 90% of the population of the planet, the Georgia Guidestones are actually meant as an instruction manual for the small band of survivors of some future cataclysm. What form the designers of the monument thought that cataclysm would take is unknown, though given the era it was built in one can assume that fears of a global nuclear war would have been a contributing factor (and perhaps offers an answer as to why it was built away from large population centers). We do know for a fact though that population increase and irrational leadership were at the forefront of the group's concerns, which might likely lead to some sort of Third World War. According to a statement by the monument's designers...

> ...The group consciousness of our race is blind, perverse, and easily distracted by trivia while it should be focused on fundamentals. We are entering a critical era. Population pressures will soon

> create political and economic crisis throughout the world. These will make more difficult and at the same time more needed the building of a rational world society.
>
> ...The approaching crisis may make mankind willing to accept a system of world law which will stress the responsibility of individual nations in regulating internal affairs, and which will assist them in the peaceful management of international frictions. With such a system we could eliminate war. We could provide every person an opportunity to seek a life of purpose and fulfillment.
>
> There are alternatives to Armageddon. They are attainable. But they will not happen without coordinated efforts by millions of dedicated people in all nations of the world.[19]

In truth, the controversial aspect of the inscription on the Georgia Guidestones is not the figure of 500 million, as the more zany conspiracy theorists would have it. As we've seen, there is little doubt that this is meant as a guide to a small group of survivors of some future disaster. The more provocative part of the inscription is the word "maintaining" – and the group are quite clear in their intended meaning on this point:

> In 1980, as these stones were being raised, the most pressing world problem was the need to control human numbers...controlling our reproduction is urgently needed. It will require major changes in our attitudes and customs.
>
> ...In these circumstances, reproduction is no longer exclusively a personal matter. Society must have a voice and some power of direction in regulating this vital function. The wishes of human couples are important, but not paramount.

> The interests of present society and the welfare of future generations must be given increasing consideration as we develop mechanisms to bring rational control to our childbearing.
>
> No person should be brought into the world unwanted and unneeded. No child should be conceived through carelessness. If each life is to have value, every conception must be part of an ordered plan of two parents who are aware of their responsibilities to that child and to society.
>
> ...Knowledge and techniques for regulating human reproduction are now in existence.[20]

Between those words, and the eugenic-sounding instruction to improve "fitness and diversity" in reproduction, the message of the Guidestones starts sounding, rather unfortunately, like a Chinese remake of *Gattaca*. To be sure, the end goal is ultimately sane, and some of the sentiments – such as having no unwanted children – are laudable, but would it justify the means? I have a sneaking suspicion that very few Western individuals would allow the government to dictate their right to have children. At least, very few pre-apocalyptic individuals...

But the message from the group acknowledges exactly that, impressing that population control would "require major changes in our attitudes and customs". It is just that they, in 1980, saw an impending population emergency. And it has to be said that time – even worse, a very short amount of time – has proven their concerns to be justified. When the Georgia Guidestones were planned and built, just three decades ago, the world population was estimated at 3.5 billion people. As of August 2009, that number has almost doubled to 6.8 billion. That sort of increase is the very definition of unsustainable. So the question should perhaps simply be framed as – are we more likely to change our customs, or rush headlong into

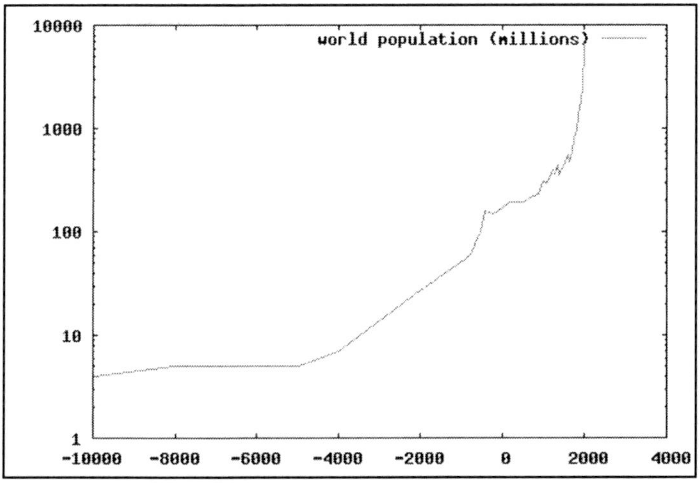

World population growth over the last 12,000 years. Note y-axis is logarithmic!

apocalypse? Perhaps the fact that the group actually decided to build the Georgia Guidestones as a lasting guide gives us an answer...

Message in a Granite Bottle

It's amusing (if you're open to black humor) to note that Graham Hancock, in the conclusion to his bestselling book *Fingerprints of the Gods,* asks what we might do if faced with impending doom. "Of course there would at first be much panic and despair," writes Hancock. "Nevertheless – if there were sufficient advance warning – steps would be taken to ensure that there would be some survivors and that some of what was most valuable in our high scientific knowledge would be preserved for the benefit of future generations."[21] He suggests that the survivors might be "blasted back into the Stone Age", so a priority would be finding a way to communicate with them and make sure they got the message "no matter what language they spoke". Amusing, because the creators of the Georgia Guidestones have done exactly that. In the same vein as the myths concerning a lost antediluvian civilization, they have inscribed messages upon granite stones, in order to pass on the 'wisdom' of our own time to future survivors of some cataclysm that is yet to occur. Whether you agree with the inscribed wisdom may be another thing, but it is hard to not be impressed with the forward-thinking behind this massive message in a bottle. Not least when we look at how most of our knowledge is currently encoded – as bits of information, stored on magnetic disks, requiring electricity to access it.

However, in terms of forward thinking to preserve knowledge for future generations, the Georgia Guidestones do not stand alone. For instance, the Rosetta Project is a modern attempt to archive all of the world's documented languages. As one aspect of their commitment to preserving this knowledge, members of the Rosetta Project have created the 'Rosetta Disk'. Made of nickel, and just 2.8 inches in diameter, the disk is meant to be a "durable archive of human languages".

> The Disk surface…is etched with a central image of the earth and a message written in eight major world languages: "Languages of the World: This is an archive of over 1,500 human languages assembled in the year 02008 C.E. Magnify 1,000 times to find over 13,000 pages of language documentation." The text begins at eye-readable scale and spirals down to nano-scale. This tapered ring of languages is intended to maximize the number of people that will be able to read something immediately upon picking up the Disk, as well as implying the directions for using it—'get a magnifier and there is more.'
>
> On the reverse side of the disk from the globe graphic are over 13,000 microetched pages of language documentation. Since each page is a physical rather than digital image, there is no platform or format dependency. Reading the Disk requires only optical magnification.[22]

The disk is "immune to water damage, able to withstand high temperatures, and unaffected by electromagnetic radiation." And the disk is housed, and protected, within a four inch spherical which is split into two hemispheres. The bottom is made of high-grade stainless steel, while the top is made of optical glass and doubles as a magnifier.

Another project to preserve knowledge is the Church of Scientology's 'Trementina Base' in New Mexico. According to the Church, the purpose of the base is as an archive to preserve the writings and recordings of the founder of Scientology, L. Ron Hubbard. The texts are said to have been engraved on stainless steel tablets and encased in titanium capsules, which reside in an underground bunker on the site.[23] I shall leave it to the reader to decide whether this is knowledge we want to transmit to our post-apocalyptic descendants...

What captivates us about the Georgia Guidestones is as much their mystery, as it is the structure itself. R.C. Christian walked into history in 1980, left his mark upon the landscape of Georgia, and then walked right back out of time. In doing so, he also left his mark upon the minds of anybody who has come across the enigmatic Georgia Guidestones. Are they the work of 'The Order of the Quest', a secret society as old as civilization and entrusted with the preservation of human wisdom? Or are they the work of a group of Nazi-inspired Illuminati wannabes, with no greater claim to knowledge than any of the rest of us? Whatever our opinion in the here-and-now, we can be sure that a future generation, rebuilding after a global cataclysm, would likely revere the message of the Guidestones – just as we have an innate feeling of respect and awe for the megaliths left behind from our predecessors, such as at Giza, Stonehenge, and Göbekli Tepe.

Lastly, in case the appearance of R.C. Christian seems more akin to a Comte de St Germain or Men in Black intervention to you, rather than a mundane project by some bored businessman, there is one story from the construction of the Georgia Guidestones which bears retelling. Sandblaster Charlie Clamp, who etched the 4,000 individual letters onto the massive granite slabs, recounted that while carving the guides he heard "strange music and disjointed voices." Readers of my article in *Darklore Volume 1,* "Her Sweet Murmur", would certainly be intrigued by that anecdote, with its suggestion of paranormal interactions.

With the Georgia Guidestones, the mystery goes on. And may continue on for millennia, beyond the apocalypse...

Greg Taylor is the owner and editor of the online alternative news portal, *The Daily Grail* (www.dailygrail.com), and is also the editor of *Darklore.* He is widely read in topics that challenge the orthodox worldview, from alternative history to the mysteries of human consciousness. Greg currently resides in Brisbane, Australia. He is the author of *The Guide to Dan Brown's The Lost Symbol,* a guidebook to the esoteric history and locations in the sequel to *The Da Vinci Code.* He is currently writing a book about the most convincing medium of modern times, Mrs. Leonora Piper.

Endnotes

Nigel Watson – Nightmares on the Edge of Reason (p. 25)

Notes

1. *Daily Express*, 18 May 1909 / *East Coast Illustrated News* (Clacton), 22 May 1909.
2. *Daily Express,* 18 May 1909.
3. Grove, Carl. "The Airship Wave of 1909?", FSR,16,6. / *Evening News*, 15 May 1909 / *East Anglian Daily Times*, 18 May 1909 / *Irish News*, 17 May 1909.
4. *East Essex Advertiser* (Clacton), 22 May 1909.
5. *Irish Times*, 19 May 1909 / *Sheffield Daily Telegraph*, 19 May 1909 / *Grimsby News*, 28 May 1909.
6. *Bath Chronicle*, 27 May 1909.
7. *Irish News*, 20 May 1909 / *Irish News*, 21 May 1909.
8. Retford, Worksop, *Isle of Axholme and Gainsborough News*, 14 May 1909.

Mention is made of other North Sea 'activities' and a rumor of an airship launching steamer in the Bristol Channel in: Screeton, Paul, "A Newspaper Looks at the Airship", MUFOB, new series 11.

9. *Grimsby News,* 14 May 1909 / *Sheffield Daily Telegraph*, 15 May 1909.
10. *The Times*, 20 May 1909 / *Grimsby News,* 21 May 1909.
11. *Sheffield Daily Telegraph*, 19 May 1909.
12. *Grimsby News*, 21 May 1909.
13. *Louth and North Lincolnshire Advertiser,* 22 May 1909.
14. *Northern Daily Mail,* 25 February 1913.
15. *Northern Daily Mail,* 25 February 1913 / *Northern Daily Mail*, 26 February 1911.
16. *Northern Daily Mail,* 5 March 1913.

Research credit to John Hind, Granville Oldroyd, David Clarke and Dirk van der Werff.

Further Reading

Dr. Robert M. Wood and Ryan S. Wood, "Majestic Documents: Evidence We Are Not Alone. Fred Crisman," www.majesticdocuments.com/personnel/crisman.php

Kenneth Arnold, "The Maury Island Episode", in *Proceedings Of The First International UFO Congress*, ed. Curtis G. Fuller, Mary Margaret Fuller, Jerome Clark, and Betty Lou White (New York: Warner Books, 1980).

Paul B. Thompson, "UFO Continuing Tales No. 5 - The Maury Island Case," www.parascope.com/nb/cautionarytales/mauryIsland.htm

Dr David Clarke, "Scareships over Britain. The Airship Wave of 1909" at: www.ufo.se/english/articles/wave.html

Peter Rogerson, "The Mythology of UFO Events and Interpretations: A New Examination" *Merseyside UFO Bulletin*, Vol. 5, No. 3, Summer 1972, at: http://magonia.haaan.com/2008/the-mythology-of-ufo-events-and-interpretations-a-new-examination-peter-rogerson/

Nigel Watson, *The Alien Deception,* Youwriteon, 2009.

Nigel Watson (ed.), *The Scareship Mystery: A Survey of Phantom Airship Scares 1909-1918*, Domra, 2000.

Airminded website at: http://airminded.org/archives/scareships-1909/

Greg McQueen – Helicopters? In Ancient Egypt? (p. 61)

References

Alford, A. (2004). The Official 'Alan Alford Website''. Retrieved August 08, 2009, from http://www.eridu.co.uk. (sourcing extracts from 'Ancient Helicopter is not a Hoax', an article in *UFO Magazine*, UK, Sept/Oct 1997, pp. 19-21).

Boyle, D. H. (2007). *The Children of the Stars - The Mathematical and Geometrical Proof We are Not Alone.* David Hugo Boyle Imprint.

Childress, D. H., & Clendenon, B. (2002). *Atlantis & the power system of the gods.*

Fanthorpe, L., & Fanthorpe, P. (2006). *Mysteries and Secrets of the Masons: The Story Behind the Masonic Order* (chapter three).

Greenberg, R. (1999). *Richard Hoagland Charged With More Plagiarism And Fraud.* From http://www.rense.com/ufo2/remedy.htm

Haughton, B. (2007). *Hidden History* (A. DeRidder, Ed.). Franklin Lakes: New Jersey.

Hoagland, R. (1999). The "Lost Tombs" Revisited: "Success Has a Thousand Fathers ..." from http://www.enterprisemission.com/tombsweb1.html

Motzer, R. F. (1999). "Hoagland's Abydos Photos? NO...They Are Mine And Ruth Hover's". From http://www.rense.com/ufo2/realowners.htm

Richardson, D. (2003). *The Rough Guide to Egypt.* Rough Guides; 5th edition. Daniel Jacobs Publisher.

Wicherink, J. (2005). *Souls of Distortion Awakening,* 5th ed. Retrieved from wejees.net/downloads/SoulsOfDistortion.pdf

Acknowledgements

With gratitude to Roz Butterworth for her support and editorial assistance. Thanks also to Bruce Rawles of www.geometrycode.com.

Neil Arnold – The Goatsucker Family Tree (p. 71)

Notes

1. http://wikipedia.org.uk
2. http://www.ufoinfo.com/humanoid/humanoid2004.shtml
3. Arnold, Neil. *Monster! The A-Z Of Zooform Phenomena*, page 229 (2007 CFZ Press)
4. http://monsters.monstrous.com/manticore.htm
5. http://www.iras.ucalgary.ca/~volk/sylvia/goatsucker.htm
6. Corrales, Scott. *Flashpoint: High Strangeness In Puerto Rico,* pages 80-82 (1998 – Amarna)
7. Shuker, Karl. *From Flying Toads to Snakes with Wings*, pages 19-21 (1997 Llewellyn)
8. http://hellhorror.com/mysteries/chupacabra/
9. Corrales, Scott. *Chupacabras & Other Mysteries*, page 74 (1997 – Greenleaf)
10. http://www.njdevilhunters.com/
11. *UFO Magazine*, Vol. 11 Issue 1 page 23
12. Farrant, David. *Beyond The Highgate Vampire* (1991 B.P.O.S.)
13. http://www.ufoinfo.com/humanoid/humanoid2008.shtml
14. http://www.thesun.co.uk/sol/homepage/news/article1555325.ece
15. http://www.ufoinfo.com/humanoid/humanoid2009.shtml
16. Published by CFZ Press 2008.
17. http://www.cfz.org.uk/beta/index.htm The world's largest cryptozoological organisation which mounts expeditions, publishes unique books and four times a year, a magazine called Animals & Men.

18. Which were introduced to some Caribbean and Hawaiian islands.

For more information on all the monsters listed in this chapter, read my 2007 book: *MONSTER! THE A-Z OF ZOOFORM PHENOMENA*.

The Emperor – Flying Saucerers (p. 93)

References

Bennett, Colin (2001) *Looking for Orthon: The story of George Adamski, the First Flying Saucer Contactee, and How he Changed the World.* Paraview Press.

Busby, Michael (2004) *Solving the 1897 Airship Mystery.* Pelican

Carter, John (2004) *Sex and Rockets: The Occult World of Jack Parsons.* Feral House.

Clancy, Susan (2005) *Abducted: How People Come to Believe They Were Kidnapped by Aliens.* Harvard University Press.

Clark, Jerome (2008) "60 Years of Fate Magazine." In *Fortean Times #237.* 44-49.

Clarke, Arthur C. (1990) *Astounding Days: A Science Fictional Autobiography.* Victor Gollancz, London

Clore, Dan. (Autumn 2001) "The Lurker on the Threshold of Interpretation: Hoax Necronomicons and Paratextual Noise." In *Lovecraft Studies #42-43.* 61-69. http://tinyurl.com/lurkerthreshold

Coleman, William Emmette (1895) "The Sources of Madame Blavatsky's Writings." In Solovyoff, Vsevolod Sergyeevich (ed.) *A Modern Priestess of Isis.* London, Longmans, Green, and Co. Appendix C. 353-366. http://tinyurl.com/colemanblavatsky

de Camp, L. Sprague (1970) *Lost Continents: The Atlantis Theme in History,* Science, and Literature. Dover Publications.

Goodrick-Clarke, Nicholas (2004) *The Occult Roots of Nazism: Secret Aryan Cults and Their Influence on Nazi Ideology.*Tauris Parke Paperbacks.

Greenfield, Allen (2006) *The Roots of Modern Magick: Glimpses of the Authentic Tradition from 1700-2000, An Anthology. Revised edition.* Manutius Press.

Greer, John Michael (2009) *The UFO Phenomenon: Fact, Fantasy and Disinformation.* Llewellyn Worldwide.

Grünschloß, Andreas (2006) "Ancient Astronaut« Narrations A Popular Discourse on Our Religious Past." In *Marburg Journal of Religion. 11 (1).* PDF: http://tinyurl.com/aanarrations HTML: http://tinyurl.com/aanarrationshtml

Hambling, David (2000) "Bring down the wrath of God on evil men." *The Guardian.*

3 February 2000. http://www.guardian.co.uk/science/2000/feb/03/technology

Hatcher Childress, David (1999) "The Shaver Mystery" in *Lost Continents and the Hollow Earth.* Adventures Unlimited Press.

Keel, John (1983) "The Man Who Invented Flying Saucers." *Fortean Times.* http://tinyurl.com/keelinvented

Kossy, Donna (2001) *Strange Creations: Aberrant Ideas of Human Origins from Ancient Astronauts to Aquatic Apes.* Feral House.

Maurer, David W. (2000) *The Big Con: The Story of the Confidence Man.* Anchor Books.

Melton, J. Gordon (1995) "The Contactees: A Survey" In Lewis, James R. (ed.) *The Gods Have Landed: New Religions from Other Worlds.* State University of New York Press, New York. Pages 1-13.

Pendle, George (2005) *Strange Angel: The Otherworldly Life of Rocket Scientist John Whiteside Parsons.* Weidenfeld & Nicolson.

Picknett, Lynn and Prince, Clive (2001) *The Stargate Conspiracy : Revealing The Truth Behind the Extraterrestrial Contact, Military Intelligence and the Mysteries of Ancient Egypt.* Warner Books.

Randle, Kevin, D., Estes, Russ & Cone, William P. (1999) *The Abduction Enigma: The Truth Behind the Mass Alien Abductions of the Late Twentieth Century.* Forge.

Russo, Gus (1998) *Live by the Sword: The Secret War Against Castro and the Death of JFK.* Bancroft Press.

Rydeen, Paul (2003) "Brother Jack Parsons: The Magickal Scientist and His Circle." *Grey Lodge Occult Review #3.* http://tinyurl.com/parsonscircle

Thomas, Kenn (1999) *Maury Island UFO: The Crisman Conspiracy.* IllumiNet Press.

Vallee, Jacques (1988) *Dimensions: A Casebook of Alien Contact.* Souvenir Press.

Vallee, Jacques (1996) *Forbidden Science: Journals 1957 - 1969.* Marlowe and Company.

Notes

1. *Darklore Volume 1*, Daily Grail Publishing.

2. "a form of theater…staged with minute naturalistic illusionism for an audience of one, who is moreover enlisted as part of the cast." "Introduction by Luc Sante" in Maurer (2000) page xxii

3. For a recent summary see Gary Lachman's Into the Interior: Discovering Swedenborg, with an overview in Fortean Times #220 (2007). What is potentially interesting for our purposes is that Melton (1995) page 3 draws parallels with the popular literary tradition of the time: "Swedenborg's Earth on Our Solar System became a first. It reads much like any other fantastic voyage novel, with the

exception that it claims to be an account of an actual trip to outer space"

4. Melton (1995) page 3 suggest the "Martian" she claimed to learn may be the languages people come out with when speaking in tongues (glossolalia): "a new language which is an infantile, cut down version of the language they speak normally"

5. Busby (2004) pages 242-243

6. *Isis Unveiled: A Master Key to the Mysteries of Ancient and Modern Science and Theology* online at: http://isisunveiled.net/

7. *The Secret Doctrine: The Synthesis of Science, Religion, and Philosophy* online at: http://secretdoctrine.net/

8. Coleman (1895) "There is not a single dogma or tenet in theosophy, nor any detail of moment in the multiplex and complex concatenation of alleged revelations of occult truth in the teachings of Madame Blavatsky and the pretended adepts, the source of which cannot be pointed out in the world's literature. From first to last, their writings are dominated by a duplex plagiarism, - plagiarism in idea, and plagiarism in language."

9. Goodrick-Clarke (2005) page 19

10. Clore (2001)

11. *A Dweller on Two Planets* http://www.sacred-texts.com/atl/dtp/index.htm

12. de Camp (1970) page 71. We met de Camp in the previous piece as a sci-fi writer and associate of Heinlein. Interestingly advanced humans living below Mt Shasta is part of Robert Heinlein's 1941 novella Lost Legacy.

13. Melton (1995) page 7

14. Melton (1995) page 6

15. Clark (2008) page46

16. Clarke (1990) page 107

17. "This was not the end of the matter, as Lovecraft also borrowed a number of occult works – as well as Charles Fort's Book of the Damned and New Lands 4 – from libraries and his friends, most notably Herman C Koenig of New York City. (Interestingly, Lovecraft actually mentions Fort by name in a couple of stories.)." http://www.forteantimes.com/features/profiles/153/hp_lovecraft.html

18. Grünschloß (2006) "It was the US-American journalist and innovative writer Charles Hoy Fort (1874–1932), who laid down the most influential modern 'foundation stone' for the idea of space alien interventions on Earth. ... Fort's books inspired many writers in the Science Fiction and fantasy genres – most prominently H.P. Lovecraft."

19. *ibid.* "Several times in his books, Fort expresses the idea that a hidden knowledge about the existence of such forces seems to be handed down only via 'esoteric ones' (who once had been in actual 'communication') and some secret

"societies" or esoteric fraternities – a topic which later was to become a strong Lovecraft motif, and which could be traced back to some core elements of the theosophic 'Secret Science' narrations in Helena P. Blavatsky's Secret Doctrine."

20. Clarke (1990) 109. For an excellent overview of Fort's influence on science fiction see "Charles Fort and Astounding Science Fiction" http://tinyurl.com/fortscifi

21. Keel (1983)

22. Hatcher Childress, David (1999) page 223

23. *ibid*

24. *ibid* page 229

25. *ibid* page 229

26. http://www.haroldsherman.com/publishedworks/greenman.htm

27. Interestingly the film is based on the 1938 novella "Who Goes There?" by John W. Campbell, who we looked at in detail in the previous piece as he went on to become the editor who launched the Golden Age of Science Fiction with Heinlein, Asimov and others, and later launched Dianetics by another protégé, L. Ron Hubbard. The 1951 film wasn't actually very accurate to the story because of technological special effects and they only really caught up with Campbell's ideas in time for the more faithful 1982 remake *The Thing* by John Carpenter (one of my favourite films) You can read the story at: http://tinyurl.com/whogoesthere

28. http://www.v-j-enterprises.com/arnold.html

29. His letter on his Shaver-like adventures was printed in the May 1947 edition of *Amazing Stories.*

30. The whole story is convoluted and complex. A good summary can be found in Thomas (1999)

31. Greer (2009) page 32. Note also that it reworks the ancient astronaut ideas.

32. It was an odd time at Lockheed: At this time Lockheed aircraft were also chasing down UFOs, they were developing a number of saucer-shaped craft and in December 1953 an engineer and his family observed a UFO which was also independently observed by a Lockheed flight (some of the crew being familiar with Van Tassel, one had visited his Giant Rock Spacecraft conventions, as Angelucci, George Hunt Williamson, Adamski and many others did in the early days of Ufology). http://conspiracy101.com/ufos/skunkworks/index.html

33. http://www.sacred-texts.com/ufo/sos/sos02.htm

34. *Gauche Encounters: Bad films and the UFO Mythos* by Martin Kottmeyer, Talking Pictures. http://www.talkingpix.co.uk/ArticleGaucheEncounters.html

35. A scanned version of which is available online: http://tinyurl.com/adamskifate

36. For a good overview see Bennett (2001)

37. Bennett (2001) page 18-19
38. Bennett (2001) page 23
39. Bennett (2001) page 24
40. Bennett (2001) page 28-29
41. Bennett (2001) page 29-30
42. Vallee (1988) page 250
43. *ibid*
44. Bennett (2001) page 38
45. Kossy (2001) page 10
46. *ibid* pages 10-11
47. *ibid* page 13
48. *ibid* page 15
49. Timothy Beckley, who recently reprinted the lost novel, said "Ray Palmer, who was one of my mentors, said several times in his *Flying Saucers From Other Worlds* magazine that he believed that Adamski was well meaning, but that his story could not be true, because Adamski had once submitted to Palmer a manuscript in which GA claimed to have voyaged into space much like he insisted he had done in his much later, frequently criticized, *Inside The Space Ships* in which Adamski speaks of traveling to the planet Saturn." http://www.ufodigest.com/news/0109/adamski.html
50. "Why I can say that Adamski was a Liar" http://tinyurl.com/adamskiliar
51. Vallee (1988) page 250: "Jack Parsons claimed to have met a Venusian in the desert in 1946." This is about all there is on this. I have passed a message on to Jacques Vallee through our noble editor, so hopefully, one day, we'll have more on this.
52. Carter (2004) page 142
53. Carter (2004) footnote 15 on page 133 says "UFO researcher Jacques Vallee says Parsons claimed to have met a Venusian in the Mojave desert during the course of 1946. The Venusian apparently was the implied source of *Liber 49*." This appears to be the extent of the published information I could find on this, all going back to Jacque Vallee. This volume's editor passed a note from me on to Vallee asking for clarification on this but, as of the time of press, there has been no reply. Worth noting that there is apparently a timeline printed at the back of Rydeen (2003) which is reproduced in a number of place which apparently says "Jan 18, 1946 - Hubbard and Parsons go to Mojave Desert, meet 'Venusian'" Which would put this date earlier and obvious he was not alone – the date is when Parsons and Hubbard went to the desert, following which they returned home and found Marjorie Cameron. See for example: http://www.lermanet2.com/scientology-and-occult/
54. Carter (2004) page 95
55. Rydeen (2003) According to *Headpress Guide to the Counter Culture,* John Carter is the Edgar Rice Burroughs-inspired pseudonym used by Paul Rydeen for

the book *Sex and Rockets*. The material quoted here comes from a pamphlet "Jack Parsons and the Fall of Babalon" which was then turned into the book *Sex & Rockets*. This information on Mount Palomar is missing from the book.

56.http://ufocon.blogspot.com/2008/01/ufos-and-scientology.html–unfortunately, I haven't yet got a definitive source for this but am still working on it.

57. Vallee (1988) page 243 for the link with Laughead. Alec Hidell has written about Laughead and associates in this period and says: "Laughead's role in that affair was basically that of agent provocateur. Without him, it is doubtful whether events would have turned out as they did. He is referred to throughout *When Prophecy Fails* as 'Dr. Armstrong.' His efforts on behalf of Mrs. Keech were rather akin to those of Thurber's Get-Ready Man, who 'used to go about shouting at people through a megaphone to prepare for the end of the world.'" http://www.excludedmiddle.com/tracks%20in%20desert.html

58. Young knew Harry Everett Smith a member of the OTO and is likely to have known Jack Parsons. Picknett & Prince (2001) page 277

59. Randle et al. (1999) and Clancy (2005). Puharich's questions included "Are you the Nine Principles that once spoke through Dr Vinod?" which is just asking for an affirmative answer.

60. Greer (2009) page 26

61. It is a big story in itself but one of the most surprising examples is the fact that one of the few things we can prove about Bob Lazar is that he was signed up with the Office of Naval Intelligence – an odd employer for someone who claims to have spent their time reverse engineering UFOs in the Nevada Desert at the airforce base better known as Area 51.

62. Randle et al. (1999) and Clancy (2005)

63. If you want to read up on this there are plenty of sites online including: http://educate-yourself.org/cn/projectbluebeam25jul05.shtml

64. Russo (1998) page 45

65. Hambling (2000)

66. Vallee (1996) page 284

67. Picknett & Prince (2001)

68. Picknett & Prince (2001) page 167: "He was Dr. Andrija Puharich, Uri Geller's mentor and the ultimate eminence gris [sic], whose disturbing talent for creating belief systems – we were to discover – helped to shape events in the last half of the twentieth century"

69. Like the way the idea that Sirius was important emerged in this period and was transmitted via Young to Robert Temple, who popularised it in his book *The Sirius Mystery*. See Picknett & Prince (2001) throughout e.g. page 275-278

70. Greer (2009) pages 203-204

71. "The Cold War Sci-Fi Parable That Fell to Earth" (2008). *The New York Times.* http://tinyurl.com/reaganufos

72. Greenfield (2006) page 130. The footnote 25 included in the quote says "Except for Mundy, the present author has met with all the pulp writers mentioned here" http://books.google.com/books?id=UM1TI_3l0GcC&pg=PA130

73. Clore (2001)

74. Clark (2008) page 48 describes the opinion of Curtis and Mary Fuller, partners in *Fate* magazine, who would eventually take over from Palmer: "As they saw him, nothing gave the reflexively deceptive Palmer more satisfaction than triumphant bamboozlement, whether the matter at issue was large or small, import or inconsequential, professional or personal" Clark himself was editor in more recent years and says of the early days of *Fate*, an apparently factual magazine, "Some of the content was surely outright fiction, though the back-up files – as I learned when I dug through them – are so thinly documented that its not possible to determine for instance, whether an actual 'Oge-Make' wrote 'Tribal Memories of Flying Saucers' (September 1949) or (more likely) an imaginative SF writer/editor in *Fate's* office. As often happened with the young *Fate's* fictions, the story has lived on in fringe literature" (page 47).

R. Schoch and O.Ghiocel - Instigating Chaos in Romania (p. 173)

Bibliography

Alexe, Dan. *Conspirația Psihotronică* [The Psychotronic Conspiracy]. Craiova: Editura Obiectiv, 2004.

Anonymous [authors blacked out in unclassified version]. Paraphysics R&D - - Warsaw Pact. Prepared by the U.S. Air Force, Air Force Systems Command, Foreign Technology Division. DST-1810S-202-78. 30 March 1978. Downloaded 22 May 2009 from: http://www.dia.mil/publicaffairs/Foia/pa_warsaw.pdf [Unclassified version with portions blacked out.]

Bearden, Thomas E. *Excalibur Briefing.* San Francisco: Strawberry Hill Press, 1980.

Becker, Robert O., and Gary Selden. *The Body Electric: Electromagnetism and the Foundation of Life.* New York: William Morrow, 1985.

Bremseth, L. R. "Unconventional Human Intelligence Support: Transcendent and Asymmetric Warfare Implications of Remote Viewing." In Robert M. Schoch and Logan Yonavjak, compilers and commentators, *The Parapsychology Revolution: A Concise Anthology of Paranormal and Psychical Research.* New York, Tarcher/Penguin, 2008, pp. 233-251 (Bremseth's paper was originally written in 2001).

CAHRA [Citizens Against Human Rights Abuse]; Cheryl Welsh, director. "Russian Book Translation Project Results, with related background information on Russian/U.S. mind control technology." Document dated September 2001. Downloaded 14 May 2009 from: http://mindjustice.org/russian.pdf

Celan, Eugen. *Serviciile Secrete şi Parapsihologia* [Secret Services and Parapsychology, Vols. I & II]. Craiova: Editura Obiectiv, 2000.

David-Neel, Alexandra. *Magic and Mystery in Tibet.* New Hyde Park, New York: University Books, 1965 (New Edition; originally published as *Mystiques et Magiciens du Thibet*, 1929, and in English as *With Mystics and Magicians in Tibet*, 1931).

Filip, Teodor. *Războiul Parapsihologic Împotriva României* (ediţia a – III – a) [The Parapsychological War Against Romania]. Craiova: Editura Obiectiv, [no date on this third edition; the first edition was published in 1998].

Gârz, Florian, Col. (r). *Istoria Interzisă* [Forbidden History]. Craiova: Editura Obiectiv, 2005.

Gârz, Florian. Col. (r). *Ghidul Spionului Român* [The Guide of the Romanian Spy]. Craiova: Editura Obiectiv, 2001.

Gârz, Florian, Col. (r). *Spionajul Total în Acţiune* [Total Espionage in Action]. Craiova: Editura Obiectiv, 2001.

Keith, Jim. *Mass Control: Engineering Human Consciousness.* Kempton, Illinois: Adventures Unlimited Press, 2003.

LaMothe, John D., Captain, Medical Service Corps. Controlled Offensive Behavior - - USSR. Defense Intelligence Agency. Prepared by U.S. Army Office of the Surgeon General, Medical Intelligence Office. ST-CS-01-169-72. July 1972. Downloaded 22 May 2009 from: http://www.dia.mil/publicaffairs/Foia/cont_ussr.pdf [Unclassified version with portions blacked out.]

Life Technology. "Psychotronics is a Czech term for parapsychology." 2006. Downloaded 22 May 2009 from: newsgroups.derkeiler.com/pdf/Archive/Soc/soc.culture.iraq/2008-06/msg00018.pdf

Maire, Louis F., III (Louis F. Maire III) and Major J. D. LaMothe, MSC. Soviet and Czechoslovakian Parapsychological Research. Defense Intelligence Agency. Prepared by U.S. Army Medical Intelligence and Information Agency, Office of the Surgeon General. DST-1810S-387-75. September 1975. Downloaded 22 May 2009 from: http://www.dia.mil/publicaffairs/Foia/sovczech.pdf [Reproduction poor with portions and various illustrations illegible.]

McMoneagle, Joseph. *Remote Viewing Secrets.* Charlottesville, Virginia: Hampton Roads Publishing, 2000.

Ostrander, Sheila, and Lynn Schroeder. *Psychic Discoveries* (Introduction by Uri Geller). New York: Marlowe and Company, 1997. (Part 1, Psychic

Discoveries Behind the Iron Curtain, abridged; Part 2, Psychic Discoveries –The Iron Curtain Lifted.)

Străinu, Emil, Gl. Bg. Dr. *Războiul Geofizic* [Geophysical Warfare]. Bucharest: Phobos Publishing House, 2008.

Străinu, Emil, Gl. Bg. Dr. *Războiul Psihotronic* [Psychotronic Warfare]. Bucharest: Phobos Publishing House, 2008.

Notes

All translations and interpretations from the Romanian used in this article are by Oana R. Ghiocel.

1. Filip, p. 38.
2. LaMothe, p. 131.
3. LaMothe, p. 137.
4. Oana R. Ghiocel witnessed this broadcast on television during the Romanian Revolution.
5. Gușă died in 1994 of cancer. He was 53 years old. Today, the general public in Romania believes that General Gușă was somehow irradiated, that his cancer was induced through some sort of psychotronic means. His physical decline was very sudden. Being a key player in the Romanian Revolution and having close ties to Ceaușescu, his mysterious cancer death seemed somewhat too convenient for the ones in power.
6. Filip, pp. 50-51.
7. Bearden, p. 93, and see the photographs on p. 95 of "foo" fighters.
8. See David-Neel.
9. Life Technology.
10. Anonymous, p. 1.
11. See Bremseth; McMoneagle.
12. See Bearden; Celan; Maire and LaMothe; Ostrander and Schroeder.
13. Străinu, Războiul Psihotronic, pp. 29-30.
14. Filip, p. 129.
15. Filip, p. 165.
16. Filip, p. 158.

Theo Paijmans – The Newhallville Terror (p. 193)

Notes

1. Alsop's account was published nationwide in America between the months of March and June 1838 in the American newspapers. Most newspapers cited the *New York Sun* as their source, following the description of Spring-heeled Jack as it was published on 22 February 1838 in *The Times* without embellishments. I have located the account in the following newspapers: 'The London Ghost', *New-York Spectator*, New York, New York, 2 April 1838; The London Ghost, *New Bedford Mercury*, New Bedford, Massachusetts, 5 April 1838; *The Southern Patriot*, Charleston, South Carolina, 12 April 1838; 'Miscellany. From the N.Y. Sun', *The Mississippian*, Jackson, Mississippi, 1 June 1838.

2. Burke, Edmund and Ivison Stevenson, *The Annual Register of World Events, A Review of the Year*, London, Longmans, Green, 1839, pages 26-27.

3. See Mike Dash's, most excellent paper 'Spring-Heeled Jack: To Victorian Bugaboo from Suburban Ghost', *Fortean Studies*, vol. 3, edited by Steve Moore, pages 7-125, of which an updated version is found online here: www.mikedash.com/investigations/investigations_jack_about.htm

4. 'The Hammersmith Ghost', *The Star*, 9 January 1804.

5. *West Kent Guardian*, 30 December 1837.

6. 'Credulity – The Ghost Story, *The Morning Chronicle*, 10 January 1838.

7. 'Ghosts In The Vicinity Of The Metropolis', *County Herald & Weekly Advertiser*, 20 January 1838.

8. Theo Paijmans, 'The Black Flash Of Cape Cod: True Heir Of Spring-heeled Jack', *The Anomalist no. 13, Intermediate States, A Nonfiction Anthology*, eds. Patrick Huyghe and Dennis Stacy, Anomalist Books 2007, pages 10-36.

9. Accounts of the Phantom of O'Donnell Heights can be found in: Mike Dash, 'Spring-Heeled Jack: To Victorian Bugaboo from Suburban Ghost', *Fortean Studies*, vol. 3, edited by Steve Moore, pages 102-108, 121, Jerome Clark, 'Springheel Jack', *The UFO Encyclopedia 2nd Edition, The Phenomenon from the Beginning*, Omnigraphics, 1998, page 880 (Clark cites Dash as source) and in Robert Damon Schneck, *The President's Vampire. Strange-but-True Tales of the United States of America*, Anomalist Books, 2005, chapter 6, 'The Horror in the Heights', pages 93-106.

10. J. Vyner, 'The Mystery Of Springheel Jack', *Flying Saucer Review*, May-June, 1961, pages 3-6.

11. J. Vyner, 'The Mystery Of Springheel Jack', *Fate Magazine*, Vol. 14 No.10, October 1961, pages 27-33.

12. Jerome Clark, 'Springheel Jack', *Unexplained!*, Visible Ink Press, 1993, pages 357-359; Phil Rife, 'Springheel Jack Invades America', *Fate Magazine*, Vol.50 No.11, No. 572, November 1997, pages 16-18; Loren Coleman, 'The Mad Gasser of Mattoon and his Kin', *Mysterious America the revised edition*, Chapter 21, Paraview Press, 2001, pages 257-261, 269; George M. Eberhart, 'Springheel Jack', *Mysterious Creatures, A Guide to Cryptozoology,* Volume two, Clio, 2002, page 517 where Spring-heeled Jack is classified as a 'flying humanoid'; W. Ritchie Benedict, Spring-Heeled Jack Does America, *Fate Magazine,* Vol. 58 No.6, June 2005, pages 19-26.

13. J. Vyner, 'The Mystery Of Springheel Jack', *Flying Saucer Review,* May-June 1961, Vol. 3 No. 7, page 6.

14. Jim Brandon, *Weird America,* Dutton, 1978, page 92.

15. E-mail correspondence with Jim Brandon, various dates, 2008. In all fairness I should mention that while discussing my solution to the mystery of the alleged Louisville event, Brandon held it plausible but maintained that he had read it somewhere other than in Vyner's article which he did not know.

16. 'A Flying Machine. What Two Louisvillians Saw Last Evening', *Louisville Courier-Journal*, Louisville, Kentucky, 29 June 1880. Also mentioned with bibliographical reference by Brandon in his *Weird America*, Dutton, 1978, page 93.

17. Theo Paijmans, 'The Black Flash Of Cape Cod: True Heir Of Spring-heeled Jack', *The Anomalist no. 13, Intermediate States, A Nonfiction Anthology,* eds. Patrick Huyghe and Dennis Stacy, Anomalist Books 2007, pages 28-36.

18. Mike Dash (ed.), *Spring-heeled Jack: Sources and Interpretation*, to be published forthcoming autumn 2009.

19. 'Newhallville's Terror. The Nightly Ghost Walking. Strange Incidents Last Night. Jennie Burton's Terrible Fright. Armed Men Hunting in Cemeteries and Highways. Mrs. Meeker's Experience. Phosphoric Gleams From Witchlike Grounds', the *New Haven Evening Register*, New Haven, Connecticut, 26 October 1881.

20. 'Various Matters', the *New Haven Evening Register*, New Haven, Connecticut, 4 November 1881, 'Various Matters', the *New Haven Evening Register*, New Haven, Connecticut, 8 November 1881.

21. 'The Ghost Identified', the *New Haven Evening Register,* New Haven, Connecticut, 9 November 1881.

22. 'More of the Ghost', the *New Haven Evening Register,* New Haven, Connecticut, 11 November 1881.

23. 'Have We A Ghost? The Reports from All Parts of the City', the *New Haven Evening Register,* New Haven, Connecticut, 16 November 1881.

24. 'The Ghost', the *New Haven Evening Register,* New Haven, Connecticut, 22 November 1881.

25. 'Two Ghosts. They are seen by two Different Policemen', the *New Haven Evening Register,* New Haven, Connecticut, 25 November 1881.

26. William H. Avis, 'Mystery Of Giant, Fence-Vaulting Ghost Of Newhallville Still remains Unsolved. Many Hamden residents Recall Wierd Wraith That Haunted Streets Fifty Years Ago', the *New Haven Evening Register,* New Haven, Connecticut, undated but probably 1933. Clipping courtesy of Neil Hogan.

27. Neil Hogan, 'Newhallville Ghost Was Terror of 1881', the *New Haven Register,* New Haven, Connecticut, 30 October 1988.

28. Joseph Citro, *Passing Strange: True Tales Of New England Hauntings and Horrors*, Houghton Mifflin, 1996, see the chapter 'When the Devil came to Provincetown', pages 176-177. Citro, with whom I communicated about the sources of his account, kindly identified Neil Hogan's article as his source.

Robert Bauval – The Sacred Landscape of Re (p. 211)

Notes

1. George Goyon, *Kheops: Le Secret des Batiseurs des Grandes Pyramides*, Pygmalion ed. Paris 1990, p. 92

2. Mirolav Verner, *Abusir: Realm of Osiris*, The American University in Cairo Press, NY 2002, p. 14.

3. J.Malek 'Orion and the Giza Pyramids' (review of Robert Bauval's book *The Orion Mystery*) in *Discussions in Egyptology* vol. 30. 1994, pp.101-114.

4. Mark Lehner, *The Complete Pyramids*, op.cit. pp.106-7.

5. See David G. Jeffreys, 'The topography of Heliopolis and Memphis: some cognitive aspects', in H Guksch & D Polz (eds), *Stationen: Beitrage zur Kulturgeschichte Agyptens.* Rainer Stadelmann Gewimdet, 63-71. Mainz. Hekakian mentioned that there was a direct line of sight joining "the South West and North Eastern Diagonals of the Soris (Cheops) Pyramid and the Obelisk'".

6. Goyon, 'Kerkasore' in BIFAO op. cit. p. 142. Also G. Goyon, 'Nouvelles Observations Relatives a l'Orientation de la Pyramide de Kheops' in *Revue D'Egyptologie* Tome 22, Paris 1970, p.85.

7. Wainwright, 'Iron in Egypt', JEA 18, 1933, p. 6-11

8. David G. Jeffreys, 'The topography of Heliopolis and Memphis: some cognitive aspects', in H Guksch & D Polz (eds), *Stationen: Beitrage zur Kulturgeschichte Agyptens.* Rainer Stadelmann Gewimdet, 63-71. Mainz

9. David G. Jeffreys, 'The topography of Heliopolis and Memphis: some cognitive aspects', in H Guksch & D Polz (eds), *Stationen: Beitrage zur Kulturgeschichte Agyptens.* Rainer Stadelmann Gewimdet, 63-71. Mainz

10. Mark Lehner, op. cit. p. 120.

11. Jeffreys, D.G, 1998. 'The topography of Heliopolis and Memphis: some cognitive aspects', in H Guksch & D Polz (eds), *Stationen: Beitrage zur Kulturgeschichte Agyptens.* Rainer Stadelmann Gewimdet, 63-71. Mainz, p. 70

12, It was at the summer solstice that the Nile's yearly flood would begin. In the Old Kingdom the summer solstice closely coincided with the heliacal rising of Sirius, the well-known marker of the New Year's Day for the ancient Egyptians. Because of this, the summer solstice originally marked the first day of the civil calendar. See *The Dawn of Astronomy,* Sir Norman Lockyer, 1894. See more recently Juan Belmonte, 'Some open questions on the Egyptian Calendar: as astronomer's view', *Trabajos de Egyptologia,* Issue 2, 2003.

13. Zahi Hawass, 'The Temples of the Rising Sun', *Horus Magazine,* April 2001

14. Labib Habachi, *The Obelisks of Egypt,* The American University in Cairo Press, 1994, p. 5.

15. "...came the occasion when the Egyptians wished to create an imposing image of their God-king, who after his death was called Horakhti --'Horus the Dweller in the Horizon'-- the Lord of Heaven. How to represent him? The idea of using the form of the lion probably occurred first, but did not quite meet the need, for the lion had come to be associated in their minds with ferocity as well as kingship, and they wished to represent a wise and powerful, but beneficent deity. It is perhaps in this manner that they evolved the form of the Sphinx, which displays the grace and terrific power of the lion and the superior intellectual power of man...In the beliefs of the Egyptians, the king was the earthly representation of this god, and we have proof that in the very early period the dead king was especially called Horakhti. When Khafra cut the Great Sphinx, it was made in his likeness, that is to say in the likeness of Horakhti, with whom he was identified (Selim Hassan, *The Sphinx, it's history in the Light of Recent Excavations,* Government Press, Cairo, 1949, p. 139-140). Egyptologist Ahmed Fakhry who also concluded that 'the stele and votive figures of sphinxes, lions, and falcons found around the Sphinx reveals the names under which it was known and worshipped. Most commonly it was called Horemakhet, "Horus-in-the-Horizon", or Horakhti, "Horus-of-the-Horizon" both are appropriate names..." (Ahmed Fakhry, *The Pyramids,* University of Chicago Press, 1969, p.164.)

16. Richard H. Wilkinson, *The Complete Gods and Goddesses of Ancient Egypt,* The American University in Cairo Press, 2003,, p. 45. Evidence of this is given in the *Gardiner Papyrus* (c.1100 BC) where it is stated: "Ramses IX Year 13, Birth of Ra-horakhti, 1st month, 1st day" (Raymond Weill, *Bases, Méthodes et Resultats de la*

Chronologie Egyptienne, Paris 1926, pp. 121-2). Also in the so-called Calendar of Edfu (100 B.C). it is stated: "Birth of Ra-Horakhti, 1st month, 1st day"(Marshall Clagett, *Ancient Egyptian Science, vol. II, Calendars, Clocks and Astronomy,* American Philosophical society 1995., Fig. III. 6a.). There is, too, a text from the so-called Cairo Calendar that describes the birth of Ra-horakhti as follows: "I Akhet 1: The Birth of Ra-horakhti; ablution throughout the entire land in the water of the beginning of the High Nile which comes forth as fresh Nun." (Abdel Mohsen Bakir, "The Cairo Calendar of Lucky an Unlucky Days' (Journal d'Entrée, no. 86637) *Annales du Service des Antiquités de l'Égypte,* Vol. 48, 1948, p. 425-31.

17. Richard H. Wilkinson, *The Complete Gods and Goddesses of Ancient Egypt,* The American University in Cairo Press, 2003,, p. 206.

John Reppion – The Mole of Edge Hill (p. 241)

Notes

1. Charles R. Hand: *Joseph Williamson – The King of Edge Hill,* Transactions of the Historical Society of Lancashire and Cheshire 1927.
2. The Story (www.williamsonstunnels.com).
3. Richard Whittington-Egan: *Joseph Williamson Maker Of Catacombs.*
4. Richard Whittington-Egan: *Joseph Williamson Maker Of Catacombs.*
5. The Story (www.williamsonstunnels.com).
6. The Story (www.williamsonstunnels.com).
7. Richard Whittington-Egan: *Joseph Williamson Maker Of Catacombs.*
8. James Stonehouse: *The Streets Of Liverpool* (1869).
9. Richard Whittington-Egan: *Joseph Williamson Maker Of Catacombs.*
10. James Stonehouse: *The Streets Of Liverpool* (1869).
11. The Story (www.williamsonstunnels.com).
12. Charles R. Hand: *Joseph Williamson – The King Of Edge Hill* (Transactions of the Historical Society of Lancashire and Cheshire 1927).
13. Charles R. Hand: *Joseph Williamson – The King Of Edge Hill* (Transactions of the Historical Society of Lancashire and Cheshire 1927).
14. Tom Slemen: *Haunted Liverpool 2,* page 59 (Bluecoat Press, Liverpool 2000).
15. Charles R. Hand:*Joseph Williamson – The King Of Edge Hill* (Transactions of the Historical Society of Lancashire and Cheshire 1927).
16. Email interview with Frank Hodges (FOWT Company Secretary and Membership Secretary).

17. The Mole newsletter #19, March 2009.

18. Email interview with Frank Hodges (FOWT Company Secretary and Membership Secretary).

19. The Story (www.williamsonstunnels.com).

20. Homa Khaleeli: 'Found! Mole's Resting Place' *Daily Post*, Monday August 24th, 2005.

21. Found! *Liverpool Echo*, Monday August 24th, 2005.

22. The Mole newsletter #19, March 2009.

Project History

First edition: *Strange Attractor Journal* volume three © the author 2006.
Second edition: Self published pamphlet to accompany the release of *800 Years of Haunted Liverpool* © the author 2008.
Third edition: *Darklore* volume four © the author 2009.

Acknowledgments

Thanks to FOWT Chairman Chris Sharples for his assistance with the original article, Johnathon Wild for his help with the 2008 revisions and Keith Hawkins for the additional information for this latest version.

Greg Taylor – Beyond the Apocalypse (p. 251)

Notes

1. *The Georgia Guidestones*, Elberton Granite and Finishing
2. http://www.wired.com/science/discoveries/magazine/17-05/ff_guidestones
3. *The Georgia Guidestones*, Elberton Granite and Finishing
4. *The Georgia Guidestones*, Elberton Granite and Finishing
5. *The Georgia Guidestones*, Elberton Granite and Finishing
6. http://www.wired.com/science/discoveries/magazine/17-05/ff_guidestones
7. http://www.wired.com/science/discoveries/magazine/17-05/ff_guidestones
8. *Phoenix Rising: The rise and fall of the American Republic*, Donald G. Lett Jr.
9. *The Final Countdown*, Billy Crone
10. http://www.wired.com/science/discoveries/magazine/17-05/ff_guidestones
11, See for example, http://forum.prisonplanet.com/index.php?topic=101678.0

12. *The Rosicrucian Enlightenment,* Frances Yates
13. *The Rosicrucian Enlightenment,* Frances Yates
14. *The Rosicrucian Enlightenment,* Frances Yates
15. *The Historical Landmarks and other evidences of Freemasonry*, George Oliver
16. *Freemasonry in Context*, Arturo de Hoyos, S. Brent Morris
17. *Fingerprints of the Gods,* Graham Hancock
18. *Fingerprints of the Gods,* Graham Hancock
19. *The Georgia Guidestones*, Elberton Granite and Finishing
20. *The Georgia Guidestones*, Elberton Granite and Finishing
21. *Fingerprints of the Gods,* Graham Hancock
22. http://rosettaproject.org/
23. http://en.wikipedia.org/wiki/Trementina_Base